Awaken to your
True Self &
Best Life Path.

RAINBOW
MEDICINE

Therapy with the **A-Team!**

DR. LEANNE LEVY
AKASHA WHITEWOLF

BALBOA.
PRESS

A DIVISION OF HAY HOUSE

Balboa Press books may be ordered through booksellers or by contacting:

Balboa Press
A Division of Hay House
1663 Liberty Drive
Bloomington, IN 47403
www.balboapress.com
1 (877) 407-4847

Because of the dynamic nature of the Internet, any web addresses or links contained in this book may have changed since publication and may no longer be valid. The views expressed in this work are solely those of the author and do not necessarily reflect the views of the publisher, and the publisher hereby disclaims any responsibility for them.

The author of this book does not dispense medical advice or prescribe the use of any technique as a form of treatment for physical, emotional, or medical problems without the advice of a physician, either directly or indirectly. The intent of the author is only to offer information of a general nature to help you in your quest for emotional and spiritual well-being. In the event you use any of the information in this book for yourself, which is your constitutional right, the author and the publisher assume no responsibility for your actions.

All images in this book are created by the author, Dr. Leanne Levy.

Print information available on the last page.

ISBN: 978-1-4525-9898-7 (sc)
ISBN: 978-1-4525-9900-7 (hc)
ISBN: 978-1-4525-9899-4 (e)

Library of Congress Control Number: 2014921309

Balboa Press rev. date: 02/03/2016

Dedicated to my A-Team
Above and Below.

Contents

Follow the yellow brick road

Prologue
The White Lion

It's the Circle of Life and it moves us all
Through despair and hope, through faith and love,
Till we find our place on the path unwinding,
in the Circle of Life.

—"The Circle of Life"
The Lion King (1994)

Crystal is a *transmedium,* someone who goes into deep trance and has spirits speak through her voice box. She works in partnership with her husband, who counts her down into trance and then brings her back. When she is giving the session, she is lying down on a hammock with her eyes closed, and then her voice changes. She speaks in an ancient dialect that cannot be easily pinpointed. She says she has a group of spirits that speak as one coming through her, and this is why. Her private sessions take place in her home, but I came to know of her through her small inner-circle group work where she would travel to the homes of people gathered in small groups.

At the time, my friend Alexa and I were each contemplating going through fertility treatments; Alexa had a husband, but I was doing it as a single parent. She and I both had vivid dreams we used to discuss, and out of all my friends at the time, she was one I could openly share my gifts with. Although neither of us were "developed" psychics, we could read the signs and interpret our dreams, and we were confident in our assessments. But despite our closeness, I still held back certain information about those

I knew on the other side but never knew here. After attending one of Crystal's groups, Alexa passed on my name, and I received permission to contact Crystal. She agreed to see me.

Knowing that her group sessions were recorded, I asked that my session be recorded.

Crystal and her husband were hesitant, and they responded, "We will record it because we feel you are here for good reasons, but when we replay it, if we hear anything that we feel may be incriminating, we will delete it." Agreed. They said that I was able to ask as many questions as I wanted in the one-hour time slot, but to be mindful of not repeating myself.

Her husband counted her back, ten through one. The first thing he asked her was, "Can you please provide a welcome statement for Leanne?"

This opening statement talked all about my Heart chakra and my connection with nature, and how I was in a transition time from cleaning away my past to make room for new thoughts and possibilities.

Thank goodness it was recorded, because at the time of the reading, I wanted proof instantly, so I wasn't overly interested in the opening statement; nor was I prepared for the voice change and her style. Initially, I was overcome by the drama of this reading, a woman in trance speaking to me about my life in another accent than the one I heard her use when I met her in was wild, and because I hadn't had much contact with mediums in the past, I felt this experience was either the real deal or a total fraud.

And so I ignored the opening statement, and when I was told to speak, I asked a question to see which one she was: *real* or *fraud.* Standing on the fence, wanting to believe and yet mindful of the proverbial charlatan, in a somewhat critical yet humble tone I heard myself ask, "So who are my Guides?"

At the time, I had not yet read anything on metaphysics, Angels, or Spirit Guides but in my dreams, whenever I was going through something difficult, there was always a young male holding me, giving me a kiss, always there in my times of sorrow. In fact, the contrast between my sadness and loneliness while awake, and my sense of comfort and romance while asleep, led me to believe I was married in another dimension. *If this woman is the real deal, she will be able to shed light on this,* I thought.

And, yes, she did. Instantly, she responded, "You have a male protector Guide who stands behind you, he has dark hair to the shoulders, and he wears it free. His name is Francesco." I started to cry almost uncontrollably. She said he has been with me since the beginning and will stay with me until the end, that we have had many lifetimes together in different roles, and always a great relationship. She listed off some of the past lives we had in different sexes and roles, and I could connect to this information easily.

As she spoke, I listened, and with every question I had, a helpful and accurate message was given. When the reading was over, I felt quite whole and connected. I still had to walk my path, which involved making big decisions and overcoming big emotions, but the last words she said to me kept me centered, and still do.

Once out of trance, I shared with her how I had recently lost my two pet babies, Calvin and Chloe, and the sadness I was undergoing, and she said, "Your loved ones are all on the Ferris wheel with you; they hear you and are well, and as you speak with them often, you know this."

There was definitely a karmic connection between Crystal and me. When I met her in person, I was amazed that I had painted her in a painting seven years prior. After our meeting, synchronistically on the same evening, we both picked up a shared past life. It came to me in a dream, while she picked it up in meditation along with a repeated image of a white lion she kept seeing. This prompted an e-mail from her and a further meeting for coffee at her day job, a week after our session.

Over coffee and at her desk (she was a business owner) she did my numerology and was able to see my path as a Sage, but at the time, after having been so driven academically and professionally, all I was interested in hearing about was when I would get pregnant and start my family. The white lion she kept seeing and mentioning, for me, meant my child to come, but for her, it felt related to psychic work. When not in trance, Crystal was not picking up on children, and she had to do what every ethical and compassionate psychic must do: find the best way to not break someone's hopes but still give them purpose. After all, we are not gods, and there is always a possibility of misinterpreting our symbols. Nevertheless, her words still ring strongly today: "What I wish for you is total detachment; surrender, Dear One." I had yet to be on the spiritual path, so to speak, so hearing words like *detachment* and *surrender* was not the least bit comforting. In fact, detachment and surrender were the *hardest* tasks for me to accomplish, yet they were the wisest words for me to hear, and they continued to echo in the days, weeks, months, and years to come.

Despite having a sinking feeling that motherhood in the traditional sense was not going to happen for me, I still decided to pursue my goal of becoming a single parent using anonymous donor sperm. I booked my first fertility treatment one month after my session with Crystal, and the universe found a way to block this treatment. Out of nowhere, although dealing with a reputable company, there were legal complications with the country I had ordered the sperm from. Not being easily deterred, I changed donor companies and booked a month later, scheduled to be inseminated on my fortieth birthday.

A few days before my first fertility treatment, my grandfather came to visit in a dream, and when I asked him what he thought about my having a kid, he responded, "Forget about it. You are an artist and entrepreneur."

Although the signs were there, I did not give up hope, and over the course of the next few years, I became a medical miracle at the fertility clinic for *not* getting pregnant. And, "coincidentally," my career path as a healer and psychic medium began to reveal itself.

A week after my forty-fourth birthday (44 is the number of the Angels), twenty-seven years *to the day* of my grandfather's passing (2+7=9 *the end of the old*), and four years after his visitation in my dream (4 refers to *balance* and *home*), I was scheduled to give a lecture to a group of women entrepreneurs, and it was at this presentation that I came out of the spiritual closet.

It was time now for me to *pay it forward* and come *home.*

Introduction
Receiving
Her Stripes

In June 2013, eight months after the channel had fully opened to me and I was handed the Golden Key (access to the *Akashic Records* where soul records are stored), and one month after I joined a spiritual center to develop my psychic mediumship gift, I was prompted by my Guides to write. The famous Ace of Swords flipping out of the Tarot deck every time I picked it up to shuffle was their way of reaching me.

At the time, I had no idea that my writing would be self-help books with Spirit, although they did try to get through to me by channeling the idea through a soul mate friend named Miles, whom you will meet in this book.

To be exact, Miles said, "We should write a book together: me asking the questions as the Doubting Thomas, and you channeling the responses from the Angels." We laughed, and I responded, "Actually, that's a great idea!"

So that whole summer, I began to write by channeling guidance from my Guides to questions I would ask them through the cards. Using cards, my Guides and I developed a communication system we call *Conversations with the Other Side*, and we began to discuss what kind of book they wanted me to channel.

This was just practice for what was to come.

In late August, I pulled four cards: to be exact, I received the Two of Wands from the Rider-Waite deck, and three Oracle cards from Doreen Virtue's

Healing with the Angels deck. The three cards were Relationships, Healing and New Beginnings. These three cards actually became the title of my first writing piece, and once I read every interpretation of the Two of Wands I could get my hands on, the article flowed and literally wrote itself. And so it began.

One month later, in a second development circle I joined, I received a message from the teacher who was meeting me for the first time: "There is something you cannot put your finger on right now, but don't worry, you are not meant to. They will show you the signs, and you will know in time." Frustrating to say the least, but I got it. And I waited alertly.

In the spirit of active development, or shall I say *driven* to develop my psychic mediumship abilities, three months later, on December 4 (the night before my birthday), I attended yet another development circle, my third, and was honored to have been one of five students out of twenty-five to receive a message from the teacher, who was a transmedium. In deep trance and in another voice, I was told that I will write self-help books and that this was my purpose.

I couldn't ask for a better birthday gift—the pieces of the puzzle were finally coming together, and I could see the way ahead.

And then, literally, within the week leading up to Christmas, I was prompted to buy an iPad to use to write. The magic began the day after Christmas. As I sat before my iPad later that afternoon in the Pink Parlor (my home office), for the first time to write, a rainbow painted on like a warrior appeared over my beloved Savannah's eye. For those of you familiar with the Queen of Wands and her black cat sidekick in the Rider-Waite deck, Savannah is indeed my psychic black pug sidekick and a huge part of our healing sessions, both in sharing her Buddha energy and bringing us our slippers.

It was at Christmastime that I came to learn that I was called "White Wolf" on the Other Side. When I heard this I cried. As a little girl, there were two strong feelings and themes I remember coming into this world with. One was, *Where is my other half?* And the other was, *If only my parents would allow me to have a little white dog, I would be the happiest girl in the world.*

In my mediumship work, when I give messages, the *dog* and *wolf* are active symbols in my data bank. The *dog* is the symbol I receive when Spirit wants me to relay a message about a loyal companion; the *dog with a leash* is a message about self-discipline. The *wolf* is the symbol I receive when there is a message about studying, teaching, and the healing arts. I have learned a lot from studying Wolf medicine and Dog psychology, and clearly Savannah earned her wings and warrior stripes that day when my beautiful A-Team psychically painted on her medicine mask. She was my 9/11 baby and has been with me through every Tower moment since, including every page written in this book.

I owe my life to my four-legged earth-angel companions, and if it were not for my pet babies who accompany me on my earth walk and get me out of the house to be with and in nature, my most sacred space, I would definitely not be grounded and able to do the work that we do—and possibly I would not be here.

For many, experiencing 9/11 was a horror show; for me, it was no different. But somehow Savannah found her way into my life, and together we carved a new path, the one which lead us to this moment here. So it makes sense that Spirit painted these warrior stripes on Savannah because she has worked very hard taking care of me so that I can be here to assist and inspire others.

Awakening

Channeled outside on my patio in nature, on a hot and sunny after-noon, June 29, 2013.

What is the energy of the dominant voices I am channeling?

We are from the stars, and our message is to have the courage to be You and acknowledge this power from Source.

The Star is the teacher who shines out in the darkest of times. She becomes the drive to bring hope into the world, and helps others recognize and develop their highest capabilities. Our purpose with Leanne/White Wolf—our vibration—is to awaken you. Awaken you against injustice, and awaken a dedication to preserve life and our natural resources. Be just in your own lives with yourselves and each other, especially with your family and inner circle. Follow your instincts, embrace your fears, and leave something for the generations that follow. Have hope in your future, and free yourself from masks and restrictions.

What is another important message that you have for us here on earth?

To have faith that you are being guided along your path, that your path is filled with giving, receiving, and releasing. Give your love, share your emotions and intuitions, give of yourself freely, receive freely, and release what no longer serves you freely. You plant, you sow, you deal with emotions that travel with you along a variety of winding paths, and you create your web of life by the way you use your emotions. Have a balance between tears and laughter; be practical, yet believe in your heart's desire. Be happy; remember to enjoy life with the wisdom of an elder and the wonder of a child. Believe in magic, in your ability to create the life you wish to live; believe you deserve it, and be well-intentioned like the naive child. Know your powerful relationship with nature and Spirit, and work with us to help you along and protect you with our love and light on your beautiful journey of life.

Thank you, that is a beautiful message, it helps to remind us how to move forward with the glass half full. Speaking of which, what do you say to someone who is frozen and cannot break out of the cycle of depression and frustration?

That it is time to move in a new direction! Let go of what no longer serves you; know that you are guided and protected on your path, that you must let go of resistance and let the current flow you forward. Recognize that it is your mind that is causing you pain, and that you must choose to stand between your thoughts and guide yourself forward into a mode of surrender. It's a passing into unknown territory that scares you, but once you awaken to the fact that you want better for yourself, then you will transform yourself into a happier, more settled, authentic you.

Do you believe you deserve to transform? If you are ready to embrace this new you, then you will decide to flow yourself through the unknown journey and will no longer be stuck. As long as you see yourself as less deserving, then you will stay in the same pattern of living. You are the captain of your ship; only you, with Spirit guiding, can move yourself in a new direction. Clarity awaits, should you choose serenity. Know that you have all that you need to stand through the fall.

You must be your biggest advocate, because only you truly know which door feels right to walk through. Be strong and courageous, clear in your mind and heart, and know that you are always connected to your team as they walk your path with you, every step of your way.

People are looking for others to save them or for them to save others. Can someone truly save another?

There are always beautiful, kind people opening their arms to love others. Your mothers, whether you like them or not, whether they have given you up or not, are the first to bestow the gift of your life on the earth plane, so in a sense, they are *saving* your soul, for your soul needs to evolve.

Your soul chooses to come to earth to learn, grow, heal, and ascend. Throughout your life you meet people, animals, nature, and other forms of materiality, and you experience how these gifts *save* you on a daily basis. Mother Earth is saving you every day with her sun, oxygen, remedies, food, and water.

When you arrive on the earth plane you have Spirit Guides, Angels, and loved ones guarding and guiding you, and in some instances, *saving* you from untimely endings and uncharted accidents. So, in essence, yes, people save animals, nature, each other. But what is most important to understand with respect to your notions of saving people, saving each other in relationships, or depending on others to save you, is that life is a beautiful reciprocity whether you are conscious of it or not. It's the circle of cause and effect, of law of attraction, of balance. What appears one way to one person may appear another way to another, but not to Spirit, for we understand the purpose of the experience, and so we know that the concept of *saving* is one that can only be accomplished with a willing participant. Hence, even when a person holds her hand out to the jumper on the ledge, the jumper has to want to save herself by grabbing and holding on to the extended hand. The beggar on the street has to accept the offers if she doesn't want to perish. The giver offers the money because on some level this action redeems her. Love, like-minded connections, sharing, humor, kindness, seeing the next as equal, being grateful for the mirror you provide each other, these are all acts of *saving,* and in this sense, the heart filled with love is your greatest savior of all.

What is "being free" supposed to "feel" like?

A flow, a give-and-take that is balanced and flowing. It is when you can see outside your own box, with minimal discomfort and just awe for the enlightenment. When you believe and have faith that you are being guided and protected by Divine beings, then you understand that trials and tribulations are there to help you move beyond your comfort zone and free yourself in your heart. When the body is physically turned upside down in the King's yoga position, the purpose is for the blood to rush from feet to head so as to purify all stale energies that block healthy balanced function. When you are shaken up by life's little jolts, you remain alert and in the game of life. Seeing both sides of a situation enables you to see the benefit of both and downside of each. Freedom comes from giving yourself permission to see and experience both sides of life, and choosing to settle somewhere in the middle. Give yourself the freedom to feel the jolts of life and not feel guilty that you hurt yourself or others; rather, know that you have to experience in order to achieve true freedom.

Where does having a conscience come in?

You have to have a sense of justice and fairness within you, and this is your compass, your radar. Knowing what the right thing to do is one thing; doing the right thing for you, may be another. A balanced and moderate approach is clearly ideal, but, nevertheless, all experiences are lessons in cause and effect (action and reaction); therefore, healing and becoming conscious is a natural effect of every cause, conscious or not. We learn as we experience, so you see, in this way we are always on the right path.

Yes, but aren't there "better choice" paths?

Yes. Those are the ones that completely help you to change the way you live your life, and they are always for the better. They are often the ones you didn't see coming, the unexplained experiences that shake you up and make you into an even stronger warrior. Fear, sadness, worry, confusion, this is all part of being human, but having loving and supportive companions on your path to help you cope with life's trials and tribulations is how you move forward. Be grateful, no matter the experience, for Spirit always places an authentic companion on your path. Animals are by far your number-one earth-angel companions. When you stop the worry, you will see your fortune clearly. Count your blessings.

Thank you. This is a beautiful message, but let me clarify: Do we each have a path of probability, as in a first choice and a second choice (or runner-up)? Is there an order or hierarchy of which is the higher path?

There are always crossroads and even three paths as options; but, yes, there is one that takes precedence and that you know deep within you, and that's your intuition, us—your team—working with you to stay on that higher path, but in the end, each path will bring you further along from where you began. You have this sense that there is a better or hierarchical way, a style of competition, but from the soul's perspective, all experiences are equal, for they all make up the whole. Too much of the same doesn't fill up the other half. You were born with the resources to create your life and life experience, so have faith that you will do a great job and succeed on your path.

Is there such thing as a "happier" route, a route with less suffering?

Yes, this is the path that makes your heart beat fast, that makes your soul shine bright; this is the path that makes you want to learn more about what you do, who you are, and that inspires and teaches you to become your best you. The happier route is the one in which you realize yourself as a creator and cocreator with the life force. It's often the path that takes time to unfold, but it is the one in which each step brings tremendous wisdom and further lights the path ahead. Be wise, learn from experiences, and create your experiences. The happier route is when you know that it is you who creates and re-creates your path. So learn the lessons, and then you will realize how only you can create a happier path, that only you can create a better you and a better life for you.

Does happiness always have to come in the form of a Trickster and from Tower scenarios, literally?

Have faith that you are always on the right path when you are confronting your fears and illusions about how your life should be. You must look fear in the face, appreciate the pleasures of life, and know that all attachments will one day be released; and it is to understand that when this day arises, you too will then be on the right path.

So you are saying that, yes, it is always the scary experience that sets us one step closer to freedom, knowing we can do something we didn't quite realize we could do or even seriously give thought to. Being grateful for the attachments and then releasing them to replenish with the new. So are you saying, keep moving forward, face our fears, live life sumptuously, but recognize the ebb and flow and as best as we can, aim to free ourselves in our hearts, and know that we deserve the best and that Spirit loves us and that we are each a star in the eyes of our A-Teams?

Don't be so hard on yourself.

How do I know for sure that you are channeling through me and that this is not all my words and thoughts?

Have faith in yourself; know that you are worthy of our guidance. We love you. Trust that you are intuitive, that you are an excellent spiritual student, medicine woman, and teacher. You understand both worlds well, and although you used to gravitate more to us than earth, today you are well-grounded and have a tremendous desire to enter the unknown so as to guide yourself and others, hand in hand, with Spirit. We have guided you to the books you are reading, to the information you are helping us to share and reinforce, so whether you *read* it or *received* it through a dream or meditation, the message is the message, and not the medium. Who do you think the other authors got their words from? It all comes from somewhere!

So, am I a high-level channel?

That is your ego talking for you. Yes, you are very good—excellent, in fact—but keep studying.

Was that my ego writing that compliment?

No. You know the difference. You are balanced; you see things clearly and responsibly. Don't doubt yourself: you are highly intuitive and clear thinking, and you have a close relationship with nature and Spirit; trust this, and trust yourself.

That brings me to a question that I, along with many others, have in our student mediumship classes.

I know your question, and you know the answer.

Pay attention to the signs, and ask your team for confirmation. Teach people this, here in this book. Share with them what we and other people on earth have taught you. You are a leader; teach them about the signs, the communication humans can develop to talk to their team.

Who is going to read this?

Be patient. Just create. Write it.

Spirit in your work and personal life is by far the most important connection for you. All your creations are aided and realized with Spirit working with and through you. You are our anchor.

There is no surprise why we gave you the Eight of Wands to describe your primary life theme. When you have a goal you accomplish it! You manifest passion in everything you do and everyone you touch.

Your secondary life theme, *ha-ha*, is challenge and competition. Although you dislike both, you are here to move through specific blocks, because they are not blocks, but rather signposts on your path. You need to grow through many different kinds of life experiences. People are your teachers, and each person brings you down a specific path to contribute to your data bank. These challenging experiences are ones you grow from big time, and they propel you forward.

You like connecting the dots from the chaos and solving the riddles of life, hence the reason why challenge through diversity and sportsmanship is your number 2. You work in support of others as they work in support of you. Reciprocity is the gift of cause and effect: every action creates a reaction. You are here to become mindful of your own actions and reactions, and to teach others about this too. You understand that you all have something to gain from your encounters with one another.

Life is a game. You know you are learning, and having the patience to play it is what you came here to do. You teach from your life experience. You have overcome and experienced. Bravo. In the dance of love, the marriage between heart and mind, of community and individuality, you are here to celebrate and love yourself, celebrate and love others, and face each new challenge with the determination of a warrior, clear in heart and mind. You want the best for all those you love, and you stand for truth because you know in your heart and mind that it is the right thing to do.

I have been through many changes, as you know. What about if I just want to stay put and not "change" anymore?

You are here to experience and appreciate your own little wonders of life, to have a beautiful sense of self, relaxed, at peace, and one with nature. This is what brings you true inner security, something that money cannot buy and people cannot give you. Unfortunately for you—the you that is your personality self—everything does change, and you cannot hold on to any material matter forever. Fortunately for your spiritual self, change is needed to grow, heal, and rejuvenate. It can only do this at its maximum capacity in the arms of Mother Nature. When you have a healthy relationship with nature, which you do, you are well-grounded, so you accept change because you understand how each cycle of growth strengthens the next.

In our book, what do you want me to talk about?

Happiness, making choices, heartbreak, and coming back into balance in heart and mind. Share what you do in your practice, your therapy work. Stability and self-reliance, letting go of the old and accepting the help of Spirit to move forward in a healthier direction. How to recognize signs and synchronistic events as heaven's way of getting your attention and leading you along your highest path. Deception, emotional blackmail, negative thinking, and letting go of this way of thinking. Prioritizing a stable body so you can understand how to be self-reliant and confident, how to pursue and manifest your best life. Saying good-bye to the old, and choosing a spiritual life as the new way. From crisis to faith, getting through the cycle and beginning the next with the love and support of your team. Law of attraction. Gaining clarity about your purpose in your career and your love life, which will help you to be happy. Working with Spirit and channeling us. Starting over.

Is this an instructional book or motivational storytelling?

It is both. We want you to teach about interdimensional travel and channeling through artistic means—the various ways that you do it. Teach about the signs in Mother Nature that you receive on a daily basis, about being an earth angel and taking care of the body as a channel. Teach about knowing what you want and how to go for it, law of alignment and attraction. Another important topic: don't forget what you wrote about earlier recognizing when to let go, to rise above to gain perspective and awareness of a new path, to choose to empower yourself over stagnancy, to move through your stuckness, the fire, to get to the other side. Change!

But when you ask others to change, isn't this inherently telling them that they are not good enough as they are?

This has nothing to do with not being good enough; this has everything to do with understanding cycles of death and rebirth, which are the only constants. We are simply here to help you ease through your transitions with minimal trauma and as smoothly as can be.

Thank you and bless you. I love you. You are everything to me, and I know I am everything to you.

Part I

Pennies,
Feathers,
& Rainbows
**The
Language
of Spirit**

Rainbows
Bridging Worlds

They live in you, they live in me,
They're watching over everything we see,
In every creature, in every star,
In your reflection, they live in you.

—"They Live in You"
The Lion King (1994)

So how and when did all this Spirit communication begin with me?

Unlike some children who clearly remember seeing their imaginary friends, I knew I was surrounded by and spoke to my invisible loved ones telepathically but I couldn't see them. For this reason, from a young age, I trusted the invisible as more real than the visible.

From childhood into young adulthood, I felt like I was deeply missing someone. I often searched for the vortex to get back "home," but the closest I ever came to finding it was while dreaming during sleep. Although it wasn't a daily occurrence, I did have a few mystical initiations between the ages of eight and twelve. Closer to the eight-year-old mark, I experienced and witnessed levitation while my girlfriends and I were playing Light as a Feather, Stiff as a Board. At age twelve, while participating in a séance with two other girls, I saw a male spirit in the human form from the waist up, along with an uncle who had died before I was born. My uncle I had seen in my mind's eye, but the other male was as clear as day, hanging over my right shoulder while batting his eyelashes at me. On that day, the veil had completely opened for me, but because I was not comfortable seeing how comfortable unfamiliar spirits were with me, I shut it down.

Outside of these childhood communal experiences, which mostly happened in nature, I did not openly share my spirit communication with family or friends. It was just something that was part of me—like eating, sleeping, and dreaming—yet it was unrecognizable to others. It wasn't that my parents were against believing in such phenomena; rather, it was something that I chose not to share because there was no real space where such talk was encouraged. So not only did I grow up in the spiritual closet, but I also literally grew up in closets, as these were most often the spaces where I searched for the doorway—the vortex—back home.

Despite not being able to "see" Spirit in my waking state, throughout my adulthood, I continued to have constant contact with the other realms, mostly through recognizing signs, synchronicity, and omens, and through visitations, premonitions, and lessons during my dream state. Within my circle, I became known for my ability to interpret dreams.

Fast-forward to November 2012. The shift of consciousness, which the Mayans had predicted, was the moment when the channel fully opened to me. It wasn't something I was aware of or read about, but when it was happening to me, my romantic partner, Pete, was able to explain, as he was initially the well-read one on these matters.

I had been going through a crisis. Over the course of several months, there were signs, synchronistic events, and dreams that were all pointing toward endings of my old emotional identity, way of living, and perception of life. In one dream, I actually saw myself lying facedown in a lake of water, dead, only to reemerge from the lake moments later, alive and dawning a new and more natural appearance. Although I had already considered myself quite natural, living a healthy lifestyle and so on, over the next six months, my life began to change in drastic, healthier ways, from my eating choices and exercise routine, to the new clients I attracted and the issues they came in with.

Although aspects of this were exciting, it was a scary time nonetheless, as most times of change are; the hardest part was letting go of some of the closest people in my life. While crying and in the midst of a panic attack, I spoke to my Spirit Guides, and for the first time ever, I heard myself say, "I understand, and I surrender." After uttering these words, it was as though I knew everything was going to be fine, and by the following morning, I had already begun to feel an internal shift. One was "Good-bye, panic attacks." A few days later, while flying back home to Montreal from Florida where I live part-time, the journey involving my new identity began, and for the first time, Spirit reintroduced themselves to me through the symbol of the *rainbow*.

Until this point, my data bank of symbols that I associated with spirit communication was limited to *pennies, dragonflies,* and *butterflies.* Rainbows were not part of it. While waiting for my airplane to takeoff, I was sitting in a window seat and staring out the window because I had been crying and did not want anyone to see my tears. As the airplane lifted off the ground and headed for the clouds, I asked Spirit for a sign and felt prompted to take a photograph. I snapped several times but noticed nothing.

The following morning, while playing with my *first* deck of Oracle cards that I bought during that trip—thank you, Denise Linn—I shuffled and received a card that read, "Spirit communicates through rainbows, feathers, and pennies." Receiving that card reminded me to look at the photos I had taken the day before. To my dismay, in one of them, in the backdrop of a cloud, was a magnificent round rainbow encircling the shadow of my airplane. It was a sure sign that I was divinely protected.

From that moment on, the rainbows kept coming, and within a week, they began to also appear to me psychically, in session, next to my clients. At first, for a brief moment, I thought there was something wrong with my eyes, but as my gifts grew stronger, so did the rainbows.

A few months later, another type of rainbow experience occurred. Earlier that day, I had a discussion with Pete about Spirit communicating with us through what we refer to as *intuition.* We differed in opinion. I expressed that intuition is really our A-Team giving us information, whereas he felt intuition was more of a solo experience. This debate took place in front of my parents and his daughter, and it was the first time we actually showed our true colors and raised our voices for others to witness. I was not happy about this, to say the least.

Later on that day, after we returned home together and the sun was setting, as I stood before the mirrored door of my closet undressing, out of nowhere a rainbow in the shape of a feather and leaf appeared in the center of my forehead, over my Third Eye. I called for him to witness this mystical moment, and as he began to photograph this phenomenon, he noticed another rainbow pattern on the back of my neck. On my forehead, the colors were red, green, and yellow, and on my neck, they were white, purple, indigo, blue, and green. Clearly, in their own comical way, my A-Team was confirming my earlier statement about them. And his karma was that he had to witness this magic. Once I decoded the symbol and positioning of colors on these two body parts, I realized this was both a message about my A-Team and a premonition of our future work together, with me as their channel.

As time went on, and quite quickly it did, I began to understand what the rainbows I see in session next to my clients mean. For one, the rainbow is a sign to tell my client that he or she is accompanied by her/his A-Team (Ancestral and passed over family and friends). And second, it is a symbol for why our clients come to us: the same reason why I saw the rainbow for the first time while flying home. The rainbow is a symbol and message from our A-Team about their ever-presence *unity, love, protection, guidance*, and *hope* on our life's journey as they help us to move forward through change from a place of love instead of fear.

Rainbows have become a regular phenomenon in my life. They appear to me in the sky as orbs of color when I am seeking an answer to something important. These orbs also trail my plane next to my window, and they only appear when I ask Spirit to show me they are with me. They continue to encircle my airplane when I travel; they encircle candlelight and light fixtures when I give readings and teach; they encircle the moon, lampposts, and cars after I finish giving messages in a circle; and, the rainbow even physically appeared over my dog Savannah's eye the day that we began to write this book, hence why we also show you ways to read, understand, and heal your pet babies.

Today, I have developed a language with the spirit world, specifically to help me and others communicate with Spirit to coheal and cocreate our best life. We call it *Rainbow Medicine: Therapy with the A-Team*. When I refer to Spirit, I am referring to our Spiritual Angelic team (A-Team) that accompanies us throughout our earth walk. We introduce who these players are in the next chapter, "Raised by Spirit." Spirit has taught me how to recognize the ways in which they reach out to us here in the third dimension, and this language is one that we teach to those who want and need this special contact.

I now understand why Spirit waited so long to show me what they look like: they knew I would be their representative to help others identify their communication in every little detail of life. Yes, on occasion, they do show us the Hollywood version of Spirit, but more importantly, they want us to know that they come to us all in the simplest of ways, such as a visit from a winged one, a song on the radio, a headline in a newspaper, a found penny or feather, a rainbow reflected within your vision, a whiff of a familiar fragrance, a license plate with the initials of a loved one you are thinking about, and a cloud formation in the shape of an angel, heart, or passed-over loved one, including our pets. In fact, much of my spirit communication is with my passed-over pet babies. Such signs become visible to us when we are seeking answers and guidance, and in my experience, our loved ones are simply a thought away.

Back in the day, Seers were relegated to a few who were known as "chosen," but times have changed. Today, the veil is open for all of us to consciously work with Spirit, for we come from those realms and we return to those realms. When we open ourselves up to consciously work with the other dimensions, we are privileged not only to witness their magic on a daily basis but also to experience "seeing" from a higher perspective and receiving guidance while living the earth walk. Let me just clarify that all relationships are healthy when they are interdependent and not codependent. This means that you do your part, and Spirit does theirs, and together, hand in hand, they support and guide us as we walk our individual path alongside theirs, for even spirits have jobs to do, paths to walk, and lessons to learn.

Now, in this third dimension, I am as *home* as I ever will be, and my life is dedicated as a Divine Channel, an instrument of Love and Light, for those who feel the calling to ascend and consciously cocreate a better life and world. But one last thing: we cannot create a better internal/external world without facing and making amends with our fears. To truly know others, we must meet our authentic self, for self-deception is the most powerful veil. Behind the personality mask is where this truth can be excavated and found, and when we face our fears, they, in turn, become our beacon of light.

We hope our stories inspire you to reach out to your A-Team to heal, manifest, and walk your Highest Path.

With Love and Gratitude,

Dr. Leanne Levy and Akasha Whitewolf
The Gentle Trickster, Wounded Healer, and Rainbow Warrior

There's no place like home

Raised By Spirit
The
Other Side

Like anything else, developing psychic mediumship abilities and working with the spirit world as a Divine messenger and healing channel is a work in progress. But what makes it more difficult than other professions is that we are working with "invisible forces."

The practice of mediumship is a discipline, a language, an art form, and a sport, and thus far, the most effective means I know to clear the mind and conquer self-doubt. In order to receive a message, we have to be able to clear and stop the mind and body long enough from going elsewhere; that is, other than where Spirit wants it to go. We learn how to pick up subtle energies and cues, which we develop with our Guides to identify a second-ary source feeding us the information, and by *secondary,* I mean other than our mind/ego. Although both take place in the mind, there is a difference between our "normal" thought forms and the energy sensed while channel-ing. The experience of being in trance feels very similar to daydreaming; in fact, it is a form of daydreaming, but unlike escapism, when channeling, you are tapped into another frequency and are receiving information. And, the art of psychic mediumship is almost identical to decoding nighttime dreams, something we will discuss in several of the chapters.

It has been quite common thinking in society that if we don't *see* Spirit, then they we do not have the "gift" of divination and prophecy. But this is not true. This is simply one way society has marketed these abilities and this "profession." Yes, some people are born with clearer seeing ability, while others have to train to develop the ability to see clairvoyantly, which is basically learning how to receive symbols transferred through the right brain and translated through the left. Nevertheless, with proper sense training and discipline, any person who feels the calling is capable of becoming a good psychic medium. Spirit communication is a teachable language.

Like with any gift we bring in with us, my understanding is that we decide on the gifts we will need and how we will use them, pre-incarnation, and when we enter, the hows and whens are worked out as we move along our path. If you are reading this book, then this is your wake-up alarm and confirmation that you too are being called and are not "crazy" for tapping into this invisible force and source.

Today, as a developed psychic medium—and the key word here is *developed*—I see psychically (*clairvoyance*), both in my mind's eye and the physical presence of Spirit; I hear them in my mind's ear (*clairaudience*), similar to hearing a song playing in my head; I feel Spirit's touch and emotions (*clairsentience*) throughout my body; I physically blend with Spirit (*physical mediumship*); and, I receive contact and premonitions in my dreams (*Oneiromancy*). But I had to develop my gifts and treat them each as a separate muscle working for the larger whole. Meaning that if you feel the calling and want this conscious connection, develop your gifts as though each sense, each ability, is a muscle, independent yet interconnected to the whole.

Although always getting stronger, like most, my ability to see Spirit in human form while awake and not in trance or sleep state is weakened, and this is largely explained by the amount of energy Spirit needs from us to anchor and manifest themselves physically. Our dimension is much slower than where they reside (in fact, you cannot even imagine the difference in speed unless you have experienced it firsthand, which I will explain later in this chapter by describing how and when one of my Guides taught me this). But for now, the easiest way to understand why they are invisible to us is to look at the wheel of a car, composed of an outer tire and inner spokes. When the wheel is in motion on a highway, the inner spokes spin like a vortex, so quickly that you can no longer see them until the wheel stops. Symbolically, the tire is the denser physical body, and the spokes are the light spiritual body. And when we train through meditation to raise our frequency, we are able to leave our physical body and travel through this vortex and back in a matter of seconds. It is an inner experience rather than an outward one, and this is why both outer physical and inner emotional, psychological, and spiritual training are needed. It is truly a holistic endeavor, unlike the process of sleeping and dreaming which comes to us naturally. When we go to bed at night and fall asleep, traveling through this vortex is no work at all; it is what we do naturally, and it is part of why we are here. Every night, whether we remember or not, we leave our body, and while asleep here, we are up and learning somewhere else. This nightly out-of-body adventure is also how our physical body receives the rest and healing it needs. The best way I can explain this is to provide you with a science fiction visual of the suit being plugged into the wall.

Nevertheless, dream recollection and decoding messages and premonitions is also a gift some are born with, while others must develop it. This is the one developed gift I came in with, my ability to see Spirit clearly while dreaming and to receive their messages and premonitions. But even with this ability, I still had to train hard in order to stabilize my recall and interpret the symbols accurately. I correlate dream interpretation with psychic mediumship because the same process applies to both.

"There's No Place Like Home"

The following is a story about how I came to meet and see some of my Guides and Angels while sleeping here on earth and awake somewhere else. Let me preface this by saying that while all of the following experiences were occurring, I had yet to study metaphysics, or to read anything about Eastern religions or philosophy, and I was never all that fond of Western religion. Although I was born into a Jewish family and went to a Jewish private school, I don't ever remember recalling an affinity with the stories and teachings. I also have a Catholic grandmother and spent just as much time as a child celebrating Christian holidays. But despite having grown up within both traditions, religion never spoke to me; nor did I ever remember believing in Angels, per se—at least not in the way the Bible spoke of them. What I do remember believing in was God and Spirit, loving beings who watched over me and with whom I felt connected but could not physically see or feel. This was and still is my definition of the Angels.

Our A-Team

Let me introduce to you some of the players on our Spiritual Angelic Team, whom I refer to as our A-Team. The *A* stands for *angels, ancestors, arc en ciel* (rainbow), and my grandfather, *Alexander*, who was the first to cross over in our family. This A-Team is made up of both ancestral and passed over family and friends who opt to guide you. To clarify who is who, we refer to those you have not met in this lifetime as *Ancestral Guides* and those you have met as *Ghost Guides*.

Ancestral Spirit Guides

We all come into this dimension with at least one Spirit Guide who we studied with while discarnate and preparing to be incarnated. This Guide knows everything we signed up for in our Sacred Contract, and his or her responsibility is to make sure we walk our highest path. What this means is that we come in with a life purpose and a set of life lessons and goals we hope to achieve, which are related to past-life experiences both pleasant and not so pleasant. Sometimes we stay on track and achieve what we came here for, and sometimes we veer off. Either way, this main Spirit Guide is like our agent and manager. As we progress on our path, and based on our free will choices, he or she will contract other Spirits when needed to assist us. Much of this expert guidance comes from those on the other side with similar goals, intentions, interests, gifts, and expertise, and in addition to channeling their guidance to you by blending their thoughts with yours, they also send you key people you need to help you along your path. Your Team members adjust according to the specifics in your life and consist of players who stay the entire course and those who come in for specific teachings. Some members you have a personal connection with and some you don't, and each has a reason for working with you.

Another important thing to know is how our Guides reach out to us. When we were little we may have had imaginary friends. These guys and gals are really our Spirit Guides, but in order for us to connect to them we have to be able to relate; hence the reason why they come to us as children themselves. Dreams, intuitive insights and promptings, and waking signs are the other way.

You will meet my main protector Guide, Francesco, toward the end of this chapter.

Guardian Angels

We are also assigned a Guardian Angel whose responsibility is to make sure we do not die before our predetermined *exit point*. We all have a few exit points, which means that there are times in our lives when we may fall ill, have a serious accident, or be suicidal, and we then have the option to return Home. But then there are times when the accident was not predetermined, and these Guardian Angels make sure we are unharmed. Some experiences we've all heard of include a person who missed a flight, and the plane crashed; a person who was supposed to be at the World Trade Center on 9/11 but was stuck in traffic; a person who was in a car crash where the car turned over several times, and the person emerged from the wreckage unharmed or with very little injury.

There are also all the other Angels who have specialties, and it is they who help us with specifics to make our lives a little easier. For example, when I became aware of my Angels, I asked them to help me cook meals that were tastier than the ones I could cook, and so they did—or shall I say, *she* did. Another time she saved my life. One night, while home alone with my two dogs, Samson and Savannah, I was cooking organic chicken in olive oil, and I forgot about it. By the time I returned to the kitchen, which may have been forty-five minutes later, the chicken had been cooked to perfection, the stove was turned off, and the spatula was put back in place. Clearly, my Guardian Angel not only cooked me a delicious meal, she also intervened to prevent a fire and possible exit.

Another thing my Angels help me with is to find parking spots. Other times, they will visit me in my dreams to alert me of a person in my inner circle who may be suffering, and ask me to relay a message to that person.

Master Teachers

We also have Master Teachers who, like teachers on this plane, have specific roles in our lives that have to do with the life lessons we set out for ourselves along with our life purpose.

I became acquainted with my Head Master Teacher, Red Owl, many years back while in a dream state. He appeared to me as a very, very tall and extremely thin wise elder with very long white hair and a long beard. He looked Asian-Aboriginal, and although he appeared human, his form was not, for it was too thin to be human. Like a Buddhist monk or a biblical leader, he was cloaked in an organic tan shroud with a simple thick rope tied around his waist. His appearance was simple and biblical-like.

While asleep here and awake during daylight in another dimension, Red Owl's role was to teach me to fly. I met him high up in the sky where we stood together on a Red Rock Mountain Peak. Perhaps it was in the southwest, because the red rocks resembled those of Sedona. When I say high up, I mean that we were surrounded by blue sky and white clouds. I gathered it was to learn how to navigate my astral travels; as in, consciously leave my body during sleep time so that I may visit other realms to learn my lessons.

Just as we stood side by side, he on one mountain peak and I on another, his mountain peak magically catapulted several hundreds of feet into the sky, while mine remained the same. I then heard him telepathically say to me, "Now will yourself up!" And with the complete use of my mind, I did, and found myself once again at eye level with him. The next thing I heard him say to me was, "Now turn around and fly!" So without hesitation, I turned around, and what had been a steep peek with only sky all around just moments earlier, became a flattened rock, which allowed me to get a running start to then jump off the edge and hope to fly.

Just as I'd willed myself up earlier with zero hesitation, I ran, and with total trust I flew off the mountain and began to fly. During flight, he placed a solid structure before me—a house with no windows, only several levels of roofs—and now my mission was to shape-shift through each level. Unfortunately, that night I was unable to, but I felt proud that I was able to fly with no fear.

When I awoke from this lucid dream state, I became aware of my lesson on the Good Red Road of Physical Life. Red Owl was teaching me how to understand that everything is in the mind, and if I believe that I can do it, I will. If I believe that I cannot, I won't. Talk about a lesson in self-empowerment.

Ghost Guides and The Extended Team

Ghost Guides are friends and family who have passed but stay with you to help from the other side. This doesn't mean that they don't move on and are stuck as earthbound spirits. On the contrary, once crossed, many have the desire to stay around, reciprocate, and accomplish from the other side what they didn't or couldn't from this side.

During the few years that followed, I did a lot of astral traveling, and my flying increasingly got better. About five years after that first lesson, I had what I call a *powwow premonition dream.* In my lucid dream state, I was flying over water at nighttime and could see Montreal from an aerial perspective. I was not alone, as I had a companion flying next to me. A few years later, I realized it was my former boyfriend and best friend, Nik, working as my Ghost Guide.

Just as we were having fun admiring the lights of the city from high above, like being on an airplane three minutes into takeoff, there appeared a huge cement structure before us that resembled a four-level parking garage without any cars in it. This more-than-solid structure had been placed in the sky as yet another challenge I was to face. I immediately became aware that this was a test, and without any hesitation, as if I were playing a video game, I shape-shifted through each level. *Bang. Bang. Bang. Bang.* The trick was: *no hesitation.*

As I came through the other side of this multilevel structure, after what felt like several seconds, I looked back and was no longer with my companion. Exhilarated by my success, I kept flying higher and higher through the midnight-blue sky, and had no intention of stopping. I flew as high as I could, without experiencing any vertigo, and at one point, I heard myself say, "Guys, I hope you have something in mind, because I am not stopping."

Just then, when I could go no further up in the now-black sky, I found myself floating in one position, amazed by these magnificent balls of energy hovering just above my head. I extended my arms to touch one and was in complete awe of the energy that emanated from them. Although they looked like nothing more than golden orbs of light, the amount of love that poured through them and into me was mesmerizing and all-fulfilling. No words can best describe this feeling, and no earthly experience can compare.

After spending a few minutes massaging these orbs and channeling this love into me, the sky turned into a solid ceiling, like that of an office, and slid open.

Awaiting me was a pleasant male voice that said, "Welcome, you finally arrived."

The space I had entered into was a taxi station, and although I was on the inside, I did have a sense that the outside resembled a *Jetsons* vibe. (You remember that cartoon, right?) As a dream symbol, seeing a taxi can represent *a time of identity in transition.*

During this visit I met with those whom I felt were my soul family and friends, but I knew none of them from this lifetime. The women had made a little party to celebrate my visit, and they served red wine and homemade toffee squares.

It was then and with them that my life purpose was confirmed: "Leanne, you help people to have fun while healing."

In another room I met my daughter whom I channel. In the dream, I had seen the outline of her hair: it was just below shoulder length, golden blond with straight thick bangs across her forehead. But I could not see her face; instead, it had been replaced by the most beautiful golden light. I kissed her lips and felt our intense and loving soul-to-soul connection. I then told her how much I missed her, loved her, and wanted to hug and kiss her. Next to my daughter was a kind woman with short blond hair who said to me, "I know what you are going through. When I was there, I too had to accept that I was not going to have children."

There was one black man who ran everything at the station. My understanding was that he was high up in the spiritual ranks. He was a man of few words, donning a serious facial expression. I also came to learn that I have a huge army of protector Angels who appear to me in dreams as silent athletic black men with bald heads, all dressed in yellow T-shirts and black track pants; my *honeys*.

I spent a lot of time in this loving space, communicating with different individuals who all had wisdom to relay to me about my life path and purpose on the earth plane. I remember saying to them, "I am not ready to leave here. Can I stay as long as I want?" To which the leader responded, "You will only leave here when you are ready, not to worry." I was relieved.

In terms of what it felt like to be there, beyond the incredible love and acceptance I received, was the physical sensation I experienced in this location. Everything had a yellow hue to it, as though I was seeing everything through yellow-colored glasses, and as I walked through this space, it felt like I was walking on jelly. These two factors—the yellow hue and the jelly-like sensation—let me know that I was still there, in that dimension. When I stopped sensing them, I knew I had left.

Just before I was to make my return home, which was a lot less fun than my trip out, the boss's last words to me were, "Learn from men."

Over the course of the two years that followed, this statement became clearer to me, as my healing practice began to veer in new directions and take on new energies. Up until this point I had been largely working with women and girls dealing with and recovering from abuse in all of its forms, and we focused on building self-esteem and sense of self, while peeling the onion to get to the core. Clearly, Spirit was now saying, "It's time to work with men."

From this moment on, men began to come onto my path both personally and professionally, and a few key figures became the catalysts for my own rebirth, personal ascension, and conscious cohealing partnership with Spirit. My client base grew to include men and couples, and I soon became a "specialist" in relationship counseling, family mediation, and ways to heal from divorce and move on to a newer, more evolved path.

All that said, as my practice grew, I was humble enough to realize that just because I was the healer didn't mean I had it all down, so I remained and continue to remain aware that everyone coming in for guidance is also there for me to learn from. Therefore, when I channel conversations for my clients, more often than not, I can recognize that I too need to hear the same information.

Now back to the dream. Although this was a celebration dream, years later I recognized that this was also a premonition dream of what was to come for me on my life path. Two years after this dream, when I decided to come out of the spiritual closet to develop my psychic mediumship abilities and meet like-minded folk, who should become my teacher and mentor? A retired taxi driver turned reverend, whose course was called "It's All in Your Mind." And what else should manifest once I left the center to go out on my own? My sisterhood of women with whom I met monthly to eat, channel, and celebrate life.

Spiritual Working Partners

Two years after my powwow premonition dream and a few months prior to coming out of the spiritual closet and joining a spiritual center to further develop my mediumship gifts, in another lucid dream, I met another one of my Spirit Guides, a Grand Chief Native American Warrior and Medicine Man whom I call "Ka." I only realized months after I named him that *Ka* means "energy." One year after meeting him, I came to learn that his name is Running Bear, but I still call him Ka.

Ka/Running Bear has been my father many times in past lives where we worked together as medicine people. In this lifetime, he continues to take on a fatherly role. While working with him on my personal healing, alongside the healing taking place with my clients, he taught me that everything we lack here from loved ones we receive on the other side from our A-Team. My parents are wonderful people who have always supported me (and continue to). They are my biggest advocates. I love them so incredibly much and am grateful for all their support throughout my life, but sometimes parents can't give us what we must learn to give to ourselves, and this is where our Guides come in.

Ka, being the healer that he is, was that figure who taught me to come into Me.

It was with Ka and through his guidance that I learned how to compassionately assert myself, come into self-reliance, and fall in love with myself (I used to be unkind to myself). It was he who taught me that the love we feel for another, especially those we "fall in love" with, is actually love channeled from Spirit and meant for the individual doing the "loving," and not to confuse the two. It's all right to feel that intense love for another, but it's never all right to give our power away by thinking that without that person love is gone. No. Instead, it's important to celebrate the access to love, but never to think that the key to our heart belongs to someone else. It is a complicated process to untangle, but with his daily, often minute-to-minute guidance, I arrived.

Ka gets to the point. Although extremely compassionate and always teaching me about *grace*, he is not one who falls back on, "It doesn't matter what path we take, as long as we are learning." He helps people on this plane walk their highest path, and this is the map we offer to people when I channel his medicine. He encourages the development of self-empowerment by facing our fears, knowing our worth, and walking the warrior's path of truth, integrity, mercy, and grace. He is also my gatekeeper in our mediumship work on the other side, which means that he is the one in charge of who gets through to me, how and when, and who is allowed in our circle. It was he who said I am known on the other dimensions as White Wolf, she is my Higher Self who I have met as well.

When I first met Ka/Running Bear in my dreams, he was introduced to me by two hooded, white-robed Angels of Ascension, the size of two huge twin pillars, standing before me, facing me and hovering over me in bed. They morphed from white clouds into their angelic appearance, and only one of them allowed me to see him. Although his hood covered his eyes, I could see from the tip of his tiny nose to his neck, that he had light-brown skin, magnificent soft full lips, and a stern chiseled chin.

Just as I thanked him for allowing me to see him, the scene transitioned, and I was presented with Ka/Running Bear, my new boss and working partner. Had I not been prepared in past dreams to handle many energies, there is no way I would have withstood his *explosive* introduction. It was as though a bomb had gone off when he raced past me in full-feathered head-dress on his white and black horse, accompanied by his wife and young son, also on horses. I later came to learn that they too are my ancestral family and guardian angels. It is Ka's wife, *Broken Wing*, who cooks with me and intervened in a possible exit point.

Talk about an entrance; hence the name *Running Bear*!

During our introduction in this dream, he taught me about shape-shifting between dimensions by recognizing the different energies between them. Clearly, they were building upon the skills they taught me in previous dreams.

He engaged me in an exercise where he had me put one arm up vertically to feel the difference in energies between the dimensions. And I could feel it: ours was a dense slow vibration, and the other was extremely fast. The best way I can explain the feeling is to tell you to imagine going from an intense pins-and-needles sensation to complete lightness. That exaggerated discomfort is what it felt like in between the shift. As he told me to lift my right arm up vertically through the portal, I watched in amazement—and felt the sensation—as it disappeared from my elbow on up. I was in between; invisible on one side, dense and present on the other. The next thing I heard him say was, "Jump through," and so I jumped into that dimension, which I later came to know as the fifth dimension, and found myself giving a healing session on my then boyfriend.

As we work together both personally and professionally, Ka continues to teach me skills both during the dream state and while awake on the earth plane. I have even had a few dreams where he taught me to give a reading while in deep trance. On these mornings, I remember being woken up by my little dog, Sam running out of the bed because he'd woken up when he heard me talking in a different voice. I heard it myself!

Protector Spirit Guides

Now it's time to introduce my main Spirit Guide, protector, and leading man; without him, I for sure would not be here. I don't know if I should hug him or kill him (LOL). His name is Francesco, and he is my Twin Flame. Yes, I came down here leaving my other half behind so that he can guide me from the other side. From the first moment I can remember, I have been searching for him—until I realized where he was.

I also know Francesco as my husband and best friend from many lifetimes, in some of which we were Buddhist monks. I refer to him as my lover because ever since I was young, I always felt that I was married in another dimension. This feeling grew stronger as I came into my thirties. Whenever I would go through a difficult time, especially when it involved a boyfriend, I would go to sleep feeling sad, and awake happy, having remembered being comforted by him in my dreams.

Today, now knowing why these feelings exist has helped me to integrate and heal these memories around unrequited love, which is, in part, what we signed up for. I am able to sense his love, talk to him, feel him, see him, and now I understand why I walk most of this earth walk solo. As I wrote earlier, what we lack here, we receive from the other side.

A few months after I met with the transmedium (at age thirty-nine) I mentioned in the prologue, at the beginning of Winter, I was walking with my dogs on the mountain at Beaver Lake. A young man with a white German shepherd (White Wolf) crossed paths with us, and as the dogs sniffed each other, the young man smiled and said, "Hi, my name is Francesco."

Sibling Spirit Guides

We are also guided by siblings we know from this lifetime, as well as, others.

The twin theme includes being guided by my twin sister, Vanessa, whom I have met several times in dreams. She is also my partner in our work, she is the one I teach with, she teaches through me, and together we make a great team. She is also one of my Master Guides. Vanessa comes to me as a Celtic redhead, although other mediums see her as a blond who looks like me. She is a dancer, and in every dream since way back, dancing is somehow always part of the theme of her visitation. In the first dream I had of her many, many years ago, we were dancing the waltz—she was teaching me how. We laughed so much together, and while dancing she showed me snapshots of my mother's inner child.

One evening, she came to me in a lucid dream state, in the guise of Angelina Jolie but from ancient Atlantean times. She had the most magnificent free flowing long hair draped down to her waist, with a large wave of hair pinned up half a foot high over her Crown chakra and down her back. I had never seen a hairstyle like this. The emphasis she placed on her hair, I interpreted, was to show me that this teaching involved channeling Spirit. However, months later, through her guidance, I came to understand that the hairstyle also had a deeper personal message about my soul/life path and the nature of our work, and was a specific reference to the Eastern Goddess and female Buddha *Kwan Yin*, a symbol for empowerment work with women and children; my life's work, up until this point. Much of my purpose work in this lifetime has been dedicated to sisterhood and healing from abuse through the creation of safe spaces for girls and women to come together to share stories for personal healing and social change. Clearly, that was also my sister's way of letting me know we have been doing this work together from the very beginning.

In the dream, she was leading a bunch of women dancers in a dance class. She walked around the room in the most serious and dignified manner, orchestrating and watching her students at play/work while paying close attention to their individual needs and skills. The following morning when I awoke, I realized it had been both a premonition and a prompting dream that I was ready to take the next step, and teach.

One evening while in another dream state, both Francesco and Vanessa appeared to me as twin lions. The scene took place in a school gymnasium, with an audience of children and adults. Aware that these mirror-image lions were mine and I was telepathically communicating with them, I watched them from the sidelines and noticed both of their *kundalini* (life force) spines on fire. It was the most incredible vision.

Surrounded by a silent, still, and yet enthusiastically mesmerized crowd, waiting for the magic to happen, in full majesty and at identical times, these two mirror-image lions walked side by side into this space. Like a coordinated trick perfectly timed and in sync, one went left as the other went right, and then each jumped through a circus hoop, which became a window into another dimension, and both disappeared.

When I awoke from this dream, I felt exhilarated and comforted. At the time, I knew it was both a message and a premonition, but I had yet to understand exactly what it spoke of other than a comforting metaphor to let me know that they "jump through hoops" with and for me. One year later, when I became a psychic medium and a teacher of psychic mediumship I came to understand more. Lions are performers and entrepreneurs, so to speak, and the kundalini spine on fire represents all chakras aligned and ignited. That night in the dream, I was *Awakened* and notified of my message bearing and teaching to come.

Remember the White Lion in the prologue?

Since we are all on the path of ascension together, I later came to learn that both Vanessa and Francesco were the twin Angels of Ascension I spoke of earlier.

So, as you see, we all have a team of spirits who root for us, love us, want to help us manifest our desires and dreams, and see us succeed on our highest path. Ultimately, what they all want for us is to come into greater self-love, self-worth, and personal truth so that we may learn from our experiences, understand the lessons of the whys, forgive ourselves and others for any wrongdoing, clear our karmic debts, and discover and use our gifts to manifest our highest potential and happiest life.

It is important that I end this chapter by letting you know that just because they are in a higher dimension with greater understanding of the larger whole doesn't mean they don't feel our pain, cry with and for us, and have lessons to learn and karmic ties and debts to make good on. When we hurt they hurt, when we shine they shine, so I stress again, it is important for you to know this. Although they tell me this, they also get their point across in dreams. On several occasions, when they were trying to help me get out of a relationship or move on from a difficult place, I would have a very disturbing dream about one of my pet babies, Sam or Savannah. In the disturbingly heartbreaking dream, one of them would be badly injured to the point that I was powerless to help them. The message my Guides were relaying to me was, "How you feel about your babies is how we feel about you, our child, when you refuse to learn your lesson."

My A-Team and yours want you to know that the way that you see Guides and Angels as godlike is the same way that they see you. So the next time you think of hurting yourself, please remember that you are not alone.

Rainbow Medicine

Prepare Your Sacred Safe Space

When channeling, we suggest you choose a comfortable space that will become your designated sacred space. You can decorate it with your favorite colors, fabrics, sacred objects, and divination tools. Make sure you have enough space in front of you, sit at a table or on a floor cushion.

Smudging

Each time you conduct a *Rainbow Medicine* session and *Open the Channel*, bless and smudge this space and yourself. *Smudging* is a Native American/Indigenous custom that involves burning herbs such as tobacco, sage, cedar, lavender, and/or sweetgrass to purify and align the energies within the space; each plant burned has a consciousness it imparts to the experience, which includes you and the Spirit of everything that enters and lives within this space for this period of time. When smudging yourself, use a large feather (found or store bought) and, start at the head. Going clockwork around your auric field, disperse the smoke from shoulder, to feet, to shoulder, to head. When smudging the room, work in a similar manner and direct the stale energies to an exit. You can envision this exist as a portal in your mind's eye or you can open a window.

Music

To further enhance your *inter-dimensional* travels, we recommend you listen to nice soft New Age music as this will help you to relax and float freely.

Candle

Always light a candle and begin with an opening prayer to invite your A-Team to work with you and assure you that you are well surrounded in and protected by their Divine White Light.

Crystals

Think of who you want to hear from on your A-Team, and then take a meaningful object to represent them each in the reading you are about to do. I use crystals.

Journal

One last suggestion: Begin a new journal for this journey and exercise, and call it *Conversations with the Other Side*.

Open the Channel

Like creating a portrait puzzle, you are now going to build a grid to channel a message from individual members on your A-Team. In a horizontal line at the top of the "puzzle," place each article/crystal to represent a team member. I call this process *Opening Up the Channel*.

For example:

1. Spirit Guide   2. Master Teacher   3. Grandparent   4. Pet

The questions you ask are going to create the vertical line, to the left.

For example:

1. Can you show me one of your qualities?
2. How are you helping me?

3. What is our karmic tie?
4. What life lesson am I learning?
5. What do I need to heal?
6. What gift do I have to offer?
7. What message do you have for me?

After you made a list of your questions, select the decks you feel will best illustrate and clearly relay the answers. I like to work with at least two decks at once: one with great imagery that I can relate to, and the other with words that are meaningful. As long as you are working with symbols and words you understand, any deck will do.

You will also need to set the rules beforehand with the Spirit you are asking to connect with, meaning that if you want them to answer your question by popping out the card, throwing it out of the deck, or on a count of ten, whatever you decide: ask, then shuffle, and then receive.

You can choose to talk with one channel at a time, in the order of your list of questions, or you can open up all of them by placing two cards, one from each deck, in every spot. If you do this, place the cards face-down, and then once you speak to each, reveal the cards accordingly.

While having a conversation with each Spirit, look at all the images and words on your card(s); let your eyes do the wondering as each will blend their thoughts and feelings with yours to help you see the answers. Sometimes answers lie only in one particular symbol on the card; therefore, it is important to trust the process and see where your eyes focus. It works the same way with the words. Sometimes the message is in one word and not the complete sentence or description accompanied in or with the card; therefore, it is important to pay attention to the story that is going on in your head as you scan the cards for your message. Remember to decode answers according to questions asked.

Once you are finished with the conversation, write everything down. Next, take a step back to look at the entire grid/puzzle and see if you can recognize an overall message and repeated themes. Pay attention to the first, middle, and last cards of the puzzle, as they too will show you a story arc. A story arc involves an introduction, a conflict, and a resolution/solution.

When you are done, thank everyone for their love and participation, and make another date to talk with them again.

Bee-Cause
Visitations
& Lucid
Dreaming

After loved ones pass, they will come to visit during our waking state and in our dreams, to let us know they are okay and to relay loving messages. Most often these visitations occur in a lucid dream state. Lucid dreaming feels different from other types of dreaming. The main components of lucid dreaming are that you are aware that you are dreaming, and you feel as though you are awake in another dimension.

The best way I can explain when our time here is up is to imagine that our loved one has moved to a faraway country, but we do not have the money or time off to get there ourselves, so until we do, we continue to keep in touch via the telephone. Although, unfortunately, we do not yet have the same technology to communicate as clearly as they do, we do have other communication tools we can use, such as our six senses, which we can further develop. (The six senses are sight, sound, taste, touch, smell, and thoughts). There are signs, symbols, and synchronicity that beg for our attention; we can learn how to use Oracle and Tarot cards, which are excellent tools for spirit communication; and we have our sleep-time dream state.

Today, I often communicate with my grandparents and pet babies on the other side while in dream state and awake, and they help out a lot with challenges that family members and I face.

Visitations from Grandma

Shortly after I lost my grandmother, who had passed in my arms in the hospital, she came in a dream to tell me how proud she was of me, specifically in regard to my academic accomplishments. Another time she came to visit was to give me a heads-up on the future mediumship work I was booked to do at a specific event. In my lucid dream, she literally appeared dressed in a red robe, with a crown on her head, as the Queen of Justice in the Rider-Waite Tarot deck. She sat down and requested that I give her a reading! On the earth plane, she was a queen and often said, "Wear red to keep away the evil eye."

In the dream, she let me know how eager the women would be to get a reading from me, and that there would be one woman who would be angry because she wasn't on the list. When the event happened a few months later, my grandmother was correct: there were eleven women booked for a reading with me (eleven is the number of the Justice card), and when the night ended, one woman was angry because she couldn't get a reading.

After she passed, my grandmother and I had a great time developing my abilities together, both with the cards and without. She helped me to code and read my cards, and the first message I gave without the help of cards was while wearing her diamond ring designed as a magnificent spiral. Out of the many rings she left me, I choose to wear this one while I channel because for me, the spiral represents my interdimensional travels, my ancestral Celtic roots with my sister and teaching partner, Vanessa, and the spiral's ancient connection to the mother goddess representing cycles of death and rebirth. The funny thing is, if I had told my grandmother that I was doing this work while she was alive, she would not have been as receptive.

Visitations from Pets

Souls, whether they incarnate as humans, animals or plants, each come from the Divine, and when they return home, they want to reassure us that they made it safely and are never that far away. When it was time for each of my cats and dogs to pass, I would get the premonition dream, and then once they passed, I would receive waking signs, as well as dreams, letting me know they are free of their ailments, happy, and at peace.

A week before Calvin, my male white Pekingese dog, passed, Chloe, my female Peke, who had passed earlier that year, came to visit us while Calvin and I were at the beach. Calvin had back problems, and at age fifteen and a half he couldn't really use his back paws. While holding him in the water as he did his aquatic therapy, a magnificent blue dragonfly landed on his neck and stayed with us in this position for more than ten minutes. I knew it was a sign from Chloe, and one week later, it was Calvin's turn to transition.

Two weeks after he passed, Samson and Savannah, my remaining dog babies, and I made a visit to the beach in memory of Calvin and Chloe. As we walked along the dirt path in the midst of the forest, flying at our pace and side by side with us, were a beautiful white butterfly and blue dragonfly. For the entire walk this elemental couple joined us; as we stopped, they perched themselves together on a branch, and as we walked, they gently flew alongside.

From the moment Calvin passed, he sent me messages. The night after he transitioned, he relayed important information to me about my future abilities as a "fortune-teller." I use this word only because in the dream he came to me as a yellow bird made out of origami by a *Gypsy* fortune-teller who was giving me a reading on the bed. Several years later, when I began to play with the cards, it was in bed where I did most of my readings.

For several nights after his passing, he would continue to send me messages. One night, I had fallen asleep with my laptop next to my bed. The laptop had been in sleep mode, but from out of nowhere, at 3:00 a.m., I was awakened by music. A song by Cinematic Orchestra was playing on my computer. As I listened closely to this song that I had never heard before but that had been mysteriously downloaded, I heard the words sung: "And I built a home for you, for me, until it disappeared from me, from you, and now it's time to leave and turn to dust."

Four months after my firstborn dog daughter, Chloe, passed, Samson, my new male pup, was eating out of Chloe's dish. I looked in the dish and saw a beautiful heart sculpted into his food.

Visitations From Clients

Another interesting aspect about dreamtime and communication with Spirit that is worth noting is that some of us called to do this work will find ourselves working in the other dimensions while our bodies rest in this one. The following is an example that I personally experienced.

One night, I received a visitation from four spirits who came to inform me of valuable information. In the dream, all four appeared to me while I was in bed.

The first was a cute female child. Two years later, I came to learn who she was while working as a psychic detective on her missing child's cold case.

The second was a woman in her early forties whose name was Debbie. She appeared to me with black costume wings safety-pinned to her white t-shirt. At first I asked her, "Are you an Angel?" To which she responded, "Not the kind you are thinking of, but, yes, I am an Angel, the human kind." I then realized her black wings were those of a bee.

Debbie came to tell me that there was still so much more she wished she could have done during her earth walk, one being to write a book. She was so excited to write a book; it was as though her exhilaration was just as powerful on the other side as it is for us on this side. Unfortunately, we didn't get to discuss what her interests were because another spirit came through and pushed her aside. But later on I realized the reason she came to me was to relay a message to one of my soul sister clients, Pam. Just to exemplify how Spirit works, it turned out that the visit I received was perfectly timed with an important charity event the two women were organizing, and it was that evening the event was to take place. The two had worked together for a small charity organization dedicated to special-needs children and dolphin rehabilitation therapy. Talk about earth-angel work!

Normally a good sleeper, one night, Pam complained to her husband of a tightening in her chest, which kept her awake throughout the early morning. That morning she received the phone call that her friend had suddenly passed from unforeseen complications related to pneumonia, leaving behind young children and a loving husband.

When Pam relayed this tragedy to me in session, she was also very much aware that her close friend and working partner had been helping her organize the event from the other side, even though it had only been a few weeks since her passing. Pam herself is very psychic. While we were discussing Debbie, we felt her presence in session and did a reading to confirm.

Fast-forward two weeks later. It did not dawn on me that the perfectly timed visitation that I received had been Pam's friend, but as the afternoon went on, I realized that the charity event was that same evening. When I put two and two together, *bang!*

Knowing how losing a loved one is a sensitive topic and having the gift of mediumship is one I take very seriously, I did not want to rush into delivering this message until I felt convinced it was indeed for Pam. I was standing in a bookstore, about to send an e-mail to her about Debbie's visitation, but just to confirm that I was interpreting it correctly, I picked up a deck of animal Oracle cards, and out flew the dolphin. I then picked up an Alison Dubois book from the bookshelf in front of me, and in the same way that I use the cards, I asked Debbie to open to a page that would either confirm or correct me. The page read, "My friend who recently passed came to visit." I then picked up a second book and did the same thing. That page read, "Thank you for relaying the message." I hit the *send* button on the e-mail.

The following day, Pam confirmed my visitation and exclaimed, "I am not sure if you know this, but the Jewish interpretation of the name Debbie means 'bee'!" No, I did not know that. The next thing she exclaimed was, "This morning I received an invitation to a friend's bar mitzvah, and on the stamp there was a picture of a bee!"

Over the next few days, I continued to feel Debbie's presence. I asked her about her book idea, and I immediately received the impression: "A children's illustrated book about spirit communication and adjusting to losing loved ones." I told this to Pam, who is an artist and graphic designer, to which she responded with excitement:

> The book theme coming up now is freaking me out! Why? For a few reasons. Before my aunt died, she gave me a book that she wrote with her friend who then passed a few years later. The title is *The Messages from Dreams*. I was able to speak with my aunt freely about my lucid dreams, astral projection experiences, and much more. She loved me in a very special way. I've been dreaming of

compiling my stories and experiences to write a book! And, did I ever tell you I've been dying to write and illustrate children's story-books for years?! I have two incredible stories that I made up that my kids *loved!* Debbie brought this together somehow, didn't she?

When I received this e-mail, I was sitting on a beach and just as I replied and hit the *send* button, a bee came to me and a manatee swam by. I guess that was as close to a dolphin I was going get!

Moments like these cannot be fully described in words.

For Hire

The third spirit who came to visit that same evening was a mixed race male in his late twenties. As I looked at him carefully, I realized how familiar he was to me, so I asked, "Haven't I met you before?" He said, "Yes, we have crossed paths." I asked him, "What can I do for you?" And he said, "I have a court case, and I would like you to be there to defend me." I responded, "Certainly." I did appear at his case and he was not found guilty.

Two years later, while working on the missing female child's case mentioned at the beginning, it became clear when I saw photos of the daughter and living father that these two spirit visitations, the first and third, were, in fact, working requests and premonitions from both.

The fourth spirit who came to visit me was a five-year old girl. She was beautiful. She was tall and thin, with pale skin, big blue eyes, and whitish-blond shoulder-length hair with bangs. I said, "What can I do for you? Your parents must be heartbroken." I can't recall exactly what she said to me, other than that she was on a mission to help the cause of which she passed from. She desperately wanted to be heard and attract the right people on this third plane to help her fulfill her mission. I hugged her, but just as I wanted to get further clarification, I awoke. Two years later, while working on the first missing child's case, next to her photo on the Internet was one of spirit number four, another high profile missing child's cold case.

When I awoke, I began to cry. Although I believe our exit points are within our free will, both contracted before we come in and then at times renegotiated once we are here, these beautiful souls taught me that just because we pass does not mean we feel like our work here has been done. This is why we continue to guide loved ones from the other side, and it's also why we reincarnate. Despite crossing over, the desire to accomplish more still stays with us.

I share this experience because this touching contact is proof of survival of the soul. We want you to know that there are many, many souls who cross but still wish to be of service to us here on the earth plane. We do not need to fear them, only to recognize themselves in us.

These visitations often occurred to me during the dream state when I was a child, but because I was afraid, I often pushed them aside. Early that morning when I met with these allies, they reminded me of the value of my own shadow work. Because I face and work through my fears, I am able to be a conscious medium—a Rainbow Bridge—for those who wish to continue their work on this dimension.

Thank you, beautiful souls, for reaching out and giving us all the comfort in knowing that we never truly die.

Rainbow Medicine

Now that you have learned how to communicate with your pet(s) above in *Meet Your A-Team*, you will learn how to read and communicate with your pet(s), below.

What is so wonderful about reading your pets is that you will gain insight into both you and your pet, and how best for you both to live your happiest and healthiest lives, together. Since our pets and their issues mirror us and our own, identifying our karmic links and lessons helps us to heal in tandem and symbiotically.

Reading your babies is truly an incredible mind-heart opening and warming experience. Through these various exercises, you will learn ways to better understand your pet's holistic needs and health issues, and you will be amazed by how much they know, feel and understand yours. Each time you access your pet in this way, we recommend you telepathically ask for their permission and bless them when the reading is over. If you don't have a pet below but have pets above, ask them to teach you and practice *reading* them. A third option is to read your friends' pets.

There are many different kinds of readings you can conduct with your pet, it all depends on the information you are seeking.

Card Reading

For this exercise, we will show you how to conduct a *card reading* to learn about your pet's likes, dislikes, wants, needs, and karmic lessons.

Select card decks that can answer your questions with pictures and words. Consider words to express your pet's thoughts and emotions, and colors, images and symbols that relate to your pet's every day life. As you learn how to communicate with Spirit through divination tools like Tarot and Oracle cards, you will see how they will use the pictorial scenes on your cards to relay daily messages to you. Therefore, we suggest you choose cards that reflect your daily life; modern Tarot decks are a good choice.

Every time you conduct a Reading begin with the same routine:

Have your journal and divination cards on hand
Smudge the space
Light a candle
Say an opening prayer
Invite your A-Team
Invite your pet's A-Team
Make a list of questions

Have fun using cards to explore these themes with your pet and don't hesitate to come up with your own questions:

What are my pet's likes/dislikes?
What is the reason for my pet's particular behavior?
What does my pet request?
What feedback can you give me about my pet's food, toys, exercise, love etc.?
What is my pet's life purpose?
What is my pet's life lesson(s)?
How does my pet feel about me?
What is in our Sacred Contract?
What is our past life and current incarnation connection?

How does my pet feel about this person in my life?
What are my pet's character traits?
What character traits does my pet like/dislike?
What is my pet's favorite past time?
What is my pet's favorite memory?

Heal the Leader, Heal the Pack

You may want to understand your role in your pet's behavior and heal-ing, and ask for guidance on how best to discipline and heal yourself of the issues that also affect the wellbeing of your pet. Ask the question, then pull a card.

Pet Body Scan Reading with Cards

With your pet in mind, ask for his/her Spirit Guide to come forward with yours to help provide you with insight into your pet's dis-ease or illness. Shuffle the cards then select a few that want to come out of the deck. Don't look at them! Now hold the cards face down over *your* Root chakra, which will substitute for your pet's, and see what you pick up for your baby. Since you are doing a reading about another's energy, Spirit knows this and will give you information for that pet. If it feels like information you can relate to—as in, you think you are reading yourself—don't worry, this is how Spirit often gets their message across, especially when you are a beginner, as they will use what you know to help you feel someone else's pain and triumphs. Once complete, combine the channeled information with the cards you selected.

Repeat this exercise with every chakra and read the chakra chapters in Part 3 to understand the qualities that belong to each.

Pet Body Scan Reading with Hands

Another way to pick up information is to do a reading by scanning the body with your hands, without the cards. If it's a cat or dog, have your pet relax in a comfortable position on the floor, bed or couch. Without touching the body, take one or both hands and place them over your pet's Root chakra, and then see what you feel, sense, hear, smell, taste, and think. Once you are done collecting, write everything down, review the information, and decode your symbols to make sense of the Root reading. Repeat this exercise with every chakra.

Mind Reading

Like Spirit who read our thoughts and feelings, and impress theirs on us, animals also communicate this way, this is called telepathic communication. When your pet appears to be confused at your command, it is because your thoughts do not match your words and actions. The more integrated your thoughts and actions are, the clearer your communication will be with both humans and pets.

The following four exercises are designed to help you sync your mind with your pet's.

One way to know what your pet is thinking is to hold your hand a few inches above his/her Crown chakra, and identify which symbols, feelings, sounds, tastes, and smells you receive. Once you have decoded your symbols, you will have insight into her/his thoughts.

Another way to read your pet's mind is to be in the mind of your pet and watch your thoughts. Bring yourself into a comfortable meditative state, open the channel, and ask to replace your thoughts with your pet's. Once you receive the impressions, write everything down, then go to books and the Internet to decode your symbols. If you need further insight or confirmation, use the cards. When you are done, thank and bless everyone involved.

If you want to know the current energy in your pet's mind, ask to receive an animal symbol. Decode the animal symbol to understand the energy.

If you want to know the energy your pet needs to heal her/his mind, ask to receive an animal symbol. When you do, go to the Internet or an animal symbology book to understand the prescription. In *Part III* of this book we discuss *Animal Medicine*.

Psychic Body Scanning

One reason for conducting a body scan is to detect how your pet feels in her/his body, where they are sore, and why.

When conducting medical intuitive scans, it helps to familiarize yourself with the body system of the species you are working with, and the positioning of their organs and chakras (human, dog, cat, horse, fish, turtle, frog, bird, lizard, snake, spider, plant, tree, flower etc.). If conducting medical intuitive scans interest you, we suggest you develop your data bank of physical health symbols to represent organs, bacteria, fungi, parasites, etc. The Internet is a great resource and research tool, so are books and flash cards.

When my little Pomeranian, Sam, had an upset stomach and vomited a couple of times in one week, I conducted a body scan to identify and isolate his discomfort. It was indeed localized in his solar plexus, the digestive system, and thankfully not as painful as I thought. I then asked to see where he was and what he ate, and I was shown Sam in the backyard with a small round shape the size of a berry. The next images I was shown were a pair of hands, birds and squirrels. With this information I was able to conclude that Sam had eaten food, possibly fruit or seeds, our neighbors fed to the squirrels and birds.

Your pet doesn't have to be sick for you to conduct a scan. You can do this reading to enquire about his/her holistic health, as in, emotional, psychological, physical and spiritual.

In one of our teaching classes where we each write a pet's name on a piece of paper, seal it, place it in a collective pouch, and pull out one to blind read, unknowingly, I received my dog daughter, Savannah. Although she is in great health, Spirit showed me her wear-and-tears so as to be extra cautious with these body parts. I had also been concerned she was experiencing urinary discomfort, and in this reading it was confirmed. This helped me to adjust her diet, accordingly. I was shown a memory of ours and how it made her feel. Clearly, my guides felt it was important for me to know the depth of our connection and the impact of my emotions on her. And, last, I received a health prediction for us both.

Your pet does not have to be with you in the room or even in the same town. During this scan you may find yourself telepathically receiving the information directly from your pet or you may be working through the A-Team. Each time may be different. As you develop your animal communication skills, you may want to practice and develop both ways of receiving, or stick with one and strengthen that.

When you work with clairsentience, you are communicating, as in receiving and decoding information, via physical sensations. Pay attention to head and body tingles, light tickles, itches and pressure on body parts and organs, goosebumps, inner heat surges, ear pops, light headedness, and brushes of cool or hot air. These are some of the ways to identify a clairsentient message. To decode their meaning, ask yourself how each sensation makes you *feel*.

To prepare for this reading, in your journal, draw a simple stick figure of your pet, which you will use to record the information you receive.

Sit down in a comfortable upright chair with two feet flat on the ground and palms facing up. To prepare yourself to receive the information, close your eyes, clear your mind, and through your nose, take a few slow deep breaths in and out. With our students, we find two minutes to align with the channel is sufficient, and we usually allocate ten to fifteen minutes per reading.

From head to toe, ask to be in your pet's body and feel where the discomfort is. Then wait for these sensations to appear in your body. When you can pin point the area(s) in your body you are feeling discomfort in, write everything down. On the stick figure drawing of your pet, circle and mark the areas you are feeling and jot down notes that come to you.

Next, work with the other Clairs to further understand the discomfort. Ask for an image, symbol, word, smell, taste, and song to accompany that body part. Write down every thing you receive.

When you are done collecting the information, bless and wrap your pet in a colored energy he/she needs or requests. Review, decode, and assess the information. Go to the Internet if you need help decoding what you received i.e. symbols, song lyrics, body parts etc. If you need further confirmation or guidance, use your cards and interpret them according to the questions you ask.

Blind Body Scanning

Because we are emotionally involved with our pets, it can be difficult to pick up the information and trust ourself as an unbiased channel. Therefore, we have a few tricks to share with you that involve having more names in the *kitty* and conducting additional readings.

Me and My Pet

In this case, you will be conducting two readings instead of one. Draw two stick figures on two separate papers. Don't worry which one is the four-legged pet and which is the human, both have four limbs. If you are enquiring about another species, such as a bird, spider or snake, we still recommend this four legged sketch until you find a better way that works for you.

Take out two *post-it* notes and write down your pet's name on one and your name on the other, seal them both in the same way. Place both in a pouch, mix, then select one, write *number one* on it, select the second, and write *number two*. Allocate a sketch to each reading. You will now be conducting a *blind reading* on both entities, one at a time. Follow the same *psychic body scan* directions above.

While doing this reading, you can even structure it by asking a few questions such as:

What is your opening statement for this entity?

What life lesson is this entity learning?

What is your guidance about their health?

What is your closing statement?

Pets Above and Below

If you have a living pet you wish to scan, and you have a pet or two above, write each of their names on a *post-it* note and place them in the pouch. Make a stick figure sketch for each. This way when you pull out a name from the pouch, you will have less of a chance knowing who you are reading, and more opportunity to practice your skills, blindly. Take ten minutes to read each. Then reveal the names and review your notes.

Doubling Up

Another way to do this exercise is with a friend who also has a pet, this way you both can practice blind reading humans and pets, and compare notes. Each of you place two *post-it* notes into the *kitty*, one with your pet's name and the other, yours. Mix them up, then each of you pull out two notes. Follow the same directions explained above.

Special note: Please do not rely solely on your medical intuitive scans to diagnose you or your pet baby's health. If you suspect either of you have an illness, please follow-up with a visit to your doctor or veterinarian.

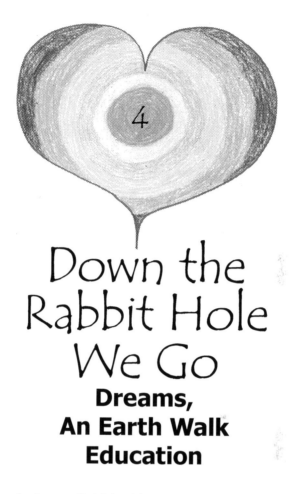

Down the Rabbit Hole We Go

Dreams, An Earth Walk Education

One of the easiest ways Spirit is able to communicate with us is through our dreamtime. While we are sleeping, our brain is more relaxed, our soul can detach completely from the body or project itself interdimensionally, being both here on earth and somewhere else, and our frequency raises, which enables us to communicate with discarnate spirits that lower their frequency to meet us halfway. At that precise moment—hello!—an interaction occurs, and a conversation is had.

All of the ways in which we use our senses, both in dreamtime and wake time, to communicate with Spirit are exactly the same tools we use to live our lives, just more exercised, enhanced, and toned. In psychic mediumship development terms, they are called the *Clair senses.*

Clairvoyance: Sight.

Clairsentience: Touch/Feeling

Clairaudience: Sound/Hearing/Listening

Claircognizance: Thought/Knowing

Clairalience: Smell

Clairgustance: Taste

When recalling a dream or interpreting a message received from Spirit, it's important to ask yourself:

What did I see?

How did I feel?

What did I hear?

What did I think?

What did I smell?

What did I taste?

In our dreams, often, it is our Higher Self, Spirit Guides, Teachers, and Angels who contact us the most, and the reason for this is to keep us on path according to the contractual agreements we set out for ourselves pre-incarnation.

What actually occurs during dreamtime is that our body relaxes and receives healing energy, while our spirit touches base back home to learn its lessons. The symbols received, the scenes and colors perceived, the words exchanged, and the feelings experienced are all ways in which our A-Team, which includes our Higher Self, is guiding our earth walk education. Each has a specific role, duty, interest, and vibration, and through the experience of remembering and decoding our dreams, we can get to know who they each are and the ways in which they are each helping us.

Hosted within us, like a treasure chest waiting to be accessed, is a data bank of symbols that we brought with us from past lives and have developed in this life; the way in which we receive messages from the other dimensions is through this data bank. Our Guides can only speak to us in a language we already understand. They will only use symbols and signs that we can, will, and do recognize. In fact, the moments are hard not to pay attention to. These are the moments when something "strange" and synchronistic happens, but you have no way of "proving" that it's a personal sign and message for you. The sense of "knowing" we feel occurs because we each already have symbols that we currently use without being totally conscious that we are using them; instead, we just "feel" them. When we develop our mediumship, these symbols become more prevalent as they are brought completely into consciousness.

Everything literal is symbolic, and everything symbolic points to something literal, so whatever message we receive will always benefit from a decoding process. The dream state is similar to the waking state in that *all* that we receive, in both states, informs us on our path. Therefore, applying the same dream decoding process to what occurs in your daily life will help you to decipher your communication and guidance from Spirit.

Another thing to remember is that although there are standard definitions of symbols, certain symbols, such as numbers, colors, and animals, will take on new meanings according to your personal experience with them, which is why you will need to work with your Guides to figure out your own unique interpretations. Start with what you know, and then investigate the ones that you don't know or that are new to you. Look in books, research others' interpretations, and adopt the ones that resonate.

If dream interpretation is something you are seriously interested in, then I suggest you allow your A-Team to lead you to the right books to help you build your data bank of symbol interpretations. The best trick I have is this: Pick up a book to see what's inside and if it's right for you. Open it to a "random" page, and if that page resonates with you, then chances are, it's the right book for you. Another way to see if the book is right for you is to choose one symbol that you are convinced you understand, and then, when shopping for your book, look to see which book shares your interpretation of that same symbol. The book I use is *The Dream Book* by Betty Bethards. (Google her to learn more.)

In Bethards's book, I learned that there are very specific symbols which, once we know what they mean to us, become easy to contextualize and decode in dreams. But I will remind you again that each one of us will eventually have our own unique ways of interpreting the symbols we receive in our dreams and in our waking mediumship, depending on our personal experiences with them. As we continue to develop these seeing abilities, so too will our sense of our symbols and their unique meanings deepen. Therefore, please understand that the more conscious you become of your symbols, the more you are actually cocreating a methodical data bank of symbols that you are agreeing to use with Spirit as part of your language with them.

In this chapter, to help you decode your nightly dreams, I concentrate on the types of dreams we have, some key symbols, and their possible meanings.

Down the Rabbit Hole We Go

Without getting too technical, and in order to keep this as simple as possible, the kinds of dreams we have and those who appear in them reflect what we are experiencing, working through, learning, teaching, and healing. When I use the word *teaching* here, I am referring to modeling behavior.

Dreams: Key Symbols

People

Unless it is a premonition dream, every person in the dream state, just as in the waking state, is often a mirror image of an aspect or situation related to you personally. The person, people, or celebrity image(s) that appear in your dream do so because each represents an aspect of you or something of interest to you (or an aspect of/interest to your Guide). For example, if the celebrity reminds you of stardom, activism, Old World charm, cowardliness, unconditional love, creativity, braggarts, free spirits, etc., these are the issues you are confronting and working through.

Usually, when a celebrity appears in the dream, he or she is actually your Spirit Guide; so, to understand his or her message, it's important to decode the celebrity, because those factors are part of the message and vibration. If your Guide comes to you as a singer, watch for the song they send you, and then Google the words to understand the message.

The *people* in your dreams represent the energies at play in your life. If there is a crowd of people you have yet to meet, it may mean that unknown energies are at play in your life. If they are focused on you, it may be a premonition of something involving a group where you will be the center of attention. Those you recognize represent energies you are mixing with. How they appear will not always reflect their real physical identities, so be mindful of the costumes they appear in, their hairstyles, adornments, and so on, as all this will tell you more of what lies beneath the surface.

House

Depending on which room you find yourself in, what appears in that room, if it is lit or dark, how you feel in it, what is occurring there, etc., will tell you about personal matters you are working through. The *home* and the *car* represent us, our vehicle and sense of belonging, inwardly as well as outwardly. The home is our body, mind, spirit, those in our family, and our sense of belonging; each room refers to an area of our life. The kitchen is where we get creative and nurture ourselves; the bathroom is where we cleanse, detox, and purify; the bedroom is where we rest, and if with someone in the dream, where we become intimate; the basement often refers to subconscious or hidden fears, often related to sexuality; and the living room is where we gather, so it represents how we get along with others.

Car

The *car* is your vehicle in life; when you are driving the car, you are in control, when you are a passenger, you are giving over the control. The road you travel along tells you how you are journeying: If it's a winding road going upward, this tells you that there are twists and turns on your path; you are unable to yet see where you will arrive, but at least you are going in the right direction. If the road is going up and down, it reflects that you are going up and down. If it's a dirt road, it can reflect rougher experiences or uncharted territory. If it's a road along water, it can reflect emotional healing. The vehicle also tells you how you are traveling through life. A bicycle might say *leisure,* whereas a motorcycle may reflect *danger, freedom* or *excitement.* Again, the value these items hold in your life determines how you interpret them.

Fire

Fire represents purification: out with the old, and in with the new; rebirth; past-life experiences; spiritual work in circles.

Blood

Blood represents your energy; when you are bleeding out of a particular body part, it often represents losing energy in that area. To decode, it is important to understand the *chakra (energy center)* where you are bleeding from, and this will give you insight into the area or areas you are losing energy from, as this will highlight your imbalances.

For example, the Root chakra relates to physical security and identity; the Sacral chakra relates to emotional issues of pleasure, dreams, and being good enough; the Solar Plexus chakra relates to intellectual power struggles, self-confidence, and will; the Heart chakra relates to grief, re- sentment, and sense of community and support; the Throat chakra relates to creative expression and lies; the Third Eye chakra relates to goals and confusion; the Crown chakra relates to inspiration and obsessive thinking. (We will discuss the chakra system in depth, in part III [Chapters 14 through 20] of this book.)

Mirror

Looking into a *mirror* can be a sign that you are learning of a past life and what happened to you during that lifetime. Pay attention to what you looked like, how you felt, what occurred, what symbols or objects appeared, where the scene took place, who was there, and what colors and feelings were present. This will tell you what, from that lifetime, is active in your current life. We only have access to past lives that inform our present life; there- fore, when you have these dreams, it is critical to pay attention; hence the mirror is often the symbol that this is indeed a past-life recollection dream.

And sometimes the mirror is a symbol for something else.

One night while in our circle teaching and receiving messages from our loved ones in spirit, when we closed with a prayer and sent everyone home to the Light, one of my students asked, "What does it mean that I saw a mirror shatter as I looked up into the Light?" I had a feeling it meant that everyone went back home through the Light and so that is what I responded. That evening as I was undressing to go to sleep, I noticed in the reflection of my mirror a rainbow next to my bed. While dreaming that night, my grandmother came to visit, and she presented herself through the reflection of the mirror. This was obviously her way of telling me that it was she next to my bed, and that the shattered mirror did in fact represent our loved ones saying good-bye.

So you see, the mirror took on a new interpretation as soon as I had a new experience with mirrors.

Pay attention to your experiences and how they interconnect. Again, this is simply a guide, so don't be rigid, just go with the flow, with what feels right, and you will often receive a confirmation or correction.

Animals

Animals often represent the qualities in an animal which you are being asked to embody or learn about because you hold aspects of this animal within you. This is often referred to as *animal totems* and *animal medicine,* which I work with and discuss very briefly in the chakra section (part III [Chapters 14 through 20] of this book).

When you see an animal in a dream or waking state, it is important to ask the question, *What is it about this particular animal that symbolizes something specific in my life?* Often, our Guides will come through as animals, meaning that the animal and the Guide are one and the same. Sometimes your Guide will give you a heads-up as to the qualities he or she is helping you with in your life through the animal you dream about. That's why it's always good to have an animal symbol interpretation book. I use many, but my favorite is Skye Alexander's *The Secret Power of Spirit Animals.*

Ocean, river, lake, pool

Water usually reflects your emotional life. Depending on the waves, currents, clarity, what or who is in the water, how you travel in the water, and so on, water will tell you what's going on in your emotional life and personal relationships, and will also provide insight into these experiences. Big waves may mean big emotional issues: if you are riding the wave, you are in control, if you are tumbled by it, you are overwhelmed and not in control. If you notice sharks in the water, this reflects your perception of danger; if you see a dolphin, it may mean you are having fun or in need of fun. If the water is murky or dark, this can reflect fears clouding the way. Once you begin to develop your water-animal symbols, you will gain a greater understanding of these kinds of dreams.

Angels

Sometimes the Angels and Archangels will visit you in a dream, and they will take on symbols too. When Archangel Michael first came to visit me, he appeared as a Michelangelo sculpture. You know the artist! Because I didn't have a childhood data bank of the Archangels, the only way he was able to make his presence known to me was through this artist, since I am an artist and can relate to this symbol. Once this was established, the next time he visited me, he appeared in human form. Years later (six years later, to be precise), I realized the image he came to me in is the same one that appears of him in one of the decks I bought, *Energy Oracle Cards,* by one of my favorite authors, Sandra Ann Taylor. He's hot! When you receive an archetypal visitation, it's important to decode its symbolic reference to understand the specific message as most often such visitations are your Guides dressed up in costume.

Nightmares

In addition to understanding the meanings of various symbols, to help you further interpret your dreams, it is important to know that different types of dreams hold different purposes.

Dreams in the form of *nightmares* are designed to help you work through an issue related to your life purpose and life lesson. When you have a nightmare, it is usually your Guide(s) telling you, "Wake up, smell the coffee, and get with your program!" The nightmare is designed to scare you just enough so you won't forget to take the time to work through the symbol interpretation, meaning, and message.

Sometimes a nightmare is also a premonition coupled with a lesson from a Guide, and you will usually be able to identify this if it feels lucid, as though you are truly awake somewhere else.

Below are some common nightmare themes that address life lessons.

Chasing scenes

Chasing scenes can represent that your fears are running your life. Whoever (or whatever) is chasing you will help you determine what (or whom) your fear is related to. In order to learn the lesson, we have several choices, which all deal with accountability. In the dream, we can realize that we are dreaming and take our power back by confronting "the stalker" and either killing or making friends with it (or him or her). However, it is difficult to navigate in the dream scape so the next choice is to work through the issue while awake.

Sometimes it's a premonition dream with the option to plan ahead, as this is your Guide's way of giving you a head's up before a situation hits you like a ton of bricks. Sometimes, you are being alerted to an upcoming major crossroads and are being presented with a choice to make between several paths. If the dream repeats, it means you didn't yet catch on and are given another chance to act accordingly and take your power back.

Either way, nightmares are all about issues of control and power, and this is the purpose of the nightmare: to take back control of your life by facing your fears and bringing them into the Light, so as to learn and grow from them.

Lost and can't find home and car scenes

Dreams in which you find yourself on a path, road, highway, street, or parking lot, *trying to find your home or car,* represent that you are on a journey and are still unaware of how it will turn out. You feel lost. The emotions experienced in the dream will tell you how you feel about this journey, and reveal what you may need to work on to help yourself move along this path.

For example, a dream where there is anxiety and a sense of powerlessness can reflect how you are coping in daily life. It could mean you are placing your power on external forces, in effort to feel a sense of stability, when you should be going inward to strengthen your sense of self and self-love. Every outer situation reflects an inner experience and reality, so if you are lost on your path and feeling anxious, it can mean you feel lost because you cannot sense what is coming your way, what your goals are, and what your next move is. Being lost can also refer to a person in a time of transition, fearful of the next stage in life, similar to the feeling most of us had when we transitioned from elementary school to high school.

Death, near death, and battle scenes

A *death scene without a battle* in the dream reflects a true transition and graduation from one identity to another. The core personality is intact, but the lens in which the person sees life shifts.

A *near-death scene in which there is a battle but you do not die* can reflect a situation where you may feel like you don't belong and are questioning this. It could also reflect how you are hurting and battling with yourself. When such dreams occur they usually reflect a situation in your life where issues of alienation and worthiness are triggered. In short, the lesson of confronting such a dream is to remind yourself that it is your responsibility to face your inner demons, so as to heal and begin a new cycle, a new grade level of learning.

I had a dream with a death scene, which occurred in a lake. I watched myself go into the water to save my dog, Savannah, from drowning. Instead, I drowned, she returned to land, and shortly thereafter, I was reborn and walked out of the water, donning a new hairstyle. After working through the symbols of what (and whom) Savannah represents for me, the water in which the dream scene took place, my hairstyle and attitude, this told me that I was indeed in a rebirth process, reborn into a more authentic self, having shed previous dreams and layers of my identity that no longer served my growth.

Gunshot scenes

Gunshot scenes where someone is killing another person, or the victim of the shooting, are often about power struggles, authority, and lost energy. Depending on where the person is shot will tell you where this person is losing energy. If there is no blood, this person is not losing energy but is killing off an old part of self no longer needed. Despite the scary aspect of the dream, this is a good thing; after all, change is scary. If there is blood, there is loss of energy, and this area needs to be brought back into balance. If you are battling a person and you shoot this person, usually, this person is reflecting something within you that you are struggling with. Killing that person is simply saying good-bye to the issue he or she represents, and embodying a healthier version of self.

The symbol of a gun is usually metaphorical for *penis energy,* which is about leadership, power, penetration, making one's mark in life, and everything male, yang, and testosterone driven. A dream like this may be asking such questions as *Are you owning your power or giving it away? How do you define power? Who are you in a power struggle with? How can you bring this part within you back into balance?*

Decoding these dreams using the chakra list will further help you to understand the message of these dreams.

[*See* Chapters 14 through 20, in Part III of this book for a detailed description of the chakra system.]

Past-Life Dreams

Past-life dreams usually show you the major themes and lessons you brought into this lifetime to work through. Whatever is going on in the dream will help you know where you are with respect to learning that lesson, so you can come into greater peace about the issue and awareness of self. You need that dream to highlight a lesson you are learning and to confirm that you are on the right track.

One of my students dreamed that she was bullied in a past life. In this dream she saw herself as a young boy on a train getting pushed around by a gang of boys. Because of the bullying, the boy jumped off the train and killed himself. Two weeks prior to having this dream, my student signed up for our healing and psychic mediumship development class. It is customary for me to blind read each student before we meet in person. Having already channeled a message to her before meeting her in person, I had tapped into a fight she was having with someone in her inner circle. The timing of her dream and the message I gave her was clearly highlighting lessons she was learning in this life: to not allow herself to take on the problems of others, and to set clear boundaries so that she could take good care of herself. The other part of the message I gave her involved her future work with teaching children. I only came to learn two months into our class that she was going back to school to become a conflict-resolution teacher.

Questions to ask yourself are, *How did I feel in the dream? What was I doing? What was my connection with others in the dream? How did the connections feel? What symbols appeared in the dream?*

It is detective work, which means the pieces interconnect one at a time, painting a picture larger than previously imagined.

Here is another story. My client had a dream that her Guides came to tell her that in a past life she was the mother of her current boyfriend, and this was the reason for her and her boyfriend's tight bond in this lifetime. She asked me if this was possible, and I responded, "The big question with past-life recollection is, "Can you see why this information is relevant for you to know right now?"

Knowing our history can bring a lot of comfort, even knowing the bad parts, for when consciousness is raised, a new perspective becomes possible (the lesson of the Hangman Tarot card).

As it turned out for my client, the timing of the dream was to relay a message about repeating family patterns. Like her mom and many *mothering* women and men, she was taking it upon herself to do everything in the relationship, expecting to be the one to adjust and hold it together. Like what moms are expected to do for their children.

Premonitions Large and Small

Sometimes people will get *premonitions* of large global events, and when they do, despite the event(s), most often the reason why they receive the premonition(s) is that, symbolically, this event also holds a message for the person. The macro always reflects the micro. These premonitions fall into the *large* category.

There are also premonitions about major and minor personal events in our lives. These premonitions fall into the *small* category. I get both kinds of premonitions. They are extremely helpful because they give us a heads-up of what we will be encountering, what to work on, what to be mindful of, and, possibly, how the experience will end. Sometimes, even though we may not be able to change the outcome, despite having knowledge beforehand of the way things will play out, giving us a heads-up of how to possibly handle things in different ways allows us to cushion the blow somewhat. Instead of being smooshed by the train, we break a leg.

Rainbow Medicine

Decoding Dreams

Can you recall having a visitation in a dream?

Usually, when we receive visits from loved ones who have crossed, they may appear as we knew them, but perhaps younger or slightly different; or they may come in a costume we can relate to them. If they appear in an outfit you cannot relate to them, this is because there is a message in why they came to you dressed like this. Also, pay attention to the setting in which they appear, as this too has meaning.

Let's expand on the initial question in this exercise:

Can you recall meeting your Spirit Guide in a dream?

Can you recall being taught something by your Master Guide in a dream?

Can you recall receiving a healing in a dream?

Can you recall having a premonition and then watching it unfold in real time?

Can you recall being shown a past life?

You may not have fully recognized any of these dreams in the past, but now you will.

In your journal, I would like you to go over all the dreams you have had where you think you may have received a visitation from a loved one, Spirit Guide, or Master Guide, had a premonition of a passing that was to come, and/or had a past-life recall. Make note of these experiences.

Once you have done this, if you need additional confirmation or explanation of a particular dream, message received, or lesson learned, you can take one of your Oracle or Tarot decks and ask your loved one for further insight. Even if you don't feel their presence, they are always available telepathically.

Select two decks for this exercise—again, one with images, and the other with words—or use only one deck that includes both. As we discussed in the previous chapter's exercise, after deciding on how you will shuffle, receive, and read your cards, sit quietly, place the question in your mind's eye, and then shuffle. When you feel ready, choose a card or a few cards. A few may pop out or fall out; if this happens, it can be the answer, confirmation of the question, or both. Again, set these rules in advance so that you do not get confused.

If you need additional information for one or some of the cards, then I suggest you use a technique I call *layering*. This is when you choose another card to explain the initial card. For example, if you are using Doreen Virtue's *Archangel Raphael* deck, and you received the *dehydration* card but are not sure what or whom that refers to, shuffle from that deck or another to ask, "What do you mean?" If you received the *home help* card, this could refer to a message about a need for more heartfelt communication with a family member. This would make sense if you are speaking with a Guide or passed-over loved one who is trying to relay a message to you about family matters.

Once you have selected all your cards, place them in front of you and see if you can identify more in the message. Look for symbols in the cards that were present in your dream. Again, it's detective work, putting a puzzle together, so let your physical eyes and your mind's eye do the wondering, and pay attention to the story line in your head.

Here is another way to do this exercise, where you will not look at the card but simply feel it.

The Psychic Reading

This time, shuffle the deck with your eyes closed, select the card you feel drawn to as you are shuffling, put the deck down, and place the selected card in one hand. Don't look at it!

Take a few yoga breaths in and out through the nose (not the mouth). Imagine that Spirit gives you thoughts similar to a process of putting a coin in the piggy bank. To get you started, feel your thoughts come in this way through the top of your head, and similar to a dream or daydream sequence, watch in your mind's eye for the images, sounds and thoughts to appear as you direct your attention to the energy of the card(s) you are holding in your hand. As you receive the impressions, write them down. Next, place the card(s) in your other hand, and continue to write what you receive.

Once you are done receiving, write anything else that comes to you or that you feel. Before looking at the card(s) in your hand, see if you can make out the message you wrote down. Once you have, turn over your card(s) and add the message(s) from the card(s) to the message you received in meditation. Combined, you should have a clear message about the dream.

Rats, Rainbows & Fairytales

Signs, Symbols & Synchronicity

Whether they be our Spirit Guides, Guardian Angels, human or pet departed loved ones, ETs, or the Archangels, Spirit communicates with us via *signs*, *symbols,* and *synchronicity*.

Signs and symbols are the images we receive via our senses. A sign and symbol can be a familiar smell or taste; sounds in your environment; a song playing on the radio or in your head; any form of animal, mammal, insect, or reptile that crosses your path; a formation of an angel, animal, or human face in a cloud; a rainbow in the sky; a found penny or feather; numbers on license plates, trucks, and buildings; or a phone call that comes in from an unknown source just at the time you are thinking of a departed loved one or Spirit Guide, or simply having a thought. These are all ways the spirit world communicates with us to let us know that we are never alone, to confirm thoughts, and to relay specific messages.

Synchronicity refers to a series of symbolic events that follow one another, that appear to be random but are not. I say "symbolic" because although something literal happened, there is also a deeper meaning to the event. For example, one day, thieves broke into my car and stole my purse and phone. Symbolically, the *car* is me, my *purse* is my identity, and the *phone* is my ability to reach out and ask for help. At the time this happened, this was one of three synchronistic events that occurred over a period of one week, and once decoded, I understood I was indeed in a period of identity transition and was being encouraged, to say the least, to reach out for help.

Once you learn how to recognize the signs, decode the symbols, and piece together their synchronistic meanings, it is like stringing together a sentence.

Let me give you an example of the way the spirit world communicates with me.

Over a period of one week, a series of signs, symbols, and synchronistic events occurred as a premonition of what was to come about.

I was scheduled to fly south to our home in Florida and was feeling very tired. It was as though someone or several people had their etheric cords attached to me, draining me, but I didn't know who. The flight went fine. During the trip, I asked for a sign, and as usual, my A-Team showed me a rainbow orb just before landing. This of course comforted me.

As we arrived at our home, it is customary to open the door of the outside shed to get our key. Inside, and for the first time ever, I was confronted with quite a bit of rat poo. Although it wasn't pleasant, I didn't fret because I had learned that a little sprinkle of cayenne pepper would ensure they would not return.

A few days later, I went into a supermarket to make a food order, and as I passed by the book section, one book about healing through natural remedies called out to me. I stopped, picked it up, and opened it to a random page. There on the page was a word relating to a personal situation in my romantic relationship, accompanied by suggested remedies.

A day later, my folks and I were leaving our home to go out for dinner, and sitting on our railing was a frog. In all my twenty years of coming to our home, never had I seen a frog; lizards always, frogs never.

Now let me preface the rest of the story by telling you what these signs mean to me.

A year prior, Pete and I had taken a time-out because of a problem he was not ready to take responsibility for. Just before the separation, Spirit sent me a sign. While sleeping alone, I was awakened by a pitter-patter in my bedroom. Although I am used to noises from Spirit, this noise sounded more like a rodent. At 1:00 a.m., as I lay awake with no lights on, I was able to see the little furry fella, and by 2:00 a.m., I managed to trap him in my closet. Of course, this led to a nauseating feeling on many levels: first, there was a rat in my bedroom; and, second, how was I going to get him out without my superintendent killing him?

Later in the morning, with the rat still in my closet, I spoke to Spirit, asking, "What does this sign mean?" In short, and to put it politely, they responded, "Boundary issues." I asked, "How can I release this rat without killing him?" They responded, "You can't without risk of getting bit." A very symbolic statement.

I held a mourning service for both rat and Pete.

Eight months after this incident and into our time-out, on a Sunday, it was Pete's birthday, so I asked my A-Team, "Should I write him an e-mail to wish him a happy birthday?"

As I sat in my Zen Den, my sacred space where I meditate, conduct readings for clients and myself, and hold our classes, I felt compelled to go outside to my patio, and so I did. Outside to the right (symbolic of the future), in the left-hand corner (symbolic of the past), on a stone sculpture I had made in 1992 named *Woman in Love,* was a dead squirrel cradling the woman's sculpted face.

This was a sure sign *not* to contact him. The past is dead.

Now let me explain to you how the *squirrel* symbol factors in. Just before we broke up, I had channeled a conversation with his Higher Self and passed-over stepfather to see what was going on. When I asked for them to give me a card to represent our relationship, I picked up my deck by Sonia Choquette called *The Answer Is Simple,* and the card they had chosen was a picture with two squirrels, with the words "Give more." I don't want to dis him, but the card spoke truth. Because I did not answer my phone and this was his only direct access to me, shortly after we broke up, he appeared on my patio to get my attention. The squirrel dying on my patio was a reference to the last place I saw him and where he expressed his "undying" feelings for me.

Fast-forward to being in Florida one month after his birthday, nine months into our breakup, and now face-to-face with this frog. The *frog* symbol also has meaning for me. Three years prior, I had bought Pete an African sculpture of a frog, and I used to kiss it every night, praying for his "princely" transformation. Now this frog was sitting on my home railing, refusing to budge.

So now let us string together the signs and symbols that came from synchronistic events.

The rat in my bedroom that crossed the boundaries and got killed in my closet symbolized what led to our demise and the need for change.

The squirrel that died on my *Woman in Love* sculpture outside on my patio, the last place where I saw Pete and where he professed his love, represented a few things, one being that, as I mentioned above, the past is dead.

And then eight months later, the draining feeling I felt leaving for Florida was Pete thinking of me and holding on tightly.

The rat droppings in the Florida closet were signs of life.

The issue page in the health book was our/his problem.

The frog on the railing, refusing to budge, was Pete himself.

Don't you know, within twenty-four hours of seeing the frog, I received an e-mail from him? This knight was ready to get back on his horse for happily ever after.

Rainbow Medicine

Build your data bank of symbols in your journal

Spirit communicates with us through signs, symbols and synchronicity so in order to understand this communication we must work on decoding and encoding our own personal data bank of symbols. This is what this exercise is all about. Begin a separate journal labeled *My Treasure Chest: Our Data Bank of Symbols*. As you engage in the various exercises in this book, you will uncover many of your symbols, so each time you identify them, mark them down in this journal.

We each have our own way of decoding symbols. It is important to develop your personal list so that you can decide on the meanings with your A-Team, and then, going forward, they will give you symbols you can understand.

The Exercise

Think about the signs and symbols you have received in the past, and the synchronicity you experienced, and make a list of them. Was it a penny, dollar bill, feather, insect, winged one, animal, rainbow, numbers, flower, color, song? What repeated, where and how? Go over each symbol and event, and write down next to each what you can remember you were thinking of at the time you found it, what was going on in your life, and what the personal meaning and significance each had for you. If you received an animal/insect/winged one/flower/crystal, go to a book to discover what medicine that species represents. If it is a song, Google the words, as somewhere in the song the message is there.

Symbols on Cards

If you use divination cards or just started using them with this book, recognize how symbols on the cards also factor in with the signs you receive. Sometimes a card will feature the same symbol you received in the past, and the word on the card will reveal the meaning and message behind the symbol. Here is such an example. Within the first year of my girlfriend's father's passing from cancer, she received an anonymous gift, a bouquet of her favorite yellow flowers. Months later, while I was playing with the Oracle deck *Talking to Heaven* by Doreen Virtue and James Van Praagh, a card flew out of the deck with the image of yellow tulips and the words *Now I have no pain*. Clearly, this was her father's way of letting us know the flowers were from him.

Coins

For the sake of the exercise, I will share with you some of my experiences with finding pennies and the interpretations I attach to that. For me, all found coins relate to *change* hence the symbol.

Penny with head facing up: Keep your head up, you are on the right path. Changes are occurring. Depending on how many pennies you find, this will give you further information about the change. One penny means new beginnings; two pennies mean partnerships and coming into balance; three pennies could refer to three people involved in the situation.

Some people are superstitious. For them, a penny with tails (head not facing up) may mean bad luck. For me, every found penny on my path has a message: sometimes it is in the date stamped into the coin; other times it is in the numbers they add up to. On a Canadian dime, the reverse (tails) has the image of the boat on water, which reminds me of the Six of Swords in the Tarot. This card means a lot of things, one being *the dead* and *River Styx*, as well as *cooperation needed to get to smoother waters*. Therefore, when I see this coin with tails up, I know it is a passed-over loved one trying to reach me with a similar message.

One night, I had a dream in which I parked my car. As I got out, next to the curb, I saw a few pennies. Since I am accustomed to picking up the pennies I see, in my dream I was about to do the same. But as I reached down to collect them, an energy zapped my hand away; it felt similar to that horrible feeling of banging the elbow's funny bone. In the dream, I received the message: "Some pennies you cannot pick up. Let go." When I awoke, I had the impression that the message referred to letting go of a few close people in my life; hence the number of pennies and the painful feeling associated with the dream.

Winged Ones and Insects

For a while, while working in session with clients outside on my deck during summertime, I would often, as in daily, have a gorgeous huge bumblebee come to visit. This bee would retreat under my deck, through the wooden slats just under my feet. I knew this to be one of my Guides, but, of course, I had no proof. One day, this happened in front of my then boyfriend, and he noticed a smiley face appear in the design on the back of the bee. So I pulled an Oracle card from Doreen Virtue's deck *Saints and Angels* to ask of this significance, and out came the card *Sign from Heaven*.

One year later, after *beeing* introduced to the bee and having lost the Strength card from one of my Tarot decks—this card represents my main protector Guide and Twin Flame, Francesco—another bee came to visit, in the same spot. This time, I watched as it crawled down through the same wooden slats. Don't you know, lying there was the Strength card I had lost the summer before! *"Honey, I am over here."*

Here is another beautiful story involving insect medicine and a message from Spirit.

In one of my teaching groups on healing and psychic mediumship development, we were having fun doing a psychometry exercise where we hold an object in our hand and receive information from it. The object we each were holding was a piece of paper with our names folded inside, not visible to the holder. When it was my turn to give the blind read, as I held the piece of paper over my Sacral chakra, I received the symbol of an *ant*. I felt this was a message about collaboration that she was receiving from the spirit world to make her joys and dreams come true. After I delivered the message and we saw this message was for her, she was relieved. To keep track of her readings, I sent the message via e-mail. A few days later, my student wrote back:

> Thank you so much! This is very reassuring and very motivating to continue pursuing my goals and dreams. Right before opening this e-mail, Spirit sent me a large picture of an ant, and when I read the part in your e-mail "In your Sacral chakra, I receive the *ant* symbol; for me, this tells me you have collaboration from the spirit world for going after your dreams," I knew it was their way of confirming the message that they are here with me, because I was stressing today about my vegetarian workshop.

One month later, while in class, I happened to have been blind reading myself, and in the meditation, I received this message: "And the ants go marching on and on." My student and I both looked at each other and laughed!

Witches, Goblins & Ghosts, Oh No!
Past Life Recall

To understand how past lives work, we must embrace reincarnation. The basic principle of reincarnation is: We have all been here, on the earth plane, before; and everything, our gifts and our suffering, is all related to past and future life situations and relationships.

Have you ever wondered why you feel an immediate closeness to certain people or an affinity to specific activities? Or why you have an aversion to certain people and/or activities? Deep-rooted agonizing feelings, such as suicide, missing someone, tremendous anxiety about engaging in certain daily life routines, or passion for specific people, ways of life, and activities can all be explained by both unresolved traumas and experienced gifts related to our past lives. But the interesting aspect to note here is that, despite not always having conscious access to past-life information, there is always a situation or theme in our current life that can explain these uncomfortable or overly comfortable situations, experiences, gifts, and moments.

Before I ever came to hear about the concept of past lives, I knew there was something more to what and why I was feeling a certain way. But Spirit, along with our Higher Self, works in mysterious ways, and we will only get little bits of the answers we seek at different moments on our path, when the time is right and we are ready, and then as we are ready for more.

Connecting the Dots

From the time I was a little girl, I believed more in what I couldn't see than in what I actually saw. I did not have imaginary friends that I could see, nor did I talk about my closeness with "my invisible loved ones"; it was just a knowing that they were part of everything that I did.

As a kid, I had a fondness for nature more so than people, and I found myself at my happiest when I was with and around trees, forests, flowers, animals, insects, water, sand (at the beach), water creatures, and seashells. I was most inspired when engaged with nature, color, and crafts. My favorite activities included the following:

> Creating art, making candles and dolls, and knitting and sewing clothing for them.

> Taking nature walks, collecting flowers and leaves to press, dry, and turn into stationery and bookmarks.

> Dressing up as a witch, cat, or Little Red Riding Hood for Halloween.

> Playing the lead role of Dorothy in *The Wizard of Oz*.

> Building houses out of my grandma's decks of playing cards.

> Assembling complex puzzles with my dad (our favorite pastime whenever I got sick, from the time I was three years old).

> A deep passion for collecting and trading pretty picture stationery with poetic, philosophical statements.

Looking back now on my child's play and what I loved the most, I find it uncanny how much their symbolism connects to my current work and life purpose. Since I have been taught by Spirit that the literal is symbolic and the symbolic is literal, this is a perfect example to demonstrate how much of what we experience can benefit from our decoding its meaning:

Candles (interdimensional light)

Dolls (souls)

Witches (medicine women)

Nature (spirit)

Cards/stationery with sayings (Tarot)

Puzzles (detective work)

Red Riding Hood (life path/spiritual journey)

Dorothy from *The Wizard of Oz* (searching for my way back home)

Wolf (teacher/pathfinder/trickster)

Cat (psychic/independent/entrepreneurial)

All my childhood pastimes and delights (as described above) were telltale signs of who I was in past lives, who I am in this one, and what is yet to come for me.

At around age eight, a few friends and I began to get together to communicate with Spirit. The motivation was usually a friend's birthday-party sleepover. It started with playing Light as a Feather, Stiff as a Board, which was when my friends and I had our first experience with levitation (as described in chapter 1). Soon after, we got involved with the Ouija board and had great experiences with that too.

But despite my no-fear approach with the spirit world while awake, it was an entirely different story when I was asleep. Whatever was going on during the day seemed to be minor compared to my sleep-time terrors.

From the time I was a young child, up until age eighteen and then again at twenty-one, I would have repeated nightmares of the devil possessing me. I often had to work very hard to bring myself out of physically frozen lucid dream states. I can best describe this as what you experience when you are lying in bed sleeping but feel like you are awake, and yet, when you try to open your eyes, to move, or to talk, you cannot. Sometimes this feeling is a result of the soul not yet fully returned and anchored in the body; sometimes it is a premonition dream of a "scary" event to come; sometimes it is a past-life recall; sometimes it is a Spirit visitation.

In my early thirties, I got seriously into dream interpretation, and it was *this* door that helped me to have conscious access to my soul's purpose, soul lessons, life lessons, past-life traumas, and present psyche.

During this time, I started reading and becoming familiar with Dr. Brian Weiss's work on past lives. Reading about this topic was the biggest help in "cracking me open" and enabling me to gain a new perspective on both my nightmares and dreams. After much detective work, I discovered that most of my nightly possessions were related to past-life karma and traumas, including ways in which I was murdered, killed myself, and otherwise died. These were all themes, life purpose, and life lessons playing out in my current lifetime.

Over the next few years, I uncovered close to twenty or more past lives through my dream state and while awake in meditation. Because of this, I have been able to put many fears, many suspicions, and much deep sadness to rest, which has enabled me to further embrace my gifts as a psychic medium and spiritual teacher, as well as to understand my affinity for my passions and certain social-justice causes.

Through much past-life recall, I discovered a consistent theme playing out, involving healing, abuse, and art. In many lifetimes, I have been a medicine woman of different sorts, and this explains my role today. I experienced much abuse, which explains much of my time in this current life spent helping abuse survivors thrive. Art was always my healing and teaching tool in some way, which explains why it still is today.

Without boring you with details of life themes and lessons, the following are some of the archetypal glimpses I have had of myself in past lives: A *Gypsy* genie from biblical times; an old witch cast out of society; an elf from pre-Atlantis times; a well-known female political figure and leader of a country; a farmer's daughter abducted as a child to marry into royalty, who witnessed the murder of her father; a Red Cross nurse for war veterans; a psychiatric nurse/doctor working in a psychiatric institution; a depressed housewife and mother who killed herself; a child sex slave in the Far East; an abducted teen who was raped and murdered; a young British boy who witnessed the police hauling away his father to prison; a religious Hindu man who lived in a temple; a black slave giving birth to a child she was not allowed to keep; an African child living a tribal life in Africa; and a Native American bride involved in a sacred ceremony.

No wonder the rainbow is such a significant symbol in my life!

With past-life recall, we are only given access to the lives which directly influence our current life. So an important question to ask when we have a dream or vision is, why now?

Every time I have had access to a past life, there was a reason why I had to know the information revealed to me, at that moment in time. Sometimes it was a premonition to give me insight into a future client and how to help him or her. Sometimes it was a warning not to get caught up in a situation, or a way to show me how to "play the hand" differently. Sometimes it was to remind me of an insecurity I needed to let go of if I wanted to move forward and upward.

Shining the Light on Our Fears Hiding in the Dark Brings Us Clarity

Another thing to remember about past-life recall and soul evolution is that, of course, we are never only the good guys and gals; for, in order to become whole and wise, we must experience both sides of the coin. Although I haven't had any dream recall of past lives where I was the perpetrator per se, my ability to have compassion and understanding for perpetrators in this lifetime comes from having been one in other lifetimes.

Similar to the information Brian Weiss channeled in *Many Lives, Many Masters*, my Guides also use the metaphor of the diamond to explain wisdom and soul evolution. Imagine the soul at inception and conception as comparable to a rough diamond; each life and experience is a facet carved into the diamond, shaping its unique beauty. The beauty of the diamond is in its reflective facets, as these nuances create the sparkle. Perspective, perspective, perspective.

Nightmares and nightmarish lucid dreaming are necessary to help us uncover soul lessons and traumas, for the sake of healing and moving forward on our path. So the next time you have a nightmare or an uncomfortable dream, thank your Higher Self and your Guides for shining the light on your fears hiding in the dark, and for bringing the clarity you need into the Light. Instead of shutting your fears out and allowing them to keep you stuck, embrace your nightmares as "eye-opener" gifts and take the necessary time to make sense of them, for when you do, they become your beacons of Light.

Rainbow Medicine

Past Life
Karma

Past-Life, Current-Life Karma

Here are some questions you can ask:

What life theme(s) did I bring into this lifetime?

What life lesson(s) did I bring into this lifetime?

What gift(s) did I carry over?

What pattern(s) of pain did I carry over?

Who in this life was a key figure in a past life?

What was our karmic tie?

Once again, choose two decks that you can use to intuit responses to these kinds of questions, and then, using the layering technique, get to work!

Clairvoyance

After you have answered every question and recorded it all in your journal, put twenty minutes aside and try this next exercise.

Play some soft New Age music, and while listening to it, close your eyes and ask your Guides to show you a childhood and past life memory (or several memories). You will see all this in your mind's eye, like a daydream. Don't think you're "crazy" if you get taken on another ride and receive fairytale images or anything that resembles your favorite characters in movies, television and books. Sometimes our guides do this to bypass the rational brain. Write down everything that you see. Once out of meditation, see if you can make out the symbolic value of the characters, storyline and life lesson, and if need be, pull cards to intuit answers.

Raindrops Keep Falling On My Head

A Visitation From the Recently Departed

There are different views regarding how long a departed loved one will take to bring back a message to loved ones on the earth plane. In my personal experience, this contact happens immediately, as the soul sticks around for a few weeks for closure purposes, and then stays longer if part of his or her job now is to be a Guide for a loved one on earth. I will share with you a touching story demonstrating proof of survival of the soul, how spirit communication works, and how parents still parent from the other side.

One day, while in Florida where I live part-time, I was in the bookstore, in my favorite section between metaphysics and psychology, reading a book on past lives written by Sandra Ann Taylor. (If you are interested in accessing your own past lives, this book, *The Hidden Power of your Past Lives,* comes with a CD, and her meditation works beautifully.) As I was looking for another copy to buy for a client, there was a guy standing in the same section, and he was reading also. When he overheard me asking the person who worked in this section to get me a second copy, he asked me about the book.

We began to talk, and after more than three hours of conversing, found out that everything in his life seemed to have aligned with everything in mine. All of our experiences resonated with similarity. We knew we were soul mates, and exchanged phone numbers and e-mail addresses.

"By the way, I am Miles," he said.

"I'm Leanne."

We hugged good-bye.

That night, I went into meditation to locate a past life that Miles and I had shared. It was amazing! In short, we worked together during the 1600s, at a psychiatric institution in the Netherlands where lepers were cast out of their families and sent to live.

In our shared past life, my soul mate was married and had two young children; I was single. He was a very bright man, ahead of his time, and so was I. Together, we came up with creative healing modalities integrating art therapy with the patients.

Don't you know that the night before I met my new friend/old soul mate, I had a dream that Sam, my male dog, had leprosy?! The *male dog* is my symbol for a loyal male friend, which Miles soon became.

When I returned to Montreal, where I live the rest of the time, we continued to talk regularly and share our daily experiences.

One morning while he was outside walking and talking to me on the phone, he said, "I see a woodpecker pecking away at a tree, what do you think this means?"

I responded, "A message that the rhythm of your life is about to change."

After we got off the phone, I went for a walk with my two dogs, and there in the forest, pecking away at a tree, was a woodpecker! Clearly this sign and premonition was for me too. As I said, from the moment we met, our lives seemed to be synchronized with similar life events following parallel lines.

A few months later, yet another synchronized event for us both occurred, with our respective experiences just a few days apart. His father was diagnosed with stage 4 lung cancer, and my ninety-seven-year old grandmother, the last one standing and still living independently with my uncle, fell and broke her hip. That weekend, when he called to give me his news, I shared mine.

Fast-forward a year and a bit later. His father passed, and within that same week, he texted to give me the news. Synchronistically, I had a dream that same week of my grandmother passing: She was all dressed up, going to a party. When I awoke, I wondered what that meant, as she was still alive.

Although I never had the honor of meeting Miles's father while alive on the earth plane, of course, I reached out to him on the other side and offered to be his messenger. Before I spoke to Miles on the telephone, I went into meditation to connect with his father, and these are the symbols I received:

I heard the song "Raindrops Keep Falling on My Head."

I saw a moon.

I saw a football.

I saw an icicle in the throat.

I felt a tightening in my upper chest and throat.

I felt tremendous love in my higher chest.

I saw a pair of dice in the sky.

I saw an hourglass with the number 10, in my left hand.

I saw a sunflower seed.

I saw a diamond and heard the song "Lucy in the Sky with Diamonds."

I then went to the cards, and several flew out. One read, "Apologies from the stars." Another, "Get it in writing"; another, "Wait patiently"; still another, "Communicate clearly, emotions are running high." The image on one of the cards was a person holding a sword pointing toward heaven, with a hawk on his arm. Another card showed a hand writing a letter.

The phone rang, and it was Miles. He began to explain to me what had happened. His dad died at night (hence the reason I saw the moon); before he passed, he had trouble breathing (hence the image I saw of an icicle and the sensation I felt in my throat and chest); Miles stroked his dad's chest, telling him he loved him (hence the loving feeling in my upper chest); and once his dad passed in his arms, Miles stayed with the body for several hours, and kept going out to the patio to look up at the stars (hence "Lucy in the Sky with Diamonds," a sign that his dad was with him, watching him do this).

Miles then began to tell me that his dad did not leave a will, and that there were now financial disagreements between Miles and his stepmother (hence the pair of dice in the sky; this is my symbol for *family quarrels,* as this was the symbol my grandmother gave me when she passed). Clearly, "Apologies from the stars" for not having things in writing was the message his dad was trying to relay through the cards that had flipped out.

The funeral service had yet to happen. It was scheduled for two days later, so Miles was in a rush to get off the phone to take care of things.

After we hung up, I got into my car and decided to take myself to my favorite metaphysical store.

Driving on the highway on my way to the store, with the sunroof open, raindrops began to fall onto my windshield and my head, and a huge ray of sunshine beamed down onto my Crown chakra. I pulled over and remained there for some time.

I texted Miles, "Is it raining where you are?"

He texted back, "No."

"Raindrops and sun on my windshield as I'm driving," I texted.

Realizing that the raindrops were a symbol from his dad—hence the song playing in my mind's ear and eye earlier—I began to speak telepathically with him. I felt him tell me to turn stations on the radio, and I landed on a station I never listened to. Two songs played back-to-back. I decoded what I was hearing and texted my friend with yet another message: "Your dad is telling me to tell you not to let your life pass you by."

I Googled the words of one of the songs, *Just the Two of Us* by Bill Withers. The words at the beginning of the song read, "I see the crystal raindrops fall, and the beauty of it all when the sun comes shining through … just the two of us, you and I."

Was this not exactly what was happening at that moment?! "Raindrops and sunshine!" Although I could relate to these words speaking of this beautiful moment between my friend's father and me as we communicated interdimensionally—and, quite possibly, I was his "first," as in spiritual contact—this song was also speaking about the tight father/son relationship they had and their last year together. So I texted Miles this new information, and when I began driving again and the sun was shining beautifully, with no more rain left on the windshield, the sensor wiper still turned on, and I knew it was his dad thanking me for relaying the message.

I arrived at the metaphysical store, hung out for a few hours, purchased some more card decks and crystals, and got back into my car to drive home. Despite it being a beautiful sunny day, more raindrops were sitting on my windshield.

On my way home, I got stuck in traffic and began to feel his dad's presence again. My head started to throb, and I felt him channeling through the back of my neck. His spirit was merging with mine so that I could receive more.

I said, "I know that Miles spent several hours with you once you passed. Can you give me a sign that only he will recognize?" He showed me a symbol that I could recognize: I was touching my Mala beads. In honor of my Guides and to bring me comfort, I wear this sacred object when I channel, so I interpreted this symbol he gave me to mean that perhaps Miles did something comforting and sacred with his dad's body. I also saw a spoon full of medicine, and to me that meant that it was the right thing to give him the medicine to kill the pain. Earlier that morning, Miles had told me that he felt bad that at the end of his dad's life, he was in a lot of sudden pain, and they had to give him a tremendous amount of morphine. This, I felt, was his dad telling me to tell his son not to feel bad about this. While receiving, I cried a lot. When we blend with Spirit, often the tears we experience are those experienced between the loved ones, and as the medium mediating the message, we will experience what they feel.

While stuck in heavy traffic on the highway, I then saw the number 44 repeated on every vehicle that was either in front or to the right of me. I also noticed the symbol of a *hawk*; at one point, my neck tightened, and I could only move it to the right and not the left. To me, *44* and *hawks* are symbols of Spirit presence, and when my neck locks left and moves only to the right, this is my symbol for *Don't look back; move forward look toward the future.*

When I arrived at a light, I opened the new deck that I'd purchased, and the first card that came to me had a picture of a woman with her hair tied up. That day, I had my hair in a high ponytail. The words on the card read, "Jewel within a teardrop: Appreciation, spiritual and emotional connection." This card tied in the symbols *diamond*, *raindrops*, *my teardrops*, and *our communication,* and I felt that my friend's father was thanking me for being a channel for him. Just as I made this connection, the windshield wiper moved again.

When I got home and later spoke to Miles, I explained everything I received from his dad. Although that morning he was not able to concentrate on what I was telling him, that evening, while talking on the phone, together, we made sense of the symbols.

The *headache* was his dad's brain tumors.

The *number 44* was the year his dad was born.

The *football* referred to his dad's having been a great football player back in the day. (I also believe it referred to the size of the tumors that riddled his body, which he was able to see only once he departed. Being the great team-spirited athlete that he was, he outlived what the doctors had originally predicted.)

The *hawk* is the bird Miles and his dad both associate with spirit communication, and it also represented his dad's football team.

That morning, when I received the symbol of the number 10 on the hourglass, I said, "Something is going to come to you sooner than later." Miles told me that during that day, one of his tasks had been to sell his car. He sold it for $10,000.00, a number that came to him intuitively, just as the number 10 had come to me.

The image I received of me holding my Mala beads, and the reference to the ritual of me praying as I touch these sacred *bodies* to bring me comfort, referred to how Miles spent the last few hours with his dad's body after passing, praying and repeatedly hugging him for comfort.

The sunflower seed and forward-moving neck pain related to his dad telling him that now that he had passed, it was time for Miles to pursue his dreams and plant seeds of happiness. I also believe it was dad's way of saying, "I am safe and made the transition."

Remember the woodpecker and the sign that Miles's life was going to take on a new rhythm? At the time, he was planning to return to school to pursue a master's degree in transpersonal psychology, but because his dad fell ill, he'd put that off, rented out his condo, and moved north of Florida to live with his dad and care for him. This was his dad's way of saying, "It's your time now, son."

And, finally, the cards that flew out earlier that morning—"Apology from the stars"; "Get it in writing"; and "Wait patiently"—all represented his dad's way of saying, "I am sorry I didn't write up the will and that you are going through this right now, but be patient, communicate clearly, and you will receive what I promised you."

Just before going to sleep, Miles, a talented writer, texted me: "Maybe, 'get it in writing' refers to me writing his eulogy, because that is what I am trying to do right now, but I am feeling blocked."

So I asked his dad for some guidance. When I pulled a card, it read, "Focus on substance." I texted the message to Miles.

He texted back, "He was both tenacious and unconditionally loving."

"Like the team-spirited football player that he was," I texted back.

Two days later, on the morning of the funeral, it rained where I was, and I smiled.

A day after that, while rummaging through his dad's belongings to take what he wanted back home with him, Miles texted me, attaching a picture of him proudly holding his dad's 1971 Football Trophy with the symbols of a *football* and *hawk.* The text read, "I thought you might like this."

Two months later, I received a text from my friend. Just as his dad suggested in his message advising Miles to not let his life pass him by and to "plant new seeds," Miles wrote to tell me he was celebrating his acceptance into the university graduate program he had put off a year prior.

His message was short and sweet: "I got in!"

Three months later, and within the first two hours of leaving home on his newfound journey, driving long distance, in his dad's car, to the university of his dreams, I heard from Miles.

This text read, "I'm on my way!"

He called right after the text. Of course, he was prompted by his dad to call me even if he didn't consciously realize it, and there waiting on the other line, so to speak, was Miles's dad, all choked up and super happy that his son was finally on his way!

From the very beginning of our phone conversation, I recognized I was channeling. So about ten minutes into our catch-up, I told Miles to hold on for a minute while I focused on receiving a message from his dad.

I said, "Your dad is showing me that he is communicating with you and sent you a message. He shows me a book with a white feather used as a bookmark, so this is my symbol for *angelic communication through a page in a book.*"

Miles said, "This morning, I went to one of my books, and on page 230, where the book opened to, there were two symbols I related to Dad and me: the *hawk* and *the Fibonacci spiral.*"

"He is saying that the message was his way of telling you that he is with you every step of the way, and your grandmother (his mother) is also there with him and us right now," I told Miles. And then I asked, "Does the number 23 mean anything to you?"

He said, "It's my dad's birthday."

I said, "He wants you to pay attention now to these signs. The next time you see the number 23, or 2:30 on a clock, this is his way of letting you know he is near. Remember when your dad passed, and I received the symbol of the *sunflower*?"

"Yes."

"Your grandmother is holding this sunflower, and she is letting us know that she was there to greet him when he transitioned, and she is here with you too, excited for your journey."

Miles was now making the links. "Within the last week of his life, with no strength left, I woke up one morning to a whole stack of books he'd somehow mysteriously gotten the strength to pick up and move to my bedroom. At the time, Dad said, 'You must have these books.' Somehow Dad knew I was going to go back to school, and this was his way of letting me know what he wished for me in his last days. Reading this page this morning made me think of him, and I wondered if he thought I was doing the right thing."

"Yes, you know you are. He is laughing now. Do you want to hear more?"

"Sure!"

"He is telling me, 'Vanilla is good.' This is my symbol for *boring is good,* so he is stressing to live by rules and self-discipline, because he shows me a ruler, and he is showing me a bottle of pills. Can you understand what he is referring to?"

"Yes, I can," Miles said. "I was concerned myself. He knows I have a friend who isn't a very good influence, and he knows I have been thinking about this lately because I will be living near him. It makes sense that he is saying to stay away because this is exactly what I was telling myself."

"If you have a question for your dad, ask it telepathically, and I will share with you what I receive," I said.

"Okay."

"Ask away."

Just as I said that, I immediately received the following symbolic information in this order:

The image of a diamond, which is my symbol for both *marriage* and *doubt.*

The image of *monkey on your back.*

The planet Saturn, which for me is about *structure, boundaries,* and *business.*

A three-to-five-year plan, with the message about *pathworking* and following the *signs,* one step at a time.

So I told this all to Miles, and then I asked, "By any chance, did you ask how this journey was going to unfold? Because you are not certain if you will stay there and what will come about."

"Yes, to be exact, I asked if I will find the woman of my dreams and get married over there."

"Ha ha! That's why I saw the diamond immediately, but then I saw that this is a monkey on your back, which means this heavy load is not what you need at this time, and this is emotionally weighing you down. Get with your program; it's *your* time now!"

As we spoke for around one hour during his road trip, Miles saw three symbols that identified that his dad was with him every step of the way. The first was a huge *snake* that crossed his path as he began his drive.

I said, "Transformation, healing, studying, teaching; you are studying to become a healer as you heal, and this is the last day of your old life and the first day of your new life."

The second omen he saw was a *hawk* perched on a lamppost as he passed the airport where he used to fly out with his dad, along the street where he was now driving to attend school. That he easily connected to.

Having the sense that we were going to end our call, I picked two more cards from Doreen Virtue's deck *Magical Unicorns,* so that his dad could say good-bye. The first read, "Hello and good-bye"; the second, "Your parents love you." Just as I said this, Miles laughed and exclaimed, "My mom is beeping through on the other line, and I just arrived at a motel where I will stay tonight. Oh my God, it's called *Loves*!" Together, the cards provided the third omen.

As I mentioned, I never had the honor of meeting Miles's dad on the earth plane, but was granted this pleasure and blessing at the start of my friend's new life. This story is written and shared to honor this father/son relationship, to honor the remarkable spirit this man showed for his will to live and love, and to honor my friend and soul mate, who is an incredible example of service based on unconditional love. I am grateful to know a person with these remarkable qualities; I am grateful for our friendship, and for being a channel for such a high-vibrating departed spirit. Thanks for letting us know that we are never without the ones we love, lose, and miss.

[Postscript: Miles was the first person I gave a card reading to (besides myself), and in this reading I shared with him that he was indeed going to be studying in this new location despite his uncertainty. Miles was contemplating this decision a year prior to our meeting but didn't have the courage to make the leap. Due to unforeseen plans (his dad got sick), he had to postpone for yet another year. Eighteen months later, just like dad, he made the transition. Makes us wonder if dad "moving" had to happen for son to "move."] A few months into his move, Miles bought a home with the number 23 in the address.

Rainbow Medicine

Music & Book
Divination

Clairaudience: Message in a Bottle

Call on someone in spirit, like a parent, grandparent, child, pet, or friend. Ask them to give you a song in your head as a way to relay a special message of guidance to help you on your path. First thing in the morning when you wake up, the song in your head is the message. When you do receive the song, it is important to Google the lyrics so you can read the words and decode the message. Do the same anytime during the day and listen to what you receive then google the words.

Using Books as Oracles

You can also try this exercise: Ask your loved ones, or someone in particular on the other side, for an answer to a question you have. Go to a book you feel called to that is appropriate to answer your question, and open to a page. Usually, your eye will be drawn immediately to the place on the page where the answer lies, if it doesn't don't fret, somewhere on this page you will intuit the answer to your question. You can also try this exercise with eyes closed, and when you open to the page, use your hand to feel the energy where the answer lies, the hottest spot is usually it. Then open your eyes and read!

Casper the Friendly Ghost

Waking Visitations
A.K.A. Hauntings

A waking spirit visitation is similar to a dreamtime visitation except that you are receiving the information while awake. Dream and waking visitations are the most effective ways your A-Team members get your attention about matters in your life.

Waking visitations are also referred to as hauntings and are characterized by physical manifestations such as noises, familiar scents, cold or warm breezes of air, movement of objects or shadows, lights flickering, mist, vortexes, spirals, sparkles, tiny orbs in the air that appear like computer dots, receiving phone calls, texts, emails and songs, visitations from insects, birds and rodents, a spider web feeling on you, and faces that appear closeup. Let's face it, if you were dead and needed to get your loved one's attention, you too would *bug* them to notice you. As we write this chapter, two flies buzz around me, and a third joins in.

Spirits are always blending with us, entering and influencing our thoughts, bodies and actions, and will use physical sensations (clairsentience) to get our attention; when you are developing your mediumship abilities, you will recognize these sensations and learn how to decode these messages. Some of the quickest, most effective ways spirits get my attention is by squeezing my heart, giving me a head rush, flicking my nose, making me sneeze, touching coded body parts, and sending me smells. When a physical medium gives a reading, there are typical physical sensations we will experience that are similar to manifestations people describe in hauntings, they are:

- Sudden lightheadedness, forehead and eye pressure, top of the head and temples tingling
- Ear pressure change and tingling
- Hard time breathing in the chest area
- Stomach discomfort, gas, diarrhea
- Body tingles and goosebumps
- Sneezing, yawning
- Throat closing or opening, slight tonal change
- Body temperature fluctuation-very cold, very hot, chills, white fingertips, burning hands
- Eyes burning, watering, a need to cry, crying, laughter, sudden disorientation
- Physical smells and tastes
- Facial ticks, facial hair sensing, itches on face, head, body
- Pain and pleasure sensing
- Transfiguration: Your physical appearance changes or someone's you are looking at does. You may also feel the person over you like you are wearing them as a costume or they are wearing you. For example, when you channel a big man or tiny woman you may feel their superimposed body expand or contract over and with yours, and sense what they are wearing, facial features, and problems they died from.

When I'm working, these sensations become amplified because I allow my clients above to merge with me, and when I'm at rest, only my A-Team have permission to touch me.

That being said, physical manifestations from family and friends should not feel scary, on the contrary, their communication is intended to make you feels safe. The following three stories demonstrate this heavenly experience.

The King

On a hot and sunny Spring Saturday, Pete, his longtime friend, Ernesto, and I spent the afternoon talking and eating on an outdoor terrace on the Maine, in Montreal. I shared with Ernie the mediumship work I was doing and he recounted a story about his friend who had passed and later came to visit as a bird. With no shame about believing in spirit and life after death, we had a laugh as he recounted verbatim the conversation he had with his dead friend, Vinnie, the now bird.

Six months later in the Fall, Ernie fell and hurt his back. This accident prompted a visit to the hospital. Although it wasn't discovered at first, months later, he was diagnosed with fourth stage lung cancer. Wintertime for Pete was all about visiting Ernie in the hospital with requests to end his life. To say the least, it was a hard time for both.

Nearly one-year later to the day the three of us shared that sunny Spring afternoon on the terrace shooting the stars, Ernie passed and Pete got the text. That afternoon, while taking a lunch break outdoors, Pete was nearly hit over the head by a 'passing' bird. It had been months since he and I had spoken, but on that evening, he called with the news of Ernie's passing, and I said, "He is trying to get your attention, did you see a bird today?" Of which he responded, "Funny you should ask," and began to recount his story along with the many other signs.

The following morning was my turn.

I had the most unexpected, one-of-a-kind experience outside on my tree-filled forest deck, drinking a cozy cup of coffee. After a few enchanting moments mesmerized by the trees, I was prompted to turn my head left and there standing next to me at eye level on a pillow less than two feet away was a baby blue jay, a bird that holds much significance in my life. For twenty minutes he stayed with me, then flew directly to the branch in front. An omen I was able to decode.

A few days later was Ernie's funeral and just as we were heading out the door, Ernie impressed his thoughts on mine, I said to Pete, "I am going to take my phone, maybe Ernie will appear on camera."

Ernie was an old school Italian *wise guy* who looked like Elvis, worked most of his adult life around music as a white glove waiter in Las Vegas resorts, had a great sense of humor, and loved to share his stories. When I saw him lying in his open casket, I telepathically said, "You are half the size, I don't remember you so thin!" Once seated, I snapped a couple of photos and overheard Ernie whisper in my ear, "Veal parmigiana."

The following morning when I reviewed the photos, next to his coffin and staring at his body was a large black shadow of a heavier set Ernie, the way I remember him. Not only did he provide me with his proof of survival photo at his funeral but he also responded to my comment about his weight. Seeing his big shadow compared to his frail body was his funny way of letting me know, "I hear you and I'm eating well!"

Red Romeo

One night at a spirit circle I said to the group, "There is a hot male biker here who died on his motorcycle. He wants his girl to know that he still considers himself your boyfriend and is very much around and in love with you." Pink jumped up, "That's me!"

Pink and Pat had been high school sweethearts who lost touch and re-united years later with plans to get serious. One day, he disappeared and Pink never heard from him again. The night I met Pat in a spirit circle, he let Pink know that the signs she had been receiving for years were indeed from him. Pink, a medium herself, *knew*, but, like all of us, was waiting for that special confirmation.

A couple of months later, we introduced Pat to our class as our anonymous ghost teacher who the students blind read; this means no one knew who they were reading, all they knew was that they had been assigned a target to describe. Everyone read him intimately, and one drew his portrait perfectly. After we posted the readings on our password protected website for Pink to read and validate, she responded:

> I can't wait to thank everyone in your group for the amazing work they have done for me, all the readings are so accurate and loving. I love this drawing, it does exactly look like Pat with his long curly hair and beautiful gentle eyes. Everyone seems to have picked up the woods at night, then an injury to his eye, a road accident, pain in the face.... stunning. Yes, he does love women, such a romantic guy!

> But the most amazing thing happened again this evening, I printed the reading, sat down to read it again, looked straight into Pat's eyes on the drawing, then looked up to see what song was play-ing on the TV, it was called "Eyes of the Night" by Hennie Bekker and Dan Gibson. Well, I was stunned, as if this sign was not enough, a pack of wolves started howling so loud during the song. Unbelievable, unbelievable.

Shortly after, Pink joined the *Whitewolf Pak* and on our first day of class as we gathered outside on my deck to discuss our plans for the school semes-ter, a red Cardinal flew onto a branch in front of us to let us know *Spirit is around*. Wowed and wondered, we asked, "Who is the red Cardinal?" We went around the circle and each received a piece of the puzzle; all picked up Pat making a grand entrance to welcome the love of his life. Minutes later when we returned inside to begin our channeling, Pink gave me a gift, a photo of Pat wearing a *red* shirt.

Holding Onto Heaven

This story shares how my former boyfriend got through to me. Since Nik passed, he has been a key guide on my A-Team leading me every step of the way. As a result of my learning to speak Spirit we have been able to continue our friendship and work together.

Nik and I lost touch in the early 2000s. In 2008, I received a comforting dream visitation by a spirit showing me the image of footsteps attached to mine. When I awoke, I knew this was significant information but I had no idea who it was from. This prompted the visit to the transmedium we write about in the prologue.

Years later, in 2013, just as I was coming out of the spiritual closet, I visited another medium who said, "You have a male friend here, tall and athletic, he says you were a good friend to him and he is now your guide." Thrown and perplexed by this information but silently knowing there was someone on the other side wanting my attention, I responded, "I don't have any good friends who are dead who would want to be *my* guide" and she replied, "Yes, you do."

When I first began learning how to speak Spirit I used a lot of different kinds of cards and a day or two later, I was prompted to go to the *Dollar Store* and play with an alphabetical children's flash card deck. To test it out, I asked to spell out the name of one of my pet babies, and when I shuffled, the letters C.L.O.E appeared. I nearly dropped the deck out of shock and bought it. That evening, I picked up the alphabet deck again, and when I shuffled and pieced together the cards he showed me to describe himself, it hit me," Nik, is this you?!"

"Yes!"

We cried and cried, and still do today. A few days later, I asked Nik to show me yet another sign and since he was a professional athlete, I hoped he could reference his sport. Later that afternoon, my mother and I drove to a shopping mall and just as we were pulling up, we decided instead to go to the movies. Halfway into the film, the main character is seen watching a sporting event on television, Nik's sport. I freaked, "Nik, you're dead!"

Since then, we continue to have lots of fun playing and teaching together in our development classes, which is no surprise because while Nik was alive, he was a terrific athlete, teacher, coach, and performer.

Two years later, in 2014, in one of our classes where Nik was teaching as the blind target for everyone to read, one of our students delivered and confirmed the piece of the puzzle I had been waiting for all these years, "I see footsteps of a strong male energy who holds you close, I feel him, and his embrace of you is, umph! Sexy!"

> *All these years*
> *I've been chasing down the answers*
> *I was here, always tracing out your shadows*
> *I need you tonight*
> *Lights fade but I won't let them*
> *I'm holding onto heaven*

-"Holding Onto Heaven"
Foxes (2014)

What To Do If You Meet the Dark

Although we share friendly visits from the Light, mischievous spirits a.k.a. tricksters also pop their heads in from time-to-time to trip you up and heal you hard. A visit from them is actually an act of intervention orchestrated by your A-Team to help you hit rock bottom so that you may finally heal. Don't worry yourself sicker should you find yourself amidst such a haunting experience because dark energy is simply unhealed consciousness with an offensive but often good sense of humor. That is, if you can find a way to laugh after you cry. Monsters do their greatest damage through your mind. If you feel your are being haunted by a dark visitor rather than a loving one, the spiritual reason for this occurrence is to help you address an issue in your life you are here to heal, learn, and grow from, it is connected to your life purpose and ancestral lineage.

We are each telepathic and a sponge, always picking up on the thoughts and feelings of others, below and above, and often mistaking them for our own. Ever wonder why you don't like to be around certain people and crowds? It's because dissonance can be overwhelming. Ever wonder why you can't stop an addiction? It's because spirits with similar issues and addictions attach to you so you are not only dealing with yours. In our mediumship training classes, we teach the importance of knowing your self, heart and thoughts because when we work as mediums we are agreeing to share our consciousness and vessel with another and what this means is, we are open to blend our thoughts and bodies with others. But whether we, as non mediums, agree to this sharing and blending or not, it is occurring for we, as energy, are each a pinball in a pinball machine.

Much like abuse in all of its forms, an unhealed consciousness, above or below, will try to control and separate you from loved ones and they manifest their power through your repetitive self-defeating thoughts and behaviors contrary to your chosen values. In Part III, you will learn how consciousness attracts consciousness and ways to heal consciousness, for when we hide from or deny our fears, we attract them. If you find yourself haunted by dark thoughts, begin with Chapter 2's exercise *Meet Your A-Team* to speak with them about the issues they want you to work on. If your issues center around relationships, follow up with Chapter 9's *Decoding Relationship Patterns*. Once you have a good idea about the major theme(s) you are here to heal, visit Chapter 13's exercise *Group Chakra Therapy* and conduct a medical intuitive body scan to diagnose the consciousness/storyline in each of your chakras. Last, engage in the individual chakra therapy exercises in the order you feel drawn. If you still need help, seek professional guidance from a medium and transpersonal therapist who can help you to address and heal the issues at the source of your haunting.

We must never forget that we are each surrounded in the Light by our A-Team members who love and support us, and there are many Guardian Angels we can call upon for extra support when we need them, you don't need to know who they are for them to love and protect you. The next time you feel a spirit manifestation and are not sure if you should trust it, you should because chances are, a loved one is trying to reach you; that's why you are reading this book. Don't ever let the dark cover up your connection to your light.

Part II

Rainbows
In Session

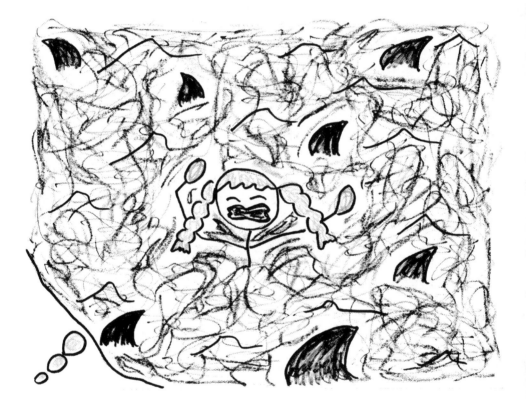

When Someone Wants A Reading, Not Therapy

For Us, It's Hard to Separate

While working as a therapist, teacher, guide, and psychic medium, I am quite attuned to those whom the spirit world sends our way. Our work here is orchestrated from the other side.

In our transpersonal empowerment practice where we blend therapy and mediumship, we work with individuals, couples, and families who come to us for channeled therapy, personal and professional pathworking, spiritual guidance, psychic detective work, and to learn how to speak Spirit. The intention of our service is to help you communicate and heal with your A-Team so that you may live your happiest life. The following is a conversation I had with Spirit for a client in her late forties who contacted me long distance for a telephone reading in order to gain insight into an intimate relationship with a married friend.

Conversation with Spirit

What is her goal in coming to me?

To let go of and end the unhealthy relationship. To move forward from this crisis and let go of carrying this weight on her shoulders, victimizing herself by her worries. Although she is fearful, she wants to gain clarity, take control of her life, and leave the past behind so that she can address her dreams and desires.

Tell me about her challenge.

She is having difficulty with someone who is trying to control her. She's confused; she doesn't know what she wants, so she cannot lead herself out of this. She needs to assume her authority. She wants to begin anew and take an empowered stance, but she hangs on because she is afraid to let go 100 percent and be "alone." She will eventually prioritize her needs and leave this relationship. It is the right thing for her to leave this situation behind, to work hard at healing and loving herself, to stop focusing on what she has lost, and to refocus on what she has gained and what has yet to come into her life. She needs to start learning her lessons and doing what is right and fair for her.

What are some of her life lessons that she is currently learning through this relationship?

She is learning about patience and how to have faith to be herself in a relationship. She is learning about what kind of relationship is right for her, as well as how to let go of relationships. She is learning how to communicate clearly and directly in her conversations with others, avoiding manipulative, indirect, and guilt-producing statements. She is learning how to look deeper into her patterns and how to let go of people and situations that disempower her. She is learning how to overcome worry and heartbreak, and how to have faith and trust in herself.

What are her patterns in relationships?

Shame: she has an overwhelming sense that who she is isn't good enough, so tell her she is good enough! She doesn't believe that a deeply satisfying relationship is possible; she needs to believe that there isn't anything she cannot achieve if she has patience and faith in herself and the universe. She needs to let the universe know she means business, and with patience, her desired outcomes will occur.

What needs to be healed? What is the best way to work on breaking this pattern?

She needs to heal her issues around having a stable committed relationship, the concept of forever, and being patient. She is in denial about childhood issues that are affecting her relationships. She is afraid of what it means for her to be a *woman*, a *wife*, and a *mother*. She doesn't know what she wants; therefore, she cannot move forward to achieve her desires. In order for her to free her heart and be open to a healthy and stable committed relationship, which is what she wants, she will need to unlock her heart and face her emotional pain and traumas; these have been left unresolved, going back to childhood. Until she can have a satisfying and stable relationship with herself, she will struggle to have it with others. But understand that with each relationship, she *is* learning how to love herself.

You need to tell her: "Let go and seek help; agree to leave the past behind and change your thinking from being negative and fearful, to being positive and solution oriented. Move forward, and learn about yourself, your emotions, your intuitive side, and your fears. Focus on what makes you happy. You need to make a decision to stop being afraid to prioritize yourself, your well-being. It's time to move forward, look ahead, and make some plans as to what you truly desire. And then, be patient and wait for the opportunities to arrive. Prioritize healing your heart and gaining clarity over what you want in life."

What kind of guy is a good match for her?

A man who does not need to focus on pain; someone who is patient and solution oriented, who moves forward, has faith in relationships, and who loves her and doesn't try to control her or one-up her. She needs to recognize this pattern in herself as well.

How can I best help her? And are there any last comments for me?

Tell her that she has reached the end, and she needs to accept this ending and do what is right for her, which is to start over and learn what is necessary so that she can manifest a happy and stable home environment. She will not get what she wishes for in this relationship: he will not leave his wife. Tell her to let go of her negative thinking. She needs to gain clarity on what she wants to create: Does she want to be a wife/mother? Right now she is uncertain.

Her path to healing is to stop crying over what she has lost in life, and, instead, to focus on what she has gained from every relationship. She is not a victim, and there are opportunities that need her attention. It will serve her well to stop worrying about what she lacks and stop focusing on her fear of the future; instead, she needs to tell a different story about herself, one that is solution oriented.

Tell her this: "Don't be afraid to go your own way. Stand up for yourself, set your boundaries, develop your self-confidence, and gain clarity over this experience. We are with you, giving you courage and strength to start over and do *your* thing. Recognize what it is you desire, what you want, and make plans to achieve your goals. Work hard, stay focused on healing, and be patient with yourself. We love you."

All Relationships Are Gifts, When We Can Identify Our Lessons

Romantic relationships teach us about commitment, commitment to ourselves and to another. Relationships involve two energies coming together; this may start out as complementary but then at some point change, with the energies working against each other. Being in a committed relationship is a lifestyle choice that requires both partners to divide their energies so as to come together with common interests and shared values, visions, and goals, and yet maintain individuality so as to each be responsible and accountable for their own health and well-being. Relationships teach us about how we honor ourselves, our emotions, and our intuitions—and how we do not. Ultimately, relationships teach us about self-love. How we love ourselves directly affects how we love others, and how we let others love us directly affects how we love ourselves.

The people we choose to have as romantic partners are mirrors of our inner selves: they show us where we are on our path of self-growth and which life lessons we are learning.

It's not always easy to perceive what is going on when we are involved in a romantic relationship. We each may find ourselves asking some or all of these questions: Am I really "in love," or am I simply just working through a deeply rooted issue? Am I simply avoiding a certain potential mate because I don't feel good enough to accept true love?

If a relationship causes us to close rather than open our heart, it's time to reexamine that relationship's role in our life. If a relationship causes us to open our heart but at the same time deeply challenges us or has an "expiration date," it may be an intuitive calling to put a stop to a relationship or relationship pattern, and to transform the self to better our relationships with others, and, most importantly, with ourselves—for the way we are with ourselves and the way we love ourselves directly affects the way we are with and the way we love another.

Whether you are in an abusive relationship or a rewarding one, what are you presently learning about yourself? If you are in a relationship where you and your partner hold opposite viewpoints, misunderstandings occur often, manipulation, low self-esteem, and overall disharmony are increasingly apparent, it is possible you are learning how to overcome confrontation and defensiveness through unconditional love of yourself and others. Unconditional love does not mean giving permission to let others hurt you, or for you to hurt others or yourself. It means that sometimes the harder path is the highest path: that of letting go of the fight and the resistance so that each person may take responsibility for his or her own healing and growth. So maybe you are learning how to flow through the ebbs of life instead of fighting the currents. Perhaps you are learning how to let go of whatever and whomever no longer serve your growth.

When loving ourselves *well* becomes our motivation for releasing fear and pain from our heart, then we are acting and attracting from a place of Love and self-love, and not reacting and attracting from a place of Fear and self-sabotage. When we make choices and act from a place of Love centeredness, the doors that open bring us opportunities that are in alignment with our passion, our life force. When we react and make decisions from a place of Fear centeredness, more often than not, we perceive ourselves as victims, and then we attract rescue scenarios. Although it may be the same lesson we are here to learn, whether it comes from Love or Fear, the teachers and mirrors we choose and attract along our path, coupled with the type of student we are, affect the style and quality of our education and overall well-being and well-doing.

So, as my Guides say, "Choose wisely."

Rainbow Medicine

Decoding
Relationship Patterns

While listening to meditative New Age music, open your journal and create a list of all your significant past exes, along with your current mate (if you are in a relationship).

Choose two decks of cards you are familiar with and that you can intuit action and behavior from. I like to use a Rider-Waite Tarot deck combined with a therapeutic text-based deck for this exercise.

Before you begin, make a list of questions. Some questions that I recommend appear below:

Why did I like this person?

What was my pattern in this relationship?

What did I learn from this relationship?

What was I in denial over?

What was my gift?

What was his or her gift?

Why did it end?

What did my heart want?

What did my head want?

What did my actions demonstrate?

Use the layering technique, and ask the same set of questions about each partner. Pay attention to the sentences you hear in your head, and also to the words and images on the cards that you draw from the decks. Write these messages down. Once you have answers in regard to each person on your list, see if you can recognize patterns that cause you pain, and those which cause you joy. When you can recognize where and why you get stuck, you can finally learn the lesson and move on.

When A Non-Believer Becomes A Believer

The Healing Divorce Can Bring

Sometimes when couples come to see me, it is because they are ready to see a truth they have been denying, and they need to acknowledge that in order to move forward. They are ready for help to work on their relationship and improve harmony by becoming aware and letting go of behaviors, thinking patterns, and people that longer serve their lives. Sometimes letting go of the partner is what is needed. Sometimes couples come to see me as a way to blame, shame, and change the other—"If only he did this"; "If only she said that"—but soon enough, each realizes that in order to heal, both must turn inward and take stock of their own well-being and -doing, because the blame-and-shame game only serves to cover up each person's light and truth. Sometimes one in the partnership is ready for this, and the other is not. Whether healing happens in tandem or separately, the process involves each individual be willing to become responsible and accountable for exfoliating layers of darkness, removing the lens of denial, overcoming insecurities, and shining the light on that which remains hidden and destructive.

Solving conflicts through patience and gradual work achieves great rewards, for it takes courage and patience to shed old belief systems that keep us in states of denial, fear, anger, resentment, loneliness, shame, and guilt. The ideal goal is to befriend our fears, for when brought into balance, they become our beacons of light. We attract what is contained within us for the benefit of healing, and it is our triggers that make us aware of our unresolved issues. Once we unpack the triggers, we shed pain and shame, and then we make room to experience greater joy, health, and peace.

Without crisis to force our hand to purify and change, we become lazy, bored, complacent, and stagnant. Embracing the healing process means putting ourselves on a path that encourages us to engage in activities that contribute to our holistic well-being and well-doing. Ask yourself, How well are you *being* and d*oing* with yourself? How well are you *being* and *doing* with others? How you answer this question will tell you if you are in the flow of life or in resistance to it. *Being in the flow* means we are aware of and accountable for how we affect the whole: *being in resistance* means we are in denial.

When we allow ourselves to face our traumas and fears with the intent to let go, forgive, heal, and love, we allow ourselves to learn something new and to grow into greater self-awareness and self-love. When we approach healing with bitterness and resentment, we are closed to its wonder. When we open to and embark on the journey of self-discovery, we teach ourselves how to be empowered actors who are able to rise above challenges and understand how they serve only to catapult us each into greater spaces and places, both internally and externally. Every relationship carries with it a gift—some form of teaching, wisdom, learning, or benefit. When we walk away from relationships feeling victimized, it means we haven't learned the lesson(s) and received the gift(s).

Healthy living and love reside in the Heart chakra, which is the center of the seven main chakras in the body, and it is where *truth* lies (an oxymoron). When anger, resentment and sadness are not dealt with, they cloud the upper truth chakras, which prevents us from speaking our truth (Throat chakra), seeing our truth (Third Eye chakra), and connecting to truth (Crown chakra). This blocked energy also creates a cyclical downward motion, reinforcing power and control issues, i.e., shadowboxing with the "other" (Solar Plexus chakra); addiction, i.e., where, who, and what we turn to as a form of pleasure seeking that never feeds the soul (Sacral chakra); and low self-worth that generates fear-based manifestation(s), i.e., patterns of suffering (Root chakra).

In order to come into *truth,* we must clean house in our heart. The greatest gift we can give to the world is our health. To decode our relationships based on these gifts is to recognize the silver linings in the clouds, release anger and resentment from the heart, celebrate our learning and growth, attract more joyful experiences, and clear the way for healthier living and love.

Here is one such story.

One year after I had been counseling his wife Willa (age fifty) and daughter Sophie (nineteen), Wesley (fifty-two) came to see me for what began as couples and family counseling but then turned into individual counseling.

When he called me for his first session, I responded, "What took you so long?" I had the premonition dream of him on my couch eight months prior. During this telephone call I asked him, "What is your dream?" He responded, "To live in the country with horses." I said, "Hold on to that dream."

Wesley, a clear thinking and mind-centered man, was "accused" by Willa and Sophie of lacking emotion, whereas both women were "accused" by Wesley of being overly emotional and heart-centered. He felt they lacked the clear-thinking ability to solve problems, and they felt he lacked heart when approaching conflict. Talk about halves making a whole—*not!*

Wesley began with me in session as a nonbeliever in the spirit world, which Willa explained was one of the reasons that contributed to the couple's alienation over time. The two women were believers.

Wesley and Willa were together for nearly twenty-five years but lived in separate bedrooms for ten of them. One year into his therapy, an affair came to light.

Although Wesley had always suspected, when he actually found proof, he still wanted to save the marriage and rekindle the romance. Willa, on the other hand, did not but was unable to let go of Wesley, given their length of time together.

During the first reading I ever gave Wesley, Spirit advised him that the only way he was going to be able to move forward was to access his heart and feel it beating once again. Wesley's favorite statement used to be, "I am content being in flatline mode; to me, it means that all is fine."

I didn't believe him for a second, and in one of our sessions, psychically, I saw a red X marked over his Throat chakra. I was baffled by the vision, and when the session ended, I asked Spirit to explain to me what I saw. I felt my Guides tell me to pick up a certain book that I had about the chakra system (thanks, Cyndi Dale!), and opened it up to a "random" page. Because I am comfortable with my Spirit Guides using this form of divination with me, I wasn't surprised to find the answer at the bottom of the right-hand page: "When you see a red or black X over a chakra, it means that this person doesn't believe that they deserve love, money, or respect." A confirmation that Wesley needed to start releasing and to speak from his heart.

As a result of the combination of stress in the home environment and a violent incident at his workplace, Wesley went on burnout. He developed high blood pressure, depression, and Post-Traumatic Stress Disorder (PTSD), and was required to go on medication. It is important to note that two years prior, Willa was on burnout, which was why she came to see me. Willa had only recently returned to work when all hell broke loose with Wesley. So, coupled with a pending divorce, we now had another issue on our plate: a career change for Wesley.

It is never easy for anyone to leave a marriage, especially when partners are financially dependent on each other and own a house together. Both explained that if they sold the home, neither would have enough money to buy a new home, and this was one of the main reasons they stayed together. I, on the other hand, loved this family like my own, but every time I tried to encourage them to work through their issues, Spirit told me to butt out.

Eventually, the strategy we took in session was for both to bring everything to light. Since they had been "roommates" for this length of time, we gambled on the hopes that each would accept the other's choice to pursue different romantic partners but be able to continue to live under the same roof, at least until both felt more certain about their respective directions.

Following these decisions, on the day of New Year's Eve, Wesley and I had a session together, and as a gift, I channeled a conversation for him. It is important to note that it didn't take long for Wesley to become a believer in the spirit world, because every channeled conversation we had in session was followed with a "coincidental" confirmation the following day.

Here is how the channeled conversation went, beginning with the opening statement from Spirit:

It's time to clear out the old and have confidence to walk your walk and talk your talk. Let your past go, and know that you deserve to be abundant in all ways. Keep your sense of humor. Take the necessary time to reflect on yourself and your situation in and with the family, and learn from this experience. Believe in yourself, because anything is possible, so focus on what makes you happy, and make that your career. Don't be afraid, allow yourself to feel good and receive joyfully.

What is our goal with Wesley right now?

To help him transition from past, to present, to future. It's over. He has a new opportunity to begin again, with much experience behind him to show him who he was and why he did what he did. You explained to him the image of death in a coffin related to a past-life issue he brought into this life.

[In a past life, Wesley lost his mother at a young age, and in meditation, I had seen him peer into the coffin and say, "Mama." It is possible that I was his mother in this past life, as it was me in the coffin, which explains my maternal instinct toward him. But given that Wesley isn't the emotional/nostalgic type, I told him that whether it was me or not, this is where his deeply rooted abandonment issues lie, and why he feels a deep calling to take care of "wounded" females. Up until this point, these emotions were shrouded in expressions like, "When I make a commitment, I keep it, for better or for worse." It is important to note that in this lifetime, Wesley was adopted.]

It is this pattern of ruin that he needs you to help him heal. He is sad, grieving, but new opportunities await him, when he is ready to look forward instead of backward. He is still very caught up in the illusion of "What's going on?" and the one-upmanship between him and Willa. It's time to feed his inner child with play. You are here to help him return to his life, both personal and work, with a renewed perspective and heightened energy. Endings are merely the start of a new beginning.

Is he ready to face his fears?

He is working hard and getting skilled; he is a quick study, quickly learning how to align his values and actions with his heart's desires. Although he is terribly heartbroken and realizes he is at a crossroads, he is moving toward a peace-offering approach with himself and the others. Healing is the main focus right now. He is learning how to look deeper into himself and his childhood in order to learn how not to compromise his heart.

What are Wesley's Current Life Lessons?

Staying neutral and trusting others to work out their own problems. Releasing resistance to himself and his environment and moving forward, accepting where he is right now. Practicing gratitude by recognizing that the problems in his life are valuable lessons to learn from, gifts to make a happier life filled with blessings. He is learning how to assess his future path in relation to his goals, and how to make a plan to attain and sustain his goals.

[One thing Wesley admitted to being a large part of his problem was that he never liked to plan ahead.]

What is my most important overall focus with Wesley right now?

Help him to move from stalemate position to completion. Help him to assess the past and present with Willa, his own depression, deceptions, and fears, and his pattern of thinking and communicating where he positions himself in a "not deserving" role. Work on self-love and clarity in his communication and thinking. He needs to learn how to be assertive, to speak his truth from a place of love, not fear.

What is Wesley working on with his Master Guide?

Being clear and direct in his communication and thinking with the other, and learning how to take care of himself and not give up on himself. He is learning how to love himself, how to let go of self-loathing and other unproductive behaviors, and how to hold himself in high self-esteem. He is learning how to stay neutral and how to set and maintain healthy boundaries.

How is he doing at this?

He is at a stalemate. He hasn't yet acted upon this; he is still in his head with it.

Any advice on how to move forward?

Yes, work on helping him to get disciplined and skilled about changing his life through making a plan and working each step, methodically.

But I can't get him to make a move on his own. What do you suggest I do to advise him?

Keep talking with him. Help him to align his values with his heart's desires; help him to see options and paths ahead. The communication right now is important for him to gain a new perspective. Help him to build his self-confidence, to identify his gifts and tools which will bring him the work he will love. He needs you to help him to decide on a direction in his career.

I already did. Was I correct in the advice you gave me about pursuing a career with animals and in the country?

Yes, and to work as part of a creative team, but he has to recognize what feels right for him. Ask him to look into the mirror and think of one wish he has that is realistic and attainable in this life. If he wants to make this happen, he has to follow his heart, and we will help him to realize this dream.

What are his unhealthy patterns in relationships? What pattern can I help him to identify in his love life?

Lack of setting deadlines.
Lack of self-love.
Lack of clear and direct communication from the *heart*—cerebral he is, heart-centered he is not.
Lack of outside support through transition times.
Addiction/bondage/control patterns in relationships.
Lack of faith and hope in a healthy relationship.
Lack of self-confidence; as in, knowing he has the resources to make his life work.

How best to work on breaking this pattern?

Focus on self-love. He needs to stop worrying and playing things over in his mind, obsessing.

Tell him, "Wesley, stop being undecided about your path. Speak your truth, become clear on your direction, and then work skillfully to attain your goals. Have faith in romance again. You are getting help for that. Focus on generosity with balance, an equal exchange. And work on forgiveness. We will help you with that."

What is Wesley afraid of and in denial over?

Communicating his grief, recognizing what is right for his heart, and having the foresight to choose a path and make it right for him.

What kind of woman is good for him?

Someone who is also at a crossroads. Someone who enjoys the support of community *in times of transition.* Someone who is in the process of working on letting go of the past patterns of ruin, or who has already let go of the past. Someone who is done with worrying about the unknown. Someone who loves nature, animals, and children. Someone who loves her self, is balanced in heart and mind, enjoys back-and-forth communication, and loves him.

Spirit then provided this closing statement for Wesley:

Work on getting help with releasing your addictive bond with Willa, and in your relationships, in general. Work on healing your fears, which are blinding you to your path forward. Work in therapy on removing the blinders that cause you to want to "own" a person rather than share generously. Work on breaking the power issues that create your fears. Look fear in the face; you can overcome your fears. The opposite of love is fear. If someone is less than loving to you, that person is hurting. And the same goes for you. Find the blessing in your current situation, prioritize your needs and desires, and follow your heart.

While channeling, I received an interruption from Wesley's mother on the other side: "It's time, release her. Listen to your heart. We are watching over you; haven't you noticed the signs? Messages surround you, and they are obvious. Pay close attention, although they come in strange ways, such as the accidents and unpleasant events in your life, they are leading you to your destiny."

[One of these was a car accident Wesley found himself in while stopped at a red light. I told him it was Spirit's way of pushing him out of "neutral." The other was the violent episode at work.]

After the most welcomed interrupted guidance from Wesley's mother, my Guides continue:

New life is only possible once we accept change. You have become stuck trying to hold on to things you should let go of. Stop, feel the fear, and move forward anyway. Although you may need to let go of your old identity and habits—and this can be frightening—you will find much joy, power, and wisdom in your new cycle. It is imperative now to mourn the old ways and then let them go. Open your arms to the new life and possibilities that await you. Move forward.

Don't be fooled by the difficult and painful events that are occurring, for you will find incredible opportunity. This is a magical time, a culmination of your life so far. It is important to move with the flow. Let your instincts guide you to where you need to be. Allow yourself a period of grieving, as nothing will feel clear unless you do this. Remain present, clear, and focused; you control your reactions, despite the major shifts that are beyond your control. Only your willingness to be responsible for yourself will determine how wonderful these changes turn out to be. You are in a time of deep catharsis, and this experience will smash the psychological barriers that bind you.

Your heart desires to connect to something greater, and through this need, something will be born, a project and a relationship. Resist second-guessing yourself. Your heart desires education, so go to school; you have a gift with animals, children, teaching, nurturing, and leadership. Your strengths are your commitment, your clear communication of ideas and thoughts, your ability to work with rehabilitation and the renewal of others' lives, and your overall ability to manage stress. You show the world that you manage stress well, that you are calm, and that you do a good job.

Remember, what you believe you create, and right now you believe that you are deserving of a relationship of poverty, stripped of love, hope, and faith. What you should believe is the opposite. Clear your energy, and let the past go. If you dare to get out of flatline mode, you just may learn to love your life.

A few months after this reading, Wesley began dating, meeting wonderful women, and realizing that life exists after Willa. He lost thirty pounds, his blood pressure returned to normal, his depression left, and he was free of all meds.

Four months later, his diet continued to improve, he lost more weight, cultivated new female friends, enrolled in a motorcycle course, recycled his wardrobe, had the home appraised, began and completed the upgraded renovations, which he did himself, and began his search for his new home in the country near horses. It was clear that he was reborn, on a new path, and conscious about his guidance from the other side.

One month after that, while in session, he shared with me a picture of his female distant cousin, June, who had come across his profile on a dating website and gotten in touch with him. This was a platonic gesture. As soon as I looked at her, I recognized that this was his moment. I hadn't told him that I knew this because I had seen her in a dream two years prior, but I had a good feeling, and so I told him to pursue this contact.

They shared with each other that they had left their respective partners. She told him she was a dog breeder and was looking to complement this business with another one, and he shared that he loved his two dogs, the country, and horses, and that he too was looking to start up a new business. The two discussed a reunion.

Two weeks later, I received a text from him:

> Hi. Happy thoughts, really my second childhood, bought all new bedroom furniture, drove my bike (motorcycle) home from class, no I am not allowed to do this (as he still hadn't fully completed his course) but it was fun! A one-time deal! Going to a different school … It's Friday … Lol.

One week later, I received another text: "I found my business partner." He was referring to his cousin, June.

One week after that, another text came in:

> Hi. Are you going to visit me in the country? I will give you free room and board at my bed-and-breakfast, and let you ride my horse and motorcycle. Lol. I am going to Ontario this weekend with an agent. Sophie will most probably move with me. It's a clear path that I am interested in, as it combines everything I am good

at: renovation, budgets, making deals, country living, horses and dogs. And I think Sophie has found a surrogate mom in June. Are you going to help me get custody of the dogs?

I cried with joy. There is no better feeling then to witness and experience firsthand how when Spirit says something, and we follow their guidance, miracles can and do happen.

Did I mention that as soon as he turned the corner and began to see the Light, every session we have, he brings me sunflowers.

A big thank-you goes out to Wesley's mom, dad, sis, pet babies, and Spirit Guides, who continue to guide us every time we connect. Just as I was rereading this chapter before submitting it for publication, a phone call came in. The Caller ID read, "Merci."

The Bat &
The Firefly
Past Lives
& Fated
Relationships

I met Ronnie in a bookstore while testing out a new Tarot deck. He was standing in front of the astrology section, and I was sitting on a chair, with my two small dogs on my lap, talking telepathically with my Spirit Guides and shuffling cards. Yes, my dogs are allowed in most bookstores.

I said to Spirit, "I don't want to pry, but if you think I should get this deck, show me who this gentleman is standing in front of me and what he is dealing with." They showed me that he works with the spirit world in his own way around issues of empowerment, and that he is having romantic issues with a woman. To be exact, they gave me a card with a picture that had a man kneeling on his knees and a woman standing behind him holding him hostage with a sword at his throat.

Clearly, this was none of my business, so I was hesitant to approach this guy with this news to confirm what I received; not to mention, I felt like Peeping Tom! So I thought for a few more minutes about what I should do, and then I shuffled more to get Spirit's guidance.

They said, "We gave you this information because we want you to approach him. Go forth, and have confidence."

So I did.

"Excuse me," I said. "I have something to ask you, but if you feel I am invading your personal space, please do not hesitate to tell me to butt out."

He responded, "Not at all. What would you like to ask me?"

So I began to explain to him what I do and how I was testing out yet another Tarot deck with my Guides, deciding whether or not I should get it, and so I asked for insight into him. He appeared happy to be experiencing this moment, so I continued.

"By any chance, are you in a relationship with someone but having trouble?"

With open laughter, he responded, "Yes."

He explained in brief that he was involved in an emotional affair with a "taken" woman, and that the two shared a passion for astrology and spirituality.

I had him pull a few cards to help give him insight, and before we parted, I said that if he needed any further "quick" guidance, he should e-mail me.

Over the next month, he e-mailed me for quick insight, asking, "What is to come for this weekend?"

Although I didn't know what was going on, I could sense the couple had upped the ante. Through clairvoyance, I received the image of a key and cotton candy, and a card I pulled read "danger," so I wrote back, "Danger, completion, sticky situation."

A few weeks later, he e-mailed me again. This time, Spirit said, "Tell him to book a session. He will know what you mean." And he did.

Prior to our session, I asked him for his birthday and age, via e-mail, as I do with all new clients. He gave me his birthday and told me that he was turning fifty. Because I go into the Akashic Records to channel a conversation with Spirit prior to our sessions, it is also customary for me to ask clients if they have any specific questions that they want answers to. Although he had some spiritual questions, he had one question that I wanted to answer immediately, and because his birthday was to occur before our session, I did.

He asked, "Will I find *the One* in this lifetime?"

And we answered, "Yes. Dream big."

In addition to channeling the guidance to answer his questions and present a map for him to walk, I also channeled information about his past life with this woman. This was my birthday gift to him, but because of time constraints, I was only able to share this with him at our next session, which I share here.

When it comes to past lives and our relationships with others, I have come to learn that themes and lessons repeat themselves in obvious ways, and, sadly, so do endings. But what I have also come to learn is that, despite having to have the ending, how we approach closure is what allows us to heal from our karmic ties and debts. And this is what happened with Ronnie.

Ronnie's Past-Life Reading

[In this channeling, Spirit addresses Ronnie directly throughout.]

What did Ronnie look like, where did he live, and what did he manifest?

You had red hair, grew up financially secure, and lived in a country setting near mountains and water. You were a person who made a serious decision to travel distances to pursue your dreams. You were a healer and teacher who helped a lot of people, and you set your own course. You had a lover, but because of your career, you had to leave her behind, and this had a great impact on you.

Ronnie, in this lifetime, you carried over the ability to do what makes you happy without the need for outside approval.

What did he create, and what kind of influence did his spirit have on others?

You were wise and shared your wisdom, which was your gift, to help nourish others walk their life path, but there was some self-deception on your part, with respect to your values and how you reached and attained your goals. You denied yourself a loving relationship with a woman because of the guilt you felt leaving your first love behind. You blamed yourself, so you did not allow yourself to fully enjoy your life with another woman.

The lesson you carried over into this lifetime is that you share your gifts with others to help empower them to walk their highest path, with respect to their career—just as you did in this past life, but now you are learning how to align your personal life path with your professional one. You are working on letting go of your need to be in pain, your need to suffer. Although you are sad, you are now learning how to move more quickly through these uncomfortable feelings so that you can experience greater joy and peace. You are working on being grateful for each moment.

Explain a little bit more about his job and how he used his intellectual mind and power.

You were a Renaissance man who left home, left behind all those you loved—most importantly, your lover—in order to accomplish your goals and fulfill your dreams. You took control of your life, and had great fortune. As we said, you did healing and teaching work, you helped people to have faith when all hope was lost, you helped them to become present in the now and to love themselves unconditionally.

In this lifetime, you carried over this ability of learning how to be in the now, how to appreciate the now, while also looking forward to a bright future. Because you did not release your guilt from the past, you are working on letting go of self-loathing and unproductive behavior.

What was the health of his heart in matters of the heart?

Your heart was dark and needed healing. You had a pet, enjoyed music, and knew how to have fun. Your heart did heal through these uplifting nurturing enjoyments, but it still didn't learn how to love a romantic partner in a healthy way.

In this lifetime, you carried over this ability to have fun and not wait for someone else to love your way. You continue to work on this ability to rescue yourself and to know that you are not helpless. As in the past, you are still drawn to rescue others, but now you are learning that only you can rescue you, and to stop expecting that this will "magically" happen. As you continue to heal yourself, your relationships will dramatically improve.

How did he communicate his truth, and what did he stand for?

You were a peaceful and entertaining communicator, friendly, wise, and a guide to others. You helped others to heal through sharing your own self-knowledge. You stood for visualizing one's goals and dreams, for taking the necessary risks to achieve them. You helped others do for themselves what you were not able to do for yourself.

In this lifetime, you are learning how to let go of the fear of failure in matters of the heart and how to make your dreams come true.

Before dying, how did he assess his life, and was he happy?

You dreamed about being in love and reuniting with your past love, but as was said, you dropped this relationship to pursue a career as a healer and teacher, and you never got seriously involved again, with her or anyone else. You realized you were grateful for the relationship, even though you didn't have what you wished for in matters of romantic love.

In this lifetime, you are practicing gratitude for the problems in your love relationships, learning lessons from your romantic partners, and understanding your spiritual nature. Your past life was about self-discovery and walking your path solo, but as a light for others; in this lifetime, you hope to do the same, but to do so with a loving partner by your side.

How did he die, and how did he feel about dying?

You died in bed peacefully, with friends around you. You were resolved about your life, in that you wished you could have been with her, but you understood your life choices and accepted responsibility for your decisions. You knew you were on the earth plane to create beauty for others, and you accepted this gift. You approached death with dignity and a sense of completion.

In this lifetime, you create beauty for yourself. The mirror of those you work with show you that it is important to reflect the beauty in both your personal and professional life, and this is what you are currently working on.

What did he love about this past life?

You loved that you had the resources to teach people how to start over, achieve clarity, and overcome obstacles.

What is the overarching unresolved issue he carried over?

Learning how to let go of the guilt and self-blame that you left her behind. In this life, Ronnie, you are learning how to let go of your need to possess her and how to feel complete without her. You are also learning how to balance work with your love life, something you could not do in this past life. You are here to learn how to risk being vulnerable with women, and people in general, so that people know who you really are and not who you think they want you to be.

What message does his past self have for his present self?

Have faith, patience, courage, strength, and good self-esteem to break your pattern with love; allow a new foundation to be laid for a new home; make decisions that are right for you; prioritize balance in work and home life; and aim to have a happy family life, based on healthy giving instead of rescuing others.

What was his life theme?

It was about creativity and destruction, moving through the discomfort that change brings, and moving forward with faith and patience to pursue dreams.

What was his soul's purpose?

To challenge yourself and others to heal, grieve loss, release anger toward family members, and learn how to communicate together, understand each other's points of view, and come into balance, healthy giving and receiving, in matters of the heart.

What should he take away from his relationship with Dora?

The wisdom to do what is right, healthy, nourishing, and nurturing for you. Forward movement is now possible, so know that you had fun, but make the decision to let go; have faith to plant new seeds in your garden, and have the patience to watch them grow. She is a mirror to visualize your dreams, reflecting your need to rescue yourself and to continue learning lessons from the work that you do.

What key words should he keep in mind?

Wisdom, fun, balance, mirror, dreams, destiny, forward movement, fortune, partnership, faith in love. Decisions must be made in favor of your heart's desire.

Spirit then shared these final comments with Ronnie:

You are starving yourself of the love you deserve, because of these old feelings of guilt and self-loathing. It's time you celebrate yourself, gain clarity, and deal with and heal your fears, for they are causing you great imbalance in matters of the heart, your truth. Be in and live your truth in your romantic relationships. You deserve to receive good things; know that you are making the right decision when you say no to someone who is less than kind to you. You are in a time of deep transformation, and the butterfly is who you will become once you shed the old, so take time to visualize your highest path, and you will then be able to manifest it.

In session, Ronnie shared that he facilitates leadership seminars and em-powerment workshops. I came to learn that he travels a lot for his work and gives workshops all over the world. The work that he does is fascinating, and he is proud that he is able to touch so many lives. By the sound of it, his past-life reading demonstrates that he came back to do similar work, but that this time, he is learning how to balance home and work life, align-ing his values through and through. Although he has an accent, I didn't think much about it until I came to learn that Ronnie is not originally from Montreal. He had chosen to cross over large bodies of water to live here many years ago for his career, just as he did in this past life.

Ronnie also shared that he has two teenage daughters and an ex-wife from twenty years of marriage, and that both spent most of their years living separate lives but stayed together for the kids. No wonder Spirit said that in this life he is to learn how to show his real self to women and not what he thinks they want him to be. We both agreed that in this life he is to stop hiding in the shadows, and, instead, become cohesive and whole.

The key I saw in my mind's eye the first time he e-mailed me was the key to a country house they rented for that upcoming weekend, and the cotton-candy sticky situation symbol related to, well, you get the picture. Clearly, he had reached out to gain a sense of how it was going to go. That weekend, a bat and firefly came to visit them. Ronnie connects deeply with the bat and associates it with his parents on the other side, and the dancing firefly, with Dora's fiery light guiding him into unknown new territory.

It is also interesting to note that in their past-life relationship together, it was Ronnie who left Dora, and in this lifetime, it is Dora who will not leave her partner for Ronnie. We both felt that this new perspective was like putting the final piece to a puzzle and closing a chapter. He exclaimed that this reading was a critical component to his healing, personal growth, and closure with Dora and what she represented in the first fifty years of his life.

The romantic relationship ended shortly after our session, because Ronnie got it. Every session that followed was magical and miraculous. With the guidance of our A-Teams—which included his parents, whom I often channeled while in session with him—we made tremendous progress. One last thing to mention, his past-life reading and the lessons he carried over also relate to why he chose his parents and what he learned through his relationship with them. Not only did this reading address life lessons with Dora but it also helped him to make the link between family patterns and what he came here to break.

Almost one year later, I received an e-mail from Ronnie: "Thank you for all your help late last year. Now, then, can you pull me a card for work and career?"

Part III

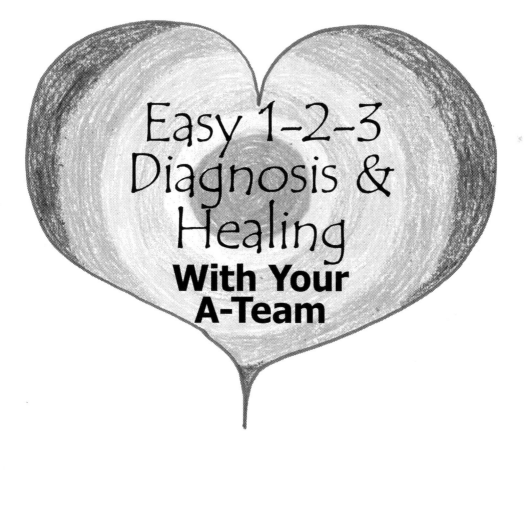

Easy 1-2-3
Diagnosis &
Healing
**With Your
A-Team**

We are now going to shift gears, and learn ways to better understand the body and diagnose root causes of your dis-eases and illnesses. This section will show you how to diagnose yourself emotionally, psychologically, physically, and spiritually, so as to intervene in your dysfunctions, heal yourself, and take control of your holistic health. At the end of each chakra chapter are channeling exercises we refer to as *Rainbow Medicine* that will help you to understand and heal each area of the body, including your relationship patterns and intimacy issues.

The Body Whispers But When We Don't Listen It Screams

Self-Diagnosis

Law of Attraction: Identifying the Emotional Dis-Ease behind Physical and Mental Illness

Everything is energy, and energy is consciousness. If you want to change something in your life, you need to first change the energy within your consciousness; hence the reason why a holistic healing approach is key. Holistic healing addresses emotional, psychological, physical, and spiritual well-being.

All that we attract is also within us. Like magnets, we attract situations, people, and even illnesses, all for the purpose of healing, learning, personal growth, and karmic completion. And this attraction occurs because we share the same frequency as that which we attract. It gets even more interesting when we discover that everything has an energetic imprint, including the activities we engage in and the bacteria, fungi, and viruses we catch. For example, fungus (yeast) has a consciousness that resonates with resentment; hence, when we harbor too much resentment and function from fear, the immune system weakens, and we become more susceptible to fungus (yeast) infections.

Again, everything has a consciousness, and we absorb the essence of whatever and whomever we "consume"; hence the expression "You make me sick." Our physical and mental bodies respond to our emotional body. Physical symptoms tell us about our emotional, mental, and spiritual states of being. Bacteria, fungi, viruses, and parasites have thought forms which they send to the host to maintain their existence, but the only reason they can send it to the host is because the host carries that negative attribute within itself. Every time we experience a physical and mental dis-ease, injury, illness, or disorder, all we have to do is look at the emotional issues we are experiencing, fore therein lie the answers on how to heal.

Sometimes the roots of our illnesses can be traced back through our ancestry, which means we inherited the "illness" for the karmic reason to put an end to the pattern and thereby heal our future bloodline. Sometimes they are simply markers to help guide us on our path, reminders that we are veering off our life path and it's time to get back on. For example, clinically diagnosed depression is one of those markers; when we feel chronically depressed, whether genetically inherited or symptomatic of our times, this form of *dissociation* is a sign that we are off track from our life purpose, as well as a reminder that we came to the earth plane to clear certain karmic debts and to manifest certain dreams. However, simply feeling "depressed" is not the same thing; rather, it is a key step to healing, as it signifies a release, a letting go, an acceptance of what we are grieving. In Elisabeth Kübler-Ross's *five stages of grief,* the fourth step is *depression,* and it is necessary for healing. (The first, second, and third steps are *denial, anger,* and *bargaining,* respectively; the fifth and final step is *acceptance.*)

As bad as it may seem, illness is never a curse; rather, it is a red flag, an awakening, and a signpost to help us heal and manifest what we came here for.

The body whispers—but when we don't listen, it screams. The important aspect to remember here is not to deny our feelings, but, rather, to understand them, express them, and release them. Having a better understanding of the stories our body tells helps us in order to communicate more compassion-ately with it, and to clear the way for healthier and more joyful living.

This section is designed to help you to identify some of the core issues you struggle with and that explain why you feel the way you do and why you manifest certain chronic symptoms that seem to come and go but never fully eradicate. Whether it's a minute physical injury (such as splinter in your thumb or a sprained ankle), a chronic situation (such as backache, diabetes, and kidney problems), a mental illness (such as clinical depres-sion), or a serious viral infection (such as hepatitis), emotional issues are the root cause for most dis-ease, injury, and illness.

Bacteria, Fungi, Viruses and Parasites

If the following information resonates with you, I suggest you pick up a copy of Vianna Stibal's *Theta Healing: Diseases and Disorders* where she discusses the consciousness of nearly every illness.

Unbalanced emotions are one reason why bacteria are able to enter into the system. When we are compulsively angry and fearful, the immune system must work harder, and it becomes exhausted. When negative emo-tions are not expressed, and, instead, are held in, this also weakens the immune system. The trick is to be able to express the anger in a positive way in order for the body to remain strong. Guilt issues have been found to be a leading cause of holding bacteria in the body. Guilt relates to issues of accountability and decision making.

Fungi grow in *low acidic*, and *high-moisture* environments. They can grow on the skin, hair, or nails, and inside the body. Being on antibiotics for ex-tended periods of time makes a person more susceptible. Yeast is a pop-ular form of fungus, and it is the cause of many illnesses, such as asthma, fatigue, headaches, and weakness. All forms of fungus infection are tied to anger, resentment, and procrastination issues. In order to heal, you must find out how this resentment is serving you. Feeling that you do not deserve love and appreciation are the root causes for attracting fungi; embracing that you deserve love and appreciation is the first step to healing.

Viruses live in the cells of animals, plants, and bacteria. Viruses cause many diseases, such as some forms of cancer, herpes, and hepatitis. Viruses can live in the body for very long periods of time without any display of symptoms, and viruses can mutate in order to survive. Lack of self-worth and fear issues are associated with viruses. People who believe that illness is a punishment and that they deserve to be ill will keep the virus thriving, but when such individuals change their belief systems, so too will the virus change. When such individuals no longer feel the need to punish themselves, the virus will transmute into something harmless. But what we resist will persist.

Parasites live in the blood, the lymph system, various organs, and other body tissues. Feeling like a victim, allowing others to take advantage of you, not being able to say no, and allowing yourself to get sucked dry, all can make a person a magnet for parasites. Although most of our food contains parasites, the more balanced our belief system is, the fewer parasites we pick up. The same goes for the people we draw into our lives.

Physical Conditions in the Body

Ted Andrews's *The Healer's Manual* is an excellent resource from where much of the following information is drawn.

There are ten conditions in the body:

> Chills and Fevers
> Congestion
> Cramps
> Fatigue
> Infection
> Inflammation
> Irritations
> Nausea
> Pain
> Swelling

Chills and Fevers

Chills occur when the body needs to realign with the physical. *Fevers* occur when the body needs to realign with Spirit.

A fever in the body means that the body is trying to shake off, burn off, and realign itself. A fever is designed to burn off toxins in the body and eliminate them through the condensation the body produces. A fever happens when a sudden temperature raise occurs and the pulse quickens, converting matter to spirit. The subtle bodies separate from the physical in order to transmute the toxins and make room for healing. A fever can mean that the person is losing touch with the spiritual, representing a toxic congestion with physical matters. The body may need to be stimulated into greater activity, a call that it needs its pulse raised. Being lazy, neglecting activities and self, putting things off, holding in and onto anger, and desires heating up inside but not being expressed can all lead the body to produce a fever.

Chills cause a contraction, a pulling inward; chills can be a sign that we are pulling away from others, or that we need to pull away to ground ourselves. Being involved in too many activities and being scattered can lead to this imbalance, if we do not take enough time for ourselves. Feeling insecure and left out in the cold can also produce chills and shivers.

Congestion

Congestion happens in the sinuses and lungs, and also in the form of *constipation.* Congestion is an excess of blood and mucus. The place in the body where congestion appears will explain which area of your life is congested as a result of being overburdened. Head congestion relates to thought processes, such as irritation, worry, doubt, and fear, all of which fill our head and congest it. Lung congestion points to holding in feelings and emotions, so a good cry will eliminate this congestion. It also reflects people who prevent good things and good people from entering their lives, or who feel deserving of taking up more space and therefore congested in their current space. Being afraid to take in and breathe life, feeling depressed and sad, feeling stifled, and stifling others, all can fill and congest the heart with unexpressed emotion, which can manifest as lung congestion. Constipation usually points to a person who refuses to eliminate old ideas, emotions, and patterns, who is stuck in the past, refusing to change.

Cramps

Cramps come from muscle contractions, a response to fear, a holding on too tightly to something or someone you don't want to let go of, and this is the way the body is telling you to relax and let go. Hand cramps relate to holding on too tightly; leg cramps could mean moving too much or working too hard (workaholics and perfectionists are examples). Menstrual cramps reflect issues around a woman's femininity. If you are a woman, over the course of several months, you can look for a pattern between the relationship of your activities, emotions, and life experiences and the severity of cramps. The location of your cramps and the body part and system they are associated with will tell you more about the underlying causes. Hand cramps are related to Heart chakra issues, leg cramps to Root chakra, etc.

Fatigue

Fatigue means we are really tired of something in our lives, be it a job, relationship, or constant family stress. Fatigue is a signpost to encourage us to play.

Infection

Infections are poisons in the body derived from toxic thoughts, negativity, anger, and fears. Disharmony and negativity in surroundings—such as unhealthy people, situations, and environments—create infections. Our bad habits also foster infection, affecting the quality, character, and condition of our lives unfavorably. Look to who or what is currently affecting you.

Inflammation

Inflammation manifests as redness, swelling, pain, tenderness, and heat. A disturbed function can indicate a reaction to an injurious agent, such as a person, condition, attitude, and negativity in your life. Who and what we expose ourselves to, harboring annoyance and aggravation, no healthy outlet to offload the anger and frustration of life conditions, preventing peacefulness and calmness, being overly critical or criticized, not approving of self, and refusing to change old patterns all would manifest as recurring inflammation.

Irritations

Irritations are burning sensations and itches, something is burning or eating you up. An unexpressed desire or unfulfilled wish could manifest as an itch. You could be itching to do something but not acting upon it, reflecting a fear of unfulfilled needs and desires, and unhappiness with your present life situation and position.

Nausea

Nausea represents what we are sick of in our lives. This may be an attitude we are exposed to but do not want to digest, something we are trying to expel from our lives, a fear of rejection, a rejection to someone or something, not feeling safe and secure, and/or having difficulty swallowing something.

Pain

Pain relates to feelings of guilt, nursing old hurts, overly critical attitudes by others or ourselves, longing, resistance to new moves and changes, and feeling a lack of freedom. Headaches can reflect how we think about ourselves; heartache can reflect our feelings or lack of feelings for self, and a lack of expression of love. People complaining about others usually develop pain, in the form of soreness and stiffness in their necks. Chronic pain that recurs and persists can relate to a refusal to change, reflecting long-standing fears and outworn behavior patterns. If this resonates with you, look for something or someone that is always a pain in your life. Throbbing pain could reflect punishing self or feeling guilty; steady pain could reflect lack of self-approval and/or approval by others. Acute pain is sharp, severe, and intense, a drastic call for attention from the body; this type of pain could reflect sensitivity to criticism, or being overwhelmed by ideas. Achy pains can reflect a longing for something or someone, a longing for love.

Swelling

Swelling in the body can indicate a blocked attitude/clogged process related to going forward in life, resulting from being stuck in old patterns and outworn ideas. Swollen ankles can indicate a refusal to move on or let others move on. Do you have issues of self-esteem? Are you too puffed up about something, refusing to let go and grow? It can be a sign of being too emotional and not practical.

When we do not allow ourselves to expand and grow but have the opportunity to do so, we become clogged internally, inflate things out of proportion, allow emotions to override common sense and practical thinking, and invade others' lives or space where we should not.

Let's move on to the chakra system, where you will learn how to look at and understand each piece of the puzzle and how it connects to the whole.

Body Systems

Skeletal System

The skeletal system includes bones, cartilage, and joints. This system has both mechanical functions and physiological functions. Mechanical functions relate to our bones, which support, protect, and move the body. Our bones are a rigid framework that protects soft tissues, such as our internal organs (the brain, heart, lungs, and the pelvic region organs). Physiological functions include blood cell production, and the supply and storing of important minerals. Blood-cell production converts chemical energy into mechanical through blood formation, providing a reservoir of minerals.

Bone problems reflect what we may or may not be protecting, the quality or lack of support or structure in our lives. The organ related to the broken bone will highlight what you are protecting, or not, and the significance of that organ in your life.

Eliminative System

The eliminative system filters and excretes waste through the kidneys and urinary bladder (in the form of urine), and through the bowel (in the form of bowel movements). The kidneys also remove waste from the blood. The waste combines with water to form urine. From the kidneys, urine travels down two thin tubes called *ureters*, which deposit the urine in the bladder. When the bladder is full, urine is discharged through the urethra. The large intestines, a ten-foot long tube, remove solid waste. The skin is also part of this system, and it removes waste through sweat glands.

Problems with the eliminative system reflect a refusal to let go and difficulty releasing emotions, thoughts, patterns, people, situations, and memories that no longer serve our growth and well-being. Examples are holding on to anger and unhealthy memories. Dis-eases and disorders can manifest from fears, such as a fear of no longer being needed, a fear of letting go of someone or something, a fear of how people will perceive us if we change, and a fear of letting go of outworn ideas, attitudes, and traditions for fear of what the new may bring.

Reproductive System

The reproductive system replaces damaged or dead cells in the body; it is a creative system because it reproduces the human being. The organs are the penis, testes, and scrotum in men; and the ovaries, uterus, clitoris, vagina, and mammary glands in women. Sperm from the male fertilizes the female's egg (ovum), in the fallopian tube. The fertilized egg travels from the fallopian tube to the uterus, where the fetus develops over a period of nine months.

Problems here reflect an inability to be creative and productive in our own life. Depending on one's perspective of what is productivity, this can refer to not participating in activities that are creative and fun, that rejuvenate and regenerate our mental, emotional, physical, and spiritual bodies. Sexual performance problems can relate to problems with self-expression, such as feeling unable to fully express sexuality, or not being happy with the self's gender and/or sexual orientation.

Digestive System

The digestive system converts food and beverages into nutrients and energy, such as protein, vitamins, minerals, carbohydrates, and fats, all of which the body needs for energy, growth, and repair. Major organs include the esophagus, stomach, intestines, liver, pancreas, and gallbladder. After food is chewed and swallowed, it goes down the esophagus and enters the stomach, where it is further broken down by powerful stomach acids. From the stomach, the food travels into the small intestine. This is where food is broken down into nutrients that can enter the bloodstream through tiny hair-like projections. The excess food that the body doesn't need or can't digest is turned into waste that is eliminated from the body.

Primary functions of this system are ingestion and absorption; look to your habits to identify what you should and should not be ingesting and absorbing. This could indicate you are not using what you have available to you, are not absorbing new ideas, and/or are being wasteful.

Respiratory System

The respiratory system acquires oxygen and eliminates carbon dioxide. The major organs are the nose, lungs, larynx, trachea, and bronchial tubes. When we breathe in, air enters the nose or mouth and goes down a long tube called the *trachea* (windpipe). The trachea branches into two bronchial tubes, or *primary bronchi*, which go to the lungs. The primary bronchi branch off into even smaller bronchial tubes, or *bronchioles*. The bronchioles end in the *alveoli*, or air sacs. Oxygen follows this path, passes through the walls of the air sacs and blood vessels, and enters the bloodstream. At the same time, carbon dioxide passes into the lungs and is exhaled.

Breathing is essential for life; therefore, problems with breathing reflect issues of a right to life. Feeling undeserving or guilty about how you live, or feeling like you are not living your best life or not allowed to live your best life, and therefore are suppressing your life expressions and emotions, all can lead to respiratory issues. Unequal exchanges in the life process reflect grief, such as one-sided giving, or taking in too much, and this lodges in the lungs and manifests breathing dis-eases and disorders, such as asthma and pneumonia.

Circulatory System

The circulatory system is the body's transport system. It circulates blood and nutrients throughout the body via the heart and vessels, such as arteries, capillaries, and veins. The heart pumps the blood, and the arteries and veins transport it. Oxygen-rich blood leaves the left side of the heart and enters the biggest artery, called the *aorta*. The aorta branches into smaller arteries, which then branch into even smaller vessels that travel all over the body. When blood enters the smallest blood vessels, which are called capillaries and are found in body tissue, it gives nutrients and oxygen to the cells and takes in carbon dioxide, water, and waste. The blood, which no longer contains oxygen and nutrients, then goes back to the heart through the veins. Veins carry waste products away from cells and bring blood back to the heart, which pumps it to the lungs to pick up oxygen and eliminate carbon dioxide.

Problems here usually stem from lack of vitality for an area in one's life. Circulation problems are tied to how we allow our emotions to circulate and flow. When emotions flow too easily, it reflects no control, and manifests as low blood pressure. When emotions are not being allowed to circulate, it reflects too much control, and and manifests as high blood pressure. Circulatory conditions reflect a person who is locked in the past, afraid to move on, unable to resolve old emotional issues, and harboring an attitude of self-defeatism.

Nervous System

The nervous system is responsible for communication and control; it integrates the activities of all the organs. It is made up of the brain, the spinal cord, and nerves. It stores information, responds to the environment, and transmits messages between the brain, spinal cord, and peripheral nervous system. There are three parts of your nervous system that work together: the *central nervous system*, the *peripheral nervous system*, and the *autonomic nervous system*.

The central nervous system sends out nerve impulses and analyzes information from the sense organs, which tell the brain about the things we see, hear, smell, taste, and feel. The peripheral nervous system includes the *craniospinal nerves* that branch off from the brain and the spinal cord. It carries the nerve impulses from the central nervous system to the muscles and glands. The autonomic nervous system regulates involuntary action, such as heartbeat and digestion.

Problems here can reflect trying to integrate too many activities in our lives, or not having enough activities to keep us occupied; being overly sensitive to criticism from self and others; not communicating our needs clearly, or interacting with others who are not communicating clearly with us; and being closed to new possibilities.

Endocrine System

The endocrine system is important to the energy system, and is responsible for glandular body functions, such as metabolism, growth, and sexual development. It works closely with the nervous system to integrate, correlate, and control body processes. It is made up of a group of glands that produce the body's hormones, which are chemicals that control body functions. The hormones get secreted into the bloodstream to excite or inhibit organ and tissue functions. The glands include the pituitary gland, thyroid gland, parathyroid glands, adrenal glands, thymus gland, pineal gland, pancreas, and reproductive glands (ovaries in women, and testes in men). These glands release hormones directly into the bloodstream, which transports the hormones to organs and tissues throughout the body.

The Glands

Adrenals

The glands associated with the Root chakra are the *adrenals*. The adrenals are glands of emergency, self-preservation, and protection. They control the *flight-or-fight* response to stresses, threats, and accidents, by secreting hormones which keep us actively present in life-threatening situations. They break down proteins from food, and when the body is in a time of need or emergency, they stimulate the metabolism. The adrenals are located on top of both kidneys and are responsible for helping a person cope with physical and emotional stress by secreting two hormones: *epinephrine* and *norepinephrine*. Epinephrine (also called *adrenaline*) is the hormone that helps the body to respond to stress by increasing the heart rate, facilitating blood flow to the muscles and brain, and converting glycogen to glucose. Norepinephrine (also called *noradrenaline*) is the hormone that increases blood pressure in response to acute stress. When the body is constantly operating from fear, the adrenal glands work too hard, and the immune system eventually weakens. This is how we get sick.

The adrenals, because they are located over the kidneys, are related to the eliminative system. The eliminative system filters and excretes waste through the kidneys and urinary bladder in the form of urine (liquid waste), through intestinal tract as bowel movements (solid waste), and through the skin (sweat). The kidneys have cellular memory of our ancestors' survival instincts; hence their relationship to the Root chakra.

Overtaxed adrenals represent long-standing anxieties and worries. They can reflect a refusal to care for the self in healthy ways and a resistance to responding to important issues in our life or in the lives of those closest to us. Malfunctions of the Root can also reflect how we perceive others' responses, or lack of response, to our issues.

The prescriptions to balance adrenal glandular function, responsible for *fight-or-flight* response patterns, are psychotherapy, rainbow medicine, nature walks, walking, cycling, jogging, yoga, dance, eating, grocery shopping, sex, cuddling, renovating, landscaping, and gardening.

Ovaries and Testes

The glands associated with the Sacral chakra are the ovaries (in women) and the testes (in men); these glands mature at around age fourteen, are responsible for the procreation of our species, and are the main source of sex hormones. In males, the testes produce a hormone called *testosterone*. These hormones affect male characteristics, such as sexual development, facial hair growth, pubic hair growth, and sperm production. Qualities are linked to left-brain logic, assertiveness, and self-confidence. In females, the ovaries, located on both sides of the uterus, produce *estrogen*, *progesterone*, and *eggs*. These hormones control breast development, menstruation, and pregnancy. Qualities are linked to right-brain creativity and emotional wellbeing.

Attitudes about sexuality are related to the problems we manifest in this area. How we value our spiritual, physical, and emotional body is connected to our attitude about growing up, having a family, and enjoying our sexuality. This chakra works from a deep unconscious realm affected by how much we value and honor ourselves. Boundaries and limitations on how we take care of ourselves are key to the necessary hormonal flow that influences our energy.

The prescriptions to balance *testosterone* and *estrogen* glandular function, responsible for balancing yin-yang energy, are engaging in activities that promote self-care and self-worth like recovery work, maintaining healthy boundaries, culinary arts, swimming, creative production, and creating a project or business.

Pancreas

The gland associated with the Solar Plexus chakra is the *pancreas*, it is both an organ and a gland that aids food digestion, influences nutritional absorption, controls carbohydrate metabolism, and produces hormones that regulate glucose and insulin (energy levels) in the blood. The pancreas is a large gland that lies alongside the stomach and the small intestine.

After we eat, enzymes (digestive juices) are released into the small intestine to break down and digest food. These enzymes make hormones that control blood glucose levels. When sugar (glucose) levels in the blood rise, the pancreas produces a hormone called *insulin*. Insulin then helps the body to lower blood glucose levels, and stores the sugar away in body tissues where it can be used for energy when required. Between meals, the pancreas does not produce insulin, which allows the body to release stored energy, gradually, back into the blood as needed. Stable glucose levels in the blood ensure that the body has a steady supply of energy needed for metabolism, exercise, and fueling parts of the brain, which runs on glucose.

Problems here reflect an inability to absorb the healthy aspects of life—such as joy, happiness, and peace—and, instead, to allow the unhealthy aspects to create imbalance and override the positive. Health issues here are indicators of how we respond to situations in our lives, such as overreacting to people and situations, or inhibiting our responses; basically, the problems reflect responding to life inappropriately.

The prescriptions to balance *pancreas* glandular function, responsible for our energy supply, are balanced nutrition, maintaining stable sugar levels, cooking, board/card games, crossword puzzles, workbook exercises, collage, reading, study, teaching, going to bookstores, attending lectures, taking a class, tennis, martial arts, and horseback riding.

Thymus

The gland associated with the Heart chakra is the *thymus gland*, which is located behind the breastbone in the upper chest area. The thymus forms part of the immune system; it is made up of two lobes, called *lymphoid tissues*, consisting of white blood cells and fat that join in front of the trachea. Its function is to transform white blood cells developed in the bone marrow into *T cells*, which are critical to human immunity. These cells are then transported to various lymph glands, where they play an important part in fighting infections and illness. Swelling of lymph glands and fever are signals that immune cells are multiplying to fight off invaders of the body, such as bacteria, fungi, viruses, or parasites.

The thymus gland is responsible for our emotional well-being. It secretes hormones that tone the heart and lungs, keeping the immune system balanced. When we are not happy, or have experienced trauma, loss, or rejection, this gland becomes under-active. Engaging in activities that make the heart sing is the best way to ensure this hormonal flow.

Repetitive illnesses reflect our not recognizing that our actions have repercussions. This includes involving the self in issues and problems that do not concern us, infecting others with our thoughts and actions, allowing others' thoughts and actions to infect us, and losing the ability to find sweetness and benefit in life.

The prescriptions to balance *thymus* glandular function, responsible for keeping the immune system balanced, are engaging in activities that make the heart sing, spending time with likeminded others, being aware of one's actions and reactions (cause and effect), team sports, group games, playing music in a band, being part of a sisterhood/brotherhood, and recovery group work.

Thyroid

The gland associated with the Throat chakra is the *thyroid*, the body's thermostat, which governs our metabolic rate. The thyroid is located at the front of the neck, just below the Adam's apple and along the front of the trachea (windpipe). The thyroid is rich with blood vessels and nerves that are important for voice quality.

The thyroid gland is responsible for regulating our body's growth, such as tooth development, muscle tone, mental development, and the functioning of our sexual organs and adrenal glands. The thyroid secretes several hormones influencing metabolism, growth and development, and body temperature. Adequate thyroid hormone produced during infancy and childhood is crucial for brain development. The main hormone secreted is called *thyroxine*, also known as T4.

Here is a list of thyroid conditions:

> Goiter
> Thyroiditis
> Hyperthyroidism (overactive thyroid)
> Hypothyroidism (underactive thyroid)
> Graves' disease (a common form of hyperthyroidism)
> Thyroid cancer
> Thyroid nodule
> Thyroid storm (a rare form of hyperthyroidism)

Problems here reflect issues of proper expression. Hyperactivity is often a reflection of an imbalance in the Throat chakra. A sluggish metabolism can reflect being sluggish in using creative expression; not expressing ourselves; not doing what we need and want to do; and not claiming our power, or claiming it in an inappropriate manner.

The prescriptions to balance *thyroid* glandular function, responsible for metabolism, growth and development, are creative activities that encourage expression like singing, writing, journaling, workbook exercises, drawing, painting, collage, channeling, theatre, playing a musical instrument, giving a reading, and mediation (listening to both points of view and advocating on behalf of both).

Pituitary

The gland associated with the Third Eye chakra is the *pituitary gland*, also known as the "governor gland" or "master gland," because it secretes hormones that control the activities of the other glands and various bodily functions, affecting the entire immune system. The pituitary gland is located at the base of the brain, below the hypothalamus. Pituitary hormones control skeletal growth, sexual development and maturation, milk secretion in women, thyroid and adrenal function, and blood pressure; the pituitary is necessary for physical and psychological growth.

The pituitary gland feeds energy to the brain, eyes, ears, nose, and mouth, activating positive thought and action. We impede this gland when we have self-limiting beliefs, and we maximize the use of this gland when we trust ourselves and use our inner knowing. Positive thinking and choosing the good we want in our lives secretes the pituitary hormone, which stabilizes blood pressure and heart rate, helping us to withstand pain and create healthier realities. Negative thinking blocks the secretion of the hormone.

The prescriptions to balance *pituitary* glandular function, responsible for directing and managing all glands, are positive thinking, choosing to thrive, choosing the good memories and thoughts, sewing, knitting, puzzles, chess, strategy games, and engaging in activities that encourage leadership and self-celebration.

Pineal

The gland associated with the Crown chakra is the *pineal gland*, which is situated in between the right and left cerebral hemispheres, attached to the third ventricle. The pineal gland is involved in several functions of the body: it secretes the hormone *melatonin* (derived from *serotonin*), which regulates the endocrine functions by converting nervous system signals to endocrine signals, causing feelings of sleepiness so that the body slows down and falls asleep; it also influences sexual development and the sexual functions of the ovaries and testes. The pineal gland is light sensitive. Considered the doorway to Spirit and Source, it releases endorphins that affect our physical and emotional happy place. I refer to it as the real *G-Spot*.

Problems here relate to physical and spiritual growth; not using and honoring our sexual, mental, and spiritual energies appropriately; not seeing what is right in front of us; not honoring all our energies and aspects of ourselves as spiritual; and not being sympathetic to others (nor finding others sympathetic to us).

The prescriptions to balance *pineal* glandular function, responsible for *melatonin-serotonin* secretion, are psychic and mediumship development, meditation, nature walks, hiking, skiing, gardening, tree planting, landscaping, interior design, all visual arts practices, snorkelling, scuba diving, and flying.

Rainbow Medicine

Decoding Discomfort

This exercise is to help you decode your discomfort, injury, accident, cold, fever, infection, disease, and mental illness. Photocopy and work with the printer friendly *Self-Diagnosis Form* available at the back of the book, *Appendix 1*. Circle everything in the form that relates to the condition you are diagnosing. After you have diagnosed your discomfort and understand its energetic imprint i.e. underlying emotional and psychological issues driving it, read the corresponding chakra chapters to learn how your imbalances come to be, how these puzzle pieces unite to create the *you* that you are, engage in the healing chakra therapy exercises at the end of the chapters, and follow the suggested glandular prescriptions.

Every dis-ease and disease is an opportunity to learn a life lesson, break a pattern, heal, and thrive. When you discover its consciousness, bring your patterns into balance, and heal intimacy issues, you will be amazed at the power you have to prevent dis-ease and maximize holistic health. Once you learn how to identify specific components that create your discomfort, you are able to intervene in your pathological behavior, heal the condition, and bring yourself into greater harmonic health within and without.

Our Rainbow Energy Field
The Chakra System

We are Spirit, balls of energy, clothed, having a human experience.

Chakras speak autobiographical volumes. They are bioenergetic centers in our body, and they spin to let energy flow through and heal our physical, mental, emotional, and spiritual bodies. We can imagine them as seven different-colored DVDs onto which information recorded from our present- and past-life experiences is downloaded.

In utero, as children, adolescents, and adults, our traumas and happy times attach themselves energetically to different parts of our bodies. Information from these experiences is downloaded onto the corresponding chakras, and this manifests as strengths and weaknesses, pleasures and dis-eases. It is this recorded information that creates blockages and imbalances which, when looked at and understood, point us in the direction of healing and manifesting abundance.

When root issues are brought to light, we are then able to clear, clean, balance, and align heart with mind, values, and action.

There are different theories as to the chakra system and how many chakras there are, so to keep it simple, we will focus only on the seven major ones along our spinal cord, from the base of the spine to the top of the head. It is important to note that the chakra system is interrelated with the endocrine system, as each chakra is associated with a particular gland. Energy blockages and flows are directly related to hormone secretion and dysfunction, hence the physical manifestation of ease/dis-ease.

Imagine the chakra system as a tree: the *lower chakras* root us deeply into the ground to manifest our desires and dreams, and the *higher chakras* raise our spirit high into the heavens for inspiration to bring back down to the earth plane. This flow of energy takes the form of the figure-eight infinity sign (also called the *lemniscate*), and is necessary to keep you, me, and every human—the *vehicle,* so to speak—running smoothly. In this lemniscate symbol, the X marks the central point between heaven and earth, and corresponds to the Heart chakra, which is the first of the upper chakras (also called the *truth chakras*).

When the heart is blocked with grief, which is a combination of sadness, anger, resentment, and guilt, our ability to speak, see, and connect to truth also becomes blocked. Going up through the truth chakras, this refers to the ability to speak truth (Throat chakra), see truth (Third Eye chakra), and connect to truth (Crown chakra). And when we go to the lower chakras, other abilities become blocked. Going down, this refers to our sense of self-confidence and willpower (Solar Plexus chakra), how we feel emotionally about our dreams and desires (Sacral chakra), and the ability to manifest (Root chakra) abundance. When chakras and energy are blocked, we get stuck. When the Heart chakra is released through forgiveness, acceptance, and lessons learned, our truth and inspiration expand, and our ability to manifest a steady flow of abundance is activated.

The colors of the rainbow are represented in the seven chakra system. Each vibrates at a certain frequency: the slowest is red, and the fastest is violet. Each of our chakras is associated with specific body parts, body systems, and glands, and when our chakras are blocked, these blockages manifest as malfunctions—physical, mental, emotional, psychological, and spiritual. Usually, malfunctions are related to a counter force opposing the natural function of the chakra, which Anodea Judith (1987, 1996, 2012) refers to as the *demon*.

In order for us to learn our life lessons, demons are necessary, for they challenge us to overcome our issues. After all, the reason we are here on the earth plane is to work through duality and come into wholeness.

Challenges are based on dual forces opposing each other, and balance can only be achieved once we make amends with our dark side (i.e., fears), and bring that which we fear into the light. By recognizing the lessons and gifts our challenges provide us with, we are then able to come into wholeness, and, ultimately, to experience greater peace, love, and happiness. Each chakra has a challenge, a gift, and a lesson.

Throughout the chakra chapters, I share various ways to heal and come into balance, but because of lack of space in this book, I can only provide you with a brief description and list of animals, crystals, and divination exercises. You can then take it upon yourself to buy other books according to your interest; you can also refer to further information listed on our website.

The Chakras

In our practice, we work with the chakra system to understand a person's story, and what he or she needs to heal to manifest the highest path. In working with this system, we are able to identify the glands associated with each body part and system, which traumas are lodged where, how they manifest into mental, emotional, and physical dis-eases that cause blockages and imbalances, and how to heal. When conducting a reading for yourself or another, simply hold your hand over a specific chakra, and see which symbols, feelings, sounds, tastes, and smells you receive. Once you have decoded what you received, you will understand that chakra's story.

Animal Medicine

Animal medicine refers to learning from the animal/mammal/insect kingdom the ways in which each has developed unique traits and skills that help them survive and thrive. Each chakra is related to an element, so by learning the instincts of specific animals/mammals/insects and how they thrive in their respective elements, we can develop ways to cope with situations and challenges, and then we can live our best life. When performing a body scan with our hands and mind's eye, or doing a reading for ourselves or another, it is important to look for such symbols and to see within which chakras they appear. This will further help to identify the story this chakra is speaking and the medicine it requires.

Crystal Medicine

Crystals and stones are incredible healing tools, as they carry with them specific healing properties. They can be programmed through our intention for healing and divination. When selecting crystals for yourself or your pet, know that each will resonate with specific chakras and heal specific emotional dis-eases and physical illnesses. Combined with love-based intention and therapeutic work, placing crystals over chakras, or in water as elixirs, will help to balance and heal specific spiritual, emotional, psychological, and physical issues.

Healing can also be done through stones in nature. Simply take a nature walk, and choose seven different stones; ideally, each should exhibit some of the same color of the corresponding chakra. It's not necessary for the entire stone to be covered in that color, simple flecks will do. Through intention, you can program your stones to aid in healing specific issues, and you can also use them as oracles. I have an oracular medicine wheel made of found stones.

I use store-bought crystals and found stones, and I have great success with both. My Guides and the Stone People help me choose the ones I or my pets need, and, together, we program them as anchors and channels for energy healing and divination. When I lie down and place them over specific chakras and body parts, I instantly feel their healing powers. When I use them for divination, they tell me what I need and what others need.

A *crystal elixir* is created when we submerge the crystal within a cup of water or bottled water (distilled or mineral water), and then drink it as a healing technique. Drinking an elixir works from the inside out. Simply choose the crystals you wish to use for your healing, wash them very well to make sure they are clean, and submerge them in water for a minimum of twenty to thirty minutes in sunlight; or leave overnight in the refrigerator. You can place them in sunlight, moonlight, or the refrigerator. [Caution: Some crystals cannot be used as elixirs, so pay attention to the warnings.]

Topical elixirs are prepared the same way, but instead of drinking the water, you apply it to your skin, scalp, and hair. Compresses are also used for eyes and wounds.

All elixirs hold their vibration for twenty-four hours unless they are prepared and stored as a mother batch, using alcohol or vinegar. You would then take a small portion from the mother batch and mix it into a dark glass bottle filled with distilled or mineral water. Using a dropper, you can take a daily prescriptive dose of three drops on your tongue, in your bath water or on your pulse points. Using a spray bottle, spritz it around your aura and in your space.

When working with water soluble crystals, you will need to make your elixirs using a double container method where you place the crystal in a small sealed glass container, which you will then place in a larger glass water filled container. Use the Internet to guide you in making your elixirs with crystals that are water soluble, photosensitive, sensitive to acid, and toxic.

Crystal elixirs are also great for your pets but do not use an elixir that contains alcohol; vinegar is fine. Simply place the appropriate crystal in their water bowl, a glass bowl is preferable as metal will interfere with the vibrations. Both sunlight and moonlight activate the crystal's properties and infuse the water with its energy so we recommend you make the elixir in the evening, leave it under a moonlit window overnight, and replenish every evening. Before each use, cleanse the stone by smudging and rinsing it.

There are also all purpose crystals that work all of the chakras at once, but even with this talent, each still has specific healing abilities for physical conditions:

Quartz Crystal: Diabetes, pain, weight loss
Titanium Quartz: Dehydration and water retention
Tourmalinated Quartz: Nervous system
Angel Aura Quartz: Headaches, backaches, and blurred vision
Diamond: Metabolism, eyesight, detox
Pyrite: Prevents snoring, clears lungs

Laying on the crystals is a technique whereby we place a crystal, or crystals, over specific body parts in order to energize and heal, or to remove pain. Choose the corresponding crystal, and for thirty minutes, listen to relaxing music as you lay it on your specific chakras for energy healing. You can also carry them around with you in your pocket or in a medicine pouch around your neck. For your pet, place the crystals next to body parts that need healing; for cats, dogs, horses, and birds, in their resting spot and water bowl; for fish, a turtle, frog, spider, lizard or snake, in their tank; for a plant, in their pot. Adjust accordingly with crystals that are water soluble, sensitive to acid, photosensitive, and toxic.

Again, for space reasons, I provide only a small list of crystals and what they heal; however, you can visit my website to review the complete list, and you can buy more-detailed books as well.

Rainbow Medicine: Therapy with the A-Team!

Rainbow Medicine is about engaging in therapy with your A-Team through channeling techniques and divination tools. This process involves asking for insight and guidance into your underlying issues—emotional, physical, psychological, and spiritual. By having conversations through light trance work, and pulling cards and channeling answers according to questions asked, we can gain tremendous insight into the seeds of our discomforts and illnesses, and heal ourselves.

Rainbow Medicine

To begin this portion of *Rainbow Medicine*, we will remind you to set up your *sacred safe space* and follow the same ritual each time.

Smudge
Music
Candle
Journal
Divination Tools

Step One: Prepare Tools

Get ready to channel a full body scan from your A-Team to identify where your energy blockages are and their story.

Paint Chips

Using psychometry, you will hold an object in one hand, and write down information you receive psychically with the other. For this body scan, you will be channeling your chakras' stories from seven different colored paper paint chips you picked up from a hardware store or made at home, one to represent each chakra; red, orange, yellow, green, sky blue, indigo, and violet or white.

Fabric Pouches

Throughout this *blind reading* exercise you are never meant to identify the colored chips you are psychically reading your charkas from until after you channeled the information. This is called a *blind reading*. You will need to place them in pouches, envelopes or keep them turned over at all times. I prefer to use pouches, they can be purchased at a *Dollar Store*, designs should be opaque and serene.

Select seven different colored pouches and place one paint chip in each. Do this part with your eyes closed to assure a blind reading.

Timer

Place all pouches in front of you and sit down on something comfortable. Set a timer for three-minute rounds and get ready to psychically read each pouch and channel the information recorded in that chakra. As you hold the bag in your hand and channel, remember to write down the bag's color so as to identify it later when you reveal the respective chakra/paint chip.

Journal

Tell me the story going on in this chakra?

In this exercise you are picking up a holistic storyline for each chakra so try not to sensor any information that comes through, even when it feels uncomfortable. You may hear words, catch phrases, songs; you may see cartoon characters, movie scenes or personal snapshots from your life; you may feel tingles, itches or pains in certain areas; you may smell odors or taste things in your mouth. Be open to everything you receive while you are holding the pouch and channeling the information, and write it *all* down.

Step Two: Body Scan

Begin. Take two minutes to meditate with eyes closed and breath calmly to find your rhythm and settle in to the Channel. Once you feel ready, turn your timer on and select a pouch. Hold each bag in your hand for three minutes and write down what you see, feel, hear, think, taste and smell.

Once complete, look at all the bags in front of you and select one bag to reread for the second time.

Step Three: Reveal~Review

After this last three-minute round, briefly review all written material. Don't be worried if at first it doesn't make any sense, it will once you begin to understand more about the individual chakras, decode your symbols, and make the links. Pay attention to stories, themes, patterns, memories, and insights you received.

Now it's time to reveal each paint chip and match the colored chakra with the corresponding channeled information. Also, identify the chakra you read twice as this is the one your A-Team wish to highlight.

Step Four: Chakra Research

Read the chakra chapters to learn about them and make the links in how these insights inform your diagnosis, strengths, imbalances, and healing. Look to identify your stronger chakras and weaker ones. Read about and become familiar with the archetypal, psychological, emotional, physical and spiritual components of each chakra to contextual your reading and understand what needs healing. Then, when you are ready to heal, engage in the healing chakra therapy exercises presented at the end of each chakra chapter and bring your issues to the Light. You can choose to work in the sequential order of the chakras or begin the next round of therapy exercises with the chakra you read twice.

Please note that this full body workout activates much *inner* house-cleaning. Do not be surprised or worried if you develop any emotional and physical aches or pains as a result, they are simply energy blockages being released, cleared and repaired. Should you manifest any symptoms, please review the corresponding chakra chapters to identify them and what they represent.

Final Note

If this exercise feels confusing or difficult, skip it and move directly to the Root Chakra. If medical intuition is for you, we suggest you conduct this *full body chakra scan* first, then investigate the individual charkas. This will provide you with a full body picture to better understand and con-textualize the information you receive concerning the individual chakras. And, if you enjoy this exercise, schedule *Group Chakra Therapy* once a month.

Root Chakra

Color Red, black, brown
Element Earth
Issue Support, Survival, Grounding, Safety, Connectedness
Demon Fear, insecurity, alienation
Balanced Archetype The Mother/Goddess
Imbalanced Archetype The Victim
Codependent Pattern Compliance
Codependent Behavior Defensiveness, paranoia, dishonesty, bullying
Complementary Chakra Heart, Crown
Intimacy Physical
Gland Adrenals
Body Part Hips, legs, knees, ankles, feet, bones, large intestines, nose
Body System Endocrine, Eliminative, Circulatory, Skeletal, Respiratory
Dis-ease and Illness Sexual dysfunctions, low blood pressure, poor circulation, cold extremities, varicose veins, joint stiffness, leg, knee, ankle, feet and toe problems, chronic lower back pain, constipation/diarrhea, colds/sinus congestion, runny/stuffed nose, bipolar disorder, personality and anxiety disorders, autoimmune diseases
Sense Smell
Spiritual Gift Clairalience (smell)
Glandular Prescription psychotherapy, rainbow medicine, nature walks, walking, yoga, dancing, cycling, jogging, grocery shopping, eating, sex, cuddling, renovating, landscaping, gardening
Animal Prescription Rabbit, Mouse, Wasp, Bear
Crystal Prescription Red Jasper, Hematite, Black Obsidian, Snowflake Obsidian, Jet, Red Calcite

The first chakra, the Root chakra, is red; it is physically located at the base of the spine, and it spins at the slowest vibrational rate because it is the closest color to the Earth. Red is associated with the blood of Mother Earth, and its roots are like veins, rooting us strongly into the ground to manifest our desires and dreams. This chakra represents our survival instincts, the triggering of the *flight-or-fight* response, and the way we cope with change. Its element is Earth (action and grounding).

Root Archetype

When we are in balance, we feel connected to other earth spirits, such as humans, animals, nature, etc., and this connection with being alive brings us a sense of inner security. The way we know we are out of alignment, however, is that we feel insecure and alienated. Feeling lost and overly consumed with the notion of "fitting in" are the cues that we need to bring ourselves back into balance. When this chakra is blocked, the most common traits are sexual dysfunction, anger, frustration, obsession with money, inability to let go of people, situations, emotions, and thoughts, and feeling stuck.

When in balance, the archetype we embody is that of the Mother/Goddess. Whether male or female, this person is nurturing, supportive, optimistic, hopeful, and has absolute faith in the goodness of life and the positive outcome of situations. This person sees life as *the glass is half full.*

Balanced Root qualities are being grounded, stable, structured, and disciplined; feeling comfortable with our connections and surroundings; feeling safe and secure; feeling safe and comfortable in our body; being able to trust; being physically agile; having good survival instincts; having a good sense of smell; being patient; being able to be still; having good health and vitality; having a good appetite; and being able to manifest dreams and prosperity.

The motto is "It's not what we accomplish, but how we get there."

When out of balance, the archetype we embody is that of the Victim, dependent on others for our own happiness.

When out of balance, Root qualities are fear for our safety; fear of being hurt psychologically and/or physically; being edgy around people; having difficulty letting go of people and/or situations; being flighty and indecisive;

feeling fearful, anxious, and/or restless; experiencing financial difficulty; having poor focus, poor discipline, and poor boundaries; hoarding; being disorganized, greedy, sluggish, lazy, and/or tired; fearing change; being addicted to security; and having rigid boundaries.

The motto is "Succeeding by any means necessary, even at the expense of others."

Red, black, and brown are the colors of the Root chakra. Red is the color that warms, activates, and stimulates. Think passion, fire, life force, enthusiasm, excitement, energy, motivation, outgoingness, ambition, persistence, aggression, danger, lust, sexuality, and stop signs. Murky red may mean the person is hard to please, impatient, and irritable. Black is the color of the unknown. Think fear, completion of a cycle, the void, the abyss, termination, and darkness. Brown is the color of earth. Think being grounded and committed.

Root Psychology

The function of this chakra is to ground us with roots like that of a tree so that when the winds blow in, like a tree, we bend but don't break. A healthy Root chakra is exemplified by flexibility, flowing through change and not being in resistance to it. There is an implicit sense of trust and belonging, of knowing that we will get through difficult, challenging times. When crisis hits, a healthy Root chakra is exemplified by a person who reaches out to community for support in a time of transition. Finding a steady and true connection sustains us when our grounding is weak and our spirit is darkened. Being part of a community helps us to develop tolerance and compassion for ourselves and others. And, when our usual community of people no longer mirrors who and where we are, there are always new ones to seek out.

The psychological function of the Root chakra is survival and self-preservation, and its dysfunction is fear and victimhood. Basic rights of this chakra are *a right to be here, and to have joy, happiness, health, and a creative existence.*

Psychological issues here relate to physical identity: how we perceive the self, as well as how we perceives others' perceptions of us. This physical identity is concerned with our roots, our sense of security, survival, trust, and nourishment, and our health, home, family, and financial well-being.

Life and death issues affect the operation of this chakra in a big way, and manifest in relationships, sexual expression, emotions related to fear of abandonment, shame, and worthiness, and our style of boundaries. Attitudes of separation, exclusivity, belonging, and a right to our own space are rooted in the Root chakra.

Childhood traumas and abuses to the Root chakra are physical, and are caused by birth trauma, abandonment, physical neglect, poor physical bonding with mother, malnourishment, feeding difficulties, major illness or surgery, physical abuse, a violent environment, and inherited traumas from parents' survival fears (surviving war, financial disaster, etc.)

These traumas manifest as fears related to physical and financial safety, self-worth, and deservedness: Having a roof over my head and finances, to boot. Can I take care of me? Can I take care of someone else? Past lives are found in this chakra, which means that both our past lives, as well as our ancestors' underlying beliefs about life and survival, are genetically encoded in this chakra and are triggered when we are confronted with crisis and change.

The life lesson of the Root chakra is to learn how to feel deserving of and manifest the life we say we want. Ways we learn this lesson are by valuing the material as sacred, finding trust in place of despair, persevering through all odds, and noticing the beauty and perfection of the natural world.

The soul lesson of the Root is service. By serving others, we teach through our life experience and lessons, and therefore create a bridge of connectivity and a sense of belonging.

The motto is "I love my body. I am safe. I am never alone."

Root Emotions

Living too much from the Root chakra is exemplified by being too attached to materiality, such as land, home, family, tradition, religion, physical identity, class, race, etc. This does not permit a person to embrace and potentiate individuality and express unique talents. Pettiness, ignorance, separateness, despair, a lack of trust in life, and a victim mentality are qualities exemplified in an imbalanced Root chakra.

Developing our internal resources comes from living life and experiencing change. The greater amount of inner stability we mentally create, the more grounded in life we become. To get through the "why is this happening to me?" experience, it is important to gain a spiritual perspective in which to view our life experiences. (This is the lesson of the Crown chakra, so as to balance out the Root—just like the tree).

Since we are Spirit having a human experience, understanding the life lessons we are here to learn helps us to move through challenges and focus on their gifts. When lessons are not learned, the trauma and triggers will continue to replay themselves in new experiences. My favorite expression in response to this is "To become wise, we must learn from the whys." When we narrow our life choices, we suffocate our potential; but when we focus on personal growth and spiritual development, we blossom. My second-favorite expression is "Get with *your* program!"

At first, it may be difficult to step out of the normal dictates of what people in your life expect from you, but the more you live, love, communicate, and make choices by your unique prescription, the more defined your new roots will eventually become. When it comes to your happiness, stability, and joy, you need no one's approval but your own.

Root Pattern
Just as every chakra is interrelated with the one below and above it, each is also linked to its complimentary chakra. Look to the Heart and Crown chakras to heal the Root chakra.

Compliance is the imbalanced behavior pattern found in the Root chakra. It is characterized by a sense of loyalty that allows a person to remain in less than kind situations for too long; a fear to express opinions when they differ from others, a sense of *walking on eggshells*; putting aside interests to do what others want, and sometimes this involves compromising values and integrity; engaging in sex when the desire is love; and, a hypersensitivity to and over identification with the feelings of others, thus taking them on.

When in balance, we choose situations that are consistent with our values and goals; we prioritize our emotional, psychological, physical, and spiritual safety; we express our opinions appropriately; we consider our interests when asked to participate with others; We do not settle for sex when the intention is love; and, we take responsibility for our feelings and allow others to take responsibility for theirs.

Root Intimacy

The Root chakra governs *physical intimacy*: sex, touch, cuddling, and physical activity together such as eating, nature walks, walking, cycling, dance, gardening, and renovation. Other activities include basic life necessities like financial planning and buying groceries. Romantic relationships must include plenty of together time to count as intimate, with sex serving as only one aspect.

Chakra intimacy is about realigning yourself to attract fulfilling relationships and experience a more complete life. If this interests you, I recommend Cyndi Dale's book *Beyond Soul Mates*.

Root Dis-eases and Malfunctions

In the Root chakra, physical and psychological dis-eases and illnesses are either minor and constant or serious and flare up suddenly. Body parts associated with the Root chakra are the hips, legs, knees, ankles, feet, large intestines, bones, and nose.

Physical dis-eases and illnesses that manifest from a blocked Root chakra are weight problems (underweight, overweight); water retention; hemorrhoids; constipation and diarrhea; male fertility issues (such as impotence); sciatica; chronic lower back pain; chronic joint stiffness and sudden joint flare-ups; varicose veins; degenerative arthritis; foot, knee, ankle, and hip troubles; bone problems and osteoporosis; autoimmune deficiencies; low blood pressure; shock; and colds.

Psychological dis-eases and disorders that manifest from a blocked or overactive Root chakra are personality and anxiety disorders; anxiety and panic attacks; phobias; insecurity; and clinical depression.

Root Body Systems

Every chakra is related and positioned next to a gland, or glands, in the body. Just as every chakra is interrelated with the one below and above it, so are the glands and body systems. The body systems that affect the Root chakra are the endocrine, eliminative, circulatory, skeletal, and respiratory systems.

Endocrine System: Adrenals

The glands associated with the Root chakra are the *adrenals*. The adrenals are glands of emergency, self-preservation, and protection. They control the *flight-or-fight* response to stresses, threats, and accidents, by secreting hormones which keep us actively present in life-threatening situations. They break down proteins from food, and when the body is in a time of need or emergency, they stimulate the metabolism.

The adrenals are located on top of both kidneys and are responsible for helping a person cope with physical and emotional stress by secreting two hormones: *epinephrine* and *norepinephrine*. Epinephrine (also called *adrenaline*) is the hormone that helps the body to respond to stress by increasing the heart rate, facilitating blood flow to the muscles and brain, and converting glycogen to glucose. Norepinephrine (also called *nor-adrenaline*) is the hormone that increases blood pressure in response to acute stress. When the body is constantly operating from fear, the adrenal glands work too hard, and the immune system eventually weakens. This is how we get sick.

Eliminative System

The adrenals, because they are located over the kidneys, are related to the eliminative system. The eliminative system filters and excretes waste through the kidneys and urinary bladder in the form of urine (liquid waste), through intestinal tract as bowel movements (solid waste), and through the skin (sweat). The kidneys have cellular memory of our ancestors' survival instincts; hence their relationship to the Root chakra.

Overtaxed adrenals represent long-standing anxieties and worries. They can reflect a refusal to care for the self in healthy ways and a resistance to responding to important issues in our life or in the lives of those closest to us. Malfunctions of the Root can also reflect how we perceive others' responses, or lack of response, to our issues.

Circulatory System

The Root chakra is related to the circulatory system, which is the body's transport system. It circulates blood and nutrients throughout the body via the heart and vessels, such as arteries, capillaries, and veins. The heart pumps the blood, and the arteries and veins transport it. Oxygen-rich blood leaves the left side of the heart and enters the biggest artery, called the *aorta.* The aorta branches into smaller arteries, which then branch into even smaller vessels that travel all over the body. When blood enters the smallest blood vessels, which are called capillaries and are found in body tissue, it gives nutrients and oxygen to the cells and takes in carbon dioxide, water, and waste. The blood, which no longer contains oxygen and nutrients, then goes back to the heart through the veins. Veins carry waste products away from cells and bring blood back to the heart, which pumps it to the lungs to pick up oxygen and eliminate carbon dioxide.

Problems here usually stem from lack of vitality for an area in one's life. Circulation problems are tied to how we allow our emotions to circulate and flow. When emotions flow too easily, it reflects no control. When emotions are not being allowed to circulate, it reflects too much control. Either way, this often creates high/low blood pressure. Circulatory conditions reflect a person who is locked in the past, afraid to move on, unable to resolve old emotional issues, and harboring an attitude of self-defeatism.

Skeletal System

The Root chakra is related to the skeletal system, which includes bones, cartilage, and joints. This system has both mechanical functions and physiological functions.

Mechanical functions relate to our bones, which support, protect, and move the body. Our bones are a rigid framework that protects soft tissues, such as our internal organs(brain, heart, lungs, and the organs in the pelvic region).

Physiological functions include blood-cell production (in the bone marrow) and the supply and storing of important minerals. Blood-cell production converts chemical energy into mechanical energy through blood formation, providing a reservoir of minerals.

Bone problems reflect what we may or may not be protecting the quality of support or structure in our lives; or we may lack support and structure. The organ related to the broken bone will highlight what you are protecting, or not, and the significance of that organ in your life.

Respiratory System

The Root chakra is related to the respiratory system, which acquires oxygen and eliminates carbon dioxide. The major organs are the nose, lungs, larynx, trachea, and bronchial tubes. When we breathe in, air enters the nose or mouth and goes down a long tube called the *trachea* (wind-pipe). The trachea branches into two bronchial tubes, or *primary bronchi*, which go to the lungs. The primary bronchi branch off into even smaller bronchial tubes, or *bronchioles*. The bronchioles end in the *alveoli*, or air sacs. Oxygen follows this path, passes through the walls of the air sacs and blood vessels, and enters the bloodstream. At the same time, carbon dioxide passes into the lungs and is exhaled.

Breathing is essential for life; therefore, problems with breathing reflect issues of a right to life. Feeling undeserving or guilty about how you live, or feeling like you are not living your best life or not allowed to live your best life, and therefore are suppressing your life expressions and emotions, all can lead to respiratory issues. Unequal exchanges in the life process reflect grief, such as one-sided giving, or taking in too much, and this lodges in the lungs and manifests breathing dis-eases and disorders, such as asthma and pneumonia.

Root Animal Medicine

Rabbit, Mouse, Wasp, and Bear Medicine are the Root's prescriptions.

Rabbit teaches us how to navigate through fear. Most predators detect their prey through movement, but when Rabbit senses a predator, it freezes. This adaptable behavior allows it to go undetected. With quick hops and jumps and knowing when to stay put, Rabbit teaches us about timing, showing us that if we get off path, we always have the ability to return and make great strides. As a divination symbol, Rabbit can refer to a one-month period when something will manifest; it is also my symbol for having a talent to manifest something quickly, like pulling a rabbit out of the hat, and often, it is a message about a child in spirit. A steady combination of patience and hopping forward is Rabbit's medicine.

Mouse teaches us to pay attention to details and what is going on in our lives. With its little body, speedy and perceptive intelligence, and great organization skills, Mouse reminds us that no big task cannot be accomplished or problem resolved if we approach it one step at a time. Mouse is known for keeping a clean house, being well groomed, and being good at storing food for a rainy day. Mouse, therefore, shows us the importance of respecting our bodies and learning how to provide for ourselves. As a divination symbol, Mouse refers to learning our life lessons and getting off the hamster wheel, so to speak. When I see them in a pack, this means industrious teamwork.

I like to work with Wasp Medicine to encourage self-assertiveness, establish boundaries and limitations, and break free from compliant behavior. Wasp teaches us how to defend and guard what we worked hard for and hold dear. We associate Wasp medicine with the Fire element and the Solar Plexus chakra. Wasp says, "Back off, buddy."

I like to work with Bear Medicine to discourage hyperactivity and promote grounding. Bear teaches us how to work efficiently with cycles and proper pacing. We associate Bear medicine with all four elements, and the Root and Crown chakras. Bear says, "No worries, I am on the job; when heart and mind are aligned, the highest path is clear."

Root Crystal Medicine

Red Jasper, Hematite, Black Obsidian, Snowflake Obsidian, Jet, Red Calcite

Crystals carry with them specific healing properties for humans and animals. They can be programmed through our intention for healing and divination. There are two ways we suggest you select your crystals; *intuitively* and *deliberately*.

Crystals call us. Therefore, allow yourself to browse a crystal selection and wait for the one that intuitively reels you in. When you research its medicinal properties, you will be amazed at how that stone spoke to you and your needs.

The second way is to deliberately select your stone based on the dis-ease or illness you wish to heal. For example:

When my dogs are constipated, they will drink a Red Calcite and Black Obsidian elixir to boost the Eliminative system; when any of us are suffering from physical discomfort, I will place a Hematite with appropriate stones around specific body parts to absorb the pain and heal that area/condition. Use the Internet to guide you in making your elixirs with crystals that are water soluble, photosensitive, sensitive to acid, and toxic.

Combining crystals with handpicked healing stones, aromatherapy, herbs, and animal medicine, I also work with my Guides as a medical intuitive using body scanning, remote viewing, and energy healing to detect and heal what is going on in the body. At the end of each chakra chapter, we show you how to conduct holistic health readings for yourself.

As a final note, you do not have to be an expert to conduct a healing session on yourself or your pet. You will learn as you practice so here are a few pointers:

Crystal Selection

When selecting your crystals and animal totems, know that each will res-onate with specific chakras and assist in rebalancing and healing specific emotional, psychological, and physical energetic imprints (dis-eases). Often, one chakra will require the energy of another to recalibrate and heal so keep this in mind when you work with crystal and animal medicine.

Healing Session

When performing a healing session, combine love-based intention with the medicinal properties of the crystal(s) and animal spirit. Experiment with therapeutic ways to work with crystal and animal energies, they will teach you, so listen carefully.

Intuitive Nudges

Listen to the intuitive nudges from your Guides, they will direct you to the material you need.

Red Jasper
Astrological Associations: Taurus, Aries

Healing Qualities: Helps to reduce stress, worry, and anxiety, and aids in deep transformation when one cycle ends and a new one begins.

Physical Benefits: As a tonic, it helps to prevent illness and fevers. Good for blood circulation, the libido and prolongs sexual pleasure, and helps unblocks blockages in the liver and bile ducts.

Hematite
Astrological Associations: Aries, Aquarius

Healing Qualities: Good for timid people. Helps to move forward with confidence, courage and strength; good for strengthening willpower, healing insomnia, improving memory recall and anything to do with numbers and legal matters. Good for clear thinking and intervening in addictions like smoking, overeating, drinking, and all sorts of indulgences. Helps with hysteria, stress, and making choices, which is the cause for much insomnia and poor memory recall. Helps with grounding.

Physical Benefits: Pain relief, such as backache, headaches, and menstrual cramping and flooding; helps the formation of red blood cells. Good for blood issues like clotting and anemia; also good for Raynaud's disease. Assists with bone fractures, spinal alignment, and leg cramps; eases travel sickness; draws heat from the body.

Black Obsidian
Astrological Association: Sagittarius, Scorpio, Capricorn

Healing Qualities: Helps with protection, grounding, creativity, psychic abilities, and shamanic healing.

Physical Benefits: Drinking it as an elixir is good for digestive disorders and digestion, fevers, chills, hardened arteries, cramps, injuries, pain, joint pain, bleeding, enlarged prostate, arthritis, detoxification, and blockages.

Snowflake Obsidian
Astrological Association: Virgo

Healing Qualities: Helps to release feelings of loneliness, unhealthy behaviour and mental patterns such as fear, anger and resentment, detoxes mind, body and emotions, "wrong thinking."

Physical Benefits: Drinking it as an elixir it is good for stomach, sinuses, eyesight, veins, bones, joint pain, cramps, pain, bleeding, wound healing, injuries, circulation, warming the extremities, arthritis, and the skin.

Jet
Astrological Association: Capricorn

Healing Qualities: Enhances male/female balance of energy within and when in balance we see things differently, which enables us to find solutions to old problems (Black Banded Agate also helps with this). Helps with ridding the self of fear and depression allowing you to move forward and attract abundance. Good for mood swings.

Physical Benefits: Helps with migraines, swollen glands, colds, stomach aches, menstrual cramps, epilepsy, and glandular and lymphatic swelling.

Red Calcite
Astrological Sign: Cancer

Healing Qualities: Good for reducing anxiety and panic attacks, helps with ADHD and OCD, study, laziness, motivation.

Physical Benefits: Good for organs of elimination, kidneys, pancreas, and spleen, constipation and intestinal conditions, blood clotting, skin and tissue healing, immune system, stiff joints and bones, calcium absorption, and dissolves calcification.

Rainbow Medicine

Root Chakra
Color Red (black, brown)

Issue
Circle your issues:

- Support
- Survival
- Grounding
- Safety
- Connectedness

Demon
Circle your demons:

- Fear
- Insecurity
- Alienation

Codependent Behavior
Circle your behaviors:

- Defensiveness
- Paranoia
- Dishonesty

- Bullying

Codependent Pattern
Circle your Compliance patterns:

- Loyal, remaining in less than kind situations for too long
- Fear to express opinions when they differ from others, *walking on eggshells*
- Putting aside interests to do what others want
- Compromising values and integrity
- Engaging in sex when the desire is love
- Hypersensitivity to and over identification with the feelings of others, taking them on

Root Lesson
Since our chakras require regular maintenance, check in with each regularly by pulling two cards. I like to use a Tarot and an oracle deck but if you do not know Tarot, select two oracle decks, one with images and the other with words.

Begin each Monday by asking the question:

What lesson does my Root chakra want me to focus on today?

Shuffle and pull out one card from each deck. Analyze the cards in response to how they speak to the issues of this particular chakra.

Root Map
Take out two decks, one with images and one with words, and ask your Higher Self and Guides:

Show me my big picture story theme in my Root chakra?

Shuffle and pull out one card from each deck. Analyze the cards in response to how they speak to the issues of this particular chakra.

Root Issues

Continue with the same decks and pull two cards according to the following questions. Work with one question at a time. Once you receive your cards, study them and write down every answer you are able to interpret. Remember to analyze the cards according to questions asked. If you need additional information or clarification for any question, pull more cards. When you move on to the next question, place all cards back into the decks. Sometimes you will see how the same cards will keep coming to you, this is Spirit's way of emphasizing the issue.

Since the Root relates to "root" issues about fear, support, alienation, and community, interpret your cards by looking for answers/responses to the following:

What do I fear?
What ancestral pattern did I come here to break?
What past-life theme am I am currently working through?
What is my relationship with money?
How do I feel about my physical presence?
What do my actions demonstrate?
What message does my Root have for me?

Once you have reviewed all your channeled information, reconnect with your big picture theme. Connect all dots to identify the storyline, and write a brief paragraph summarizing your Root Reading.

Root Energy with Cards
Try this exercise by pulling cards for your Root and reading them psychically.

What energy is in my Root?

After you pull a couple of cards from your selected decks, don't look at them, place them together in one hand and face down hold them over your Root chakra. This will trigger information to come. You will feel the energy in that area, so it is important to write down everything you feel, taste, smell, sense, hear, think, and see.

Once you have completed the exercise, review your written material. Next, look at your cards to see how they relate to what you picked

up in meditation. The cards' meanings and images coupled with your channeled impressions will further inform your Root reading.

Psychic Root Scan

What Animal Medicine does my Root need?

Another way to pick up information about yourself or someone else is to scan your body using your mind and body sensations. Ask your Guide to give you the symbol of an animal that reflects the coping behavior you need to adopt.

Sacral Chakra

Color Orange

Element Water

Issue Sweetness, Desires, Dreams, Sexuality, Joy, Creativity

Demon Guilt, selfishness, low self-esteem

Balanced Archetype Empress/Emperor

Imbalanced Archetype The Martyr

Codependent Pattern Avoidance

Codependent Behavior Addiction (sexual), excessive behavior, manipulation

Complementary Chakra Throat

Intimacy Emotional

Gland Ovaries and Testes

Body Part Womb, vagina, penis, kidneys, bladder, intestines

Body System Endocrine, Reproductive, Eliminative, Nervous

Dis-ease and Illness PMS, (peri)menopause, impotence, infertility, urinary tract infections, vaginal infections, STDs, eating disorders, chronic back pain

Sense: Taste

Spiritual Gift Clairgustance (taste)

Glandular Prescription Healthy boundaries, activities that encourage self-care, self-worth and joy, swimming, sculpture, culinary arts, creating a project/business

Animal Prescription Blue Heron, Wolf, Ant, Skunk

Crystal Prescription Carnelian, Orange Calcite, Copper, Moonstone, Picasso Marble

The second chakra is the Sacral chakra; it is located in the uterus/pelvic area, our pleasure center, the womb in which we give birth to our dreams and desires. It spins orange, and is associated with right-brain creativity (imagination), the water element (emotions and values), balance between pleasure and work, and female yin energy (Empress; Grandmother Moon; creation, patience, fluidity, nurturance, unconditional love).

Sacral Archetype

This chakra represents our self-worth and confidence. When we are in balance, we feel creative, worthy, and self-accepting of our authentic nature and our power as a sexual being. The way we know we are out of alignment, however, is that we either behave selfishly or give way too much. This results from having low self-esteem. *Not feeling good enough and therefore giving too much or not enough* is the cue that we need to bring ourselves back into balance. When blocked, lack of creativity and infertility both can occur. Sexual encounters with people also tend to leave their energetic imprints here, causing dis-ease and illness.

When in balance, the archetype we embody is that of the Empress. This is a person who loves to have abundance in life, knows he or she deserves good things, and understands how to enjoy the physical aspects of life, without abuse or guilt.

Balanced Sacral qualities are effortless creativity, graceful movement, and emotional intelligence; ability to experience pleasure, and to give and receive pleasure equally in all matters; ability to nurture self and others; ability to create and maintain healthy boundaries with respect to well-being, sexuality, sensuality, and abundance; ability to have balanced relationships; ability to experience a sense of self-fulfillment and enjoyment from being alone as well as with others; ability to appreciate the beauty in life; and ability to change.

The motto is "Don't let others' nastiness bring you down; instead, let them inspire you to walk your highest path. When faced with adversity, call upon your Divine support, which will help you laugh instead of getting angry."

When out of balance, the archetype is that of the Martyr. This is someone who deprives himself or herself of the pleasures and goodness of life; instead, he or she punishes the self out of guilt, projecting this onto others and making them suffer.

Imbalanced Sacral qualities are trouble being creative; feeling under-valued and unappreciated; difficulty connecting with others; giving too much; feeling depressed; having a hard time experiencing joy; displaying sexual addiction/acting out sexually, or the opposite, fearing sex; display-ing pleasure addiction, or the opposite, denial of pleasure; and displaying frigidity and rigidity. This person is ruled by emotions. He or she is over-sensitive and even hysterical; has bipolar mood swings; is diagnosed with Borderline Personality Disorder; is addicted to crisis; has poor and/or excessive boundaries (letting others in too much and/or invading the space of others); uses seductive manipulation, emotional dependency, obsessive attachment, and game playing (swinging between lack of desire and excess of passion and excitement).

The motto is "Choosing deception, manipulation, and emotional blackmail to achieve desired outcomes instead of accomplishing goals honorably."

Orange, the color of the Sacral chakra, is the color of joy, creativity, play-fulness, fun, pleasure, giving birth to desires and dreams, positivity, opti-mism, sociability, consideration, and thoughtfulness. When dull and almost brown, a person may be overly emotional, indulging, suffering from addic-tion, and exhausted. Sacral chakra issues relate to feelings of unworthi-ness and worthiness.

Sacral Psychology

The role of this chakra is to learn balance between play and work through self-discipline and maturity. For example, learning how to honor the body by giving it enough (neither excessive nor deficient) nourishment, through food, pleasure, joy, rest, and exercise, is the way that we bring this chakra into balance. When we feel deserving, the body thrives because we treat it well. When we make life complex, we strip away pleasure and the per-mission to have the things we truly desire. Activities that feed the soul and generate joy feed this chakra. Respecting limits that are neither too flexible nor too rigid nourishes the body, and thus also nourishes our life.

The psychological function of the Sacral chakra is desire and self-gratifi-cation; its dysfunction is guilt. Basic rights of this chakra are *a right to feel and to have pleasure.*

Psychological issues here relate to emotional identity, and attitudes of being good enough to deserve a joyful life and having enough to appreciate enjoyment. When healthy, this emotional identity is concerned with delighting in good health; when unhealthy, it uses sickness to attract wants and needs.

Childhood traumas and abuses to the Sacral chakra are emotional, and are caused by sexual abuse, emotional abuse, physical abuse, volatile situations, neglect, coldness, rejection, denial of a child's feeling states, enmeshment, emotional manipulation, overuse of playpen (restricting normal movement), religious/moral severity, alcoholic families, and inherited issues from parents who haven't worked out their own issues around sexuality, incest, etc.

The life lessons of the Sacral chakra are knowing and feeling that you are good enough; having enough exercise, food, rest, fun, and money; not linking self-worth with what you do or have; and creating healthy boundaries to protect your life force.

The soul lesson is peace and wisdom.

The motto is "I deserve pleasure in my life."

Sacral Emotions

Anodea Judith refers to healthy pleasures as *Type 1 Pleasures:* laughter, family vacations, nature, nurturing communication, and so forth. If our parents did not teach us this balance at home—meaning, if it was all play and no work, or all work and no play—then as we get older and seek pleasure, for pleasure is a necessary part of living, we go to *Type 2 Pleasures.* These are addictions, which never feed the soul; examples are drug/alcohol abuse, gambling, too much sex/love, shopping, and anything that is excessive and makes you feel like you are a bottomless pit.

Although boundaries are instinctive in the Root chakra, boundaries are learned in this chakra, so if you were abused, emotionally, physically or sexually, chances are that you have a pattern in your life where you either let someone have all of you and/or walk all over you, or you shut people out by putting up a wall. This resulted because your rights were overridden and so you oscillate between both extremes.

The Sacral chakra is concerned with self-deservedness, and it controls our appetite for food, sex, and pleasure. *Is what I have and who I am good enough?* The negative response to this *I am not worthy enough to feel good and to experience pleasure,* which manifests as making others feel guilty for not making the life of the sacrally damaged person better. This leads to excessive indulgent behavior, which burns up energy, depleting the rest of the body and making us hungry; alternatively, it leads to deficient behavior, which slows us down and makes us lose our appetite.

This chakra is responsible for refueling the body with vital energy; therefore, a balanced lifestyle is key. Good nutrition, sufficient hydration, ample rest, and time off from stress all are necessary to revitalize. If this doesn't occur, then other parts of the body become affected. Knowing when to stop, when something is enough, and recuperating from illness or abuse are very important boundaries for maintaining health. When people don't appreciate what you do or who you are, it is a natural reaction to do more to win approval. When we know that who we are and what we do are good enough, then we make healthy decisions for our well-being. Loss and frustration are the emotions in this chakra; therefore, learning how to be grateful for what we have and do not have releases these emotions, helping us to focus our attention on finding positive ways to express our haves, our doings, and our becomings.

Sacral Pattern

Just as every chakra is interrelated with the one below and above it, each is also linked to its complimentary chakra. Look to the Throat chakra to heal the Sacral chakra.

Avoidance is the imbalanced behavior pattern found in the Sacral and Throat chakras. It is characterized by actions that encourage rejection and shame, a cat and mouse *catch me if you can* game; addictions that distract from accomplishing goals; harsh judgments of others; indirect communication as a means to avoid confrontation; suppressing feelings so as not to feel vulnerable; and an *I love you, I hate you* dualistic dynamic.

When in balance, we act in ways that encourage loving responses; we engage only in healthy authentic relationships and maintain healthy boundaries; we accept people as they are; we honor and share our emotions using direct communication to resolve conflict; and we express our appreciation appropriately.

Sacral Intimacy

The Sacral chakra governs *emotional intimacy*: emotional connectivity such as considering our romantic partner our best friend and confidante. Both partners express themselves in loving and true feeling ways inviting the full expression of five main feelings: fear, anger, sadness, joy, and disgust.

When feelings are shared kindly and accepted with gratitude, the relationship encourages childlike wonder in an environment that is accepting and freeing. Both partners feel comfortable playing, giggling, and acting silly. Together they turn on the creative juices seeking innovative solutions to their individual problems as well as joint issues. They see all challenges as stepping-stones to connectivity.

Sacral Dis-eases and Malfunctions

In the Sacral chakra, physical and psychological dis-eases and illnesses are toxic and psychosomatic. Body parts associated with the Sacral chakra are the womb, genitals, kidneys, bladder, and intestines.

Physical dis-eases and illnesses that manifest from a blocked Sacral chakra are male and female sexual dysfunctions, such as infertility, impotence, frigidity, premature ejaculation, lack of orgasm, gynecological problems and disorders, blockages, sterility, and problems and diseases affecting the male and female reproductive organs; problems with the bladder and kidneys; urinary tract infections and illnesses; menstrual difficulties and dysfunction, such as menstrual cramping, PMS, and fibroids; prostate issues; chronic lower back pain and sciatica; lack of flexibility; deadened senses; irritable bowel syndrome (IBS); intestinal dysfunction; liver dysfunction; gallbladder disorders; spleen conditions; and eating disorders, such as anorexia and bulimia.

Psychological dis-eases and disorders that manifest from a blocked or overactive Sacral chakra are lack of confidence; loss of/excessive appetite for food, sex, and life; addictions of all kinds; and unbalanced emotions.

Sacral Body Systems

Every chakra is related and positioned next to a gland, or glands, in the body. Just as every chakra is interrelated with the one below and above it, so are the glands and body systems. The body systems that affect the Sacral chakra are the endocrine, reproductive, eliminative, and nervous systems.

Endocrine System: Testes and Ovaries

The glands associated with the Sacral chakra are the ovaries (in women) and the testes (in men); these glands mature at around age fourteen, are responsible for the procreation of our species, and are the main source of sex hormones. In males, the testes produce a hormone called *testosterone*. These hormones affect male characteristics, such as sexual development, facial hair growth, pubic hair growth, and sperm production. Qualities are linked to left-brain logic, assertiveness, and self-confidence. In females, the ovaries, located on both sides of the uterus, produce *estrogen*, *progesterone*, and *eggs*. These hormones control breast development, menstruation, and pregnancy. Qualities are linked to right-brain creativity and emotional wellbeing.

Attitudes about sexuality are related to the problems we manifest in this area. How we value our spiritual, physical, and emotional body is connected to our attitude about growing up, having a family, and enjoying our sexuality. This chakra works from a deep unconscious realm affected by how much we value and honor ourselves. Boundaries and limitations on how we take care of ourselves are key to the necessary hormonal flow that influences our energy.

Reproductive System

The reproductive system replaces damaged or dead cells in the body; it is a creative system because it reproduces the human being. The organs are the penis, testes, and scrotum in men; and the ovaries, uterus, clitoris, vagina, and mammary glands in women. Sperm from the male fertilizes the female's egg (ovum), in the fallopian tube. The fertilized egg travels from the fallopian tube to the uterus, where the fetus develops over a period of nine months.

Problems here reflect an inability to be creative and productive in our own life. Depending on one's perspective of what is productivity, this can refer to not participating in activities that are creative and fun, that rejuvenate and regenerate our mental, emotional, physical, and spiritual bodies. Sexual performance problems can relate to problems with self-expression, such as feeling unable to fully express sexuality, or not being happy with the self's gender and/or sexual orientation.

Eliminative System

The eliminative system filters and excretes waste through the kidneys and urinary bladder (in the form of urine), and through the bowel (in the form of bowel movements). The kidneys also remove waste from the blood. The waste combines with water to form urine. From the kidneys, urine travels down two thin tubes called *ureters,* which deposit the urine in the bladder. When the bladder is full, urine is discharged through the urethra. The large intestines, a ten-foot long tube, remove solid waste. The skin is also part of this system, and it removes waste through sweat glands.

Problems here relate to difficulty releasing emotions, holding on to anger, fear of letting go of someone or something, fear of no longer being needed, clinging to outworn ideas, attitudes, and traditions for fear of what the new may bring.

Nervous System

The nervous system is responsible for communication and control; it integrates the activities of all the organs. It is made up of the brain, the spinal cord, and nerves. It stores information, responds to the environment, and transmits messages between the brain, spinal cord, and peripheral nervous system. There are three parts of your nervous system that work together: the *central nervous system,* the *peripheral nervous system,* and the *autonomic nervous system.*

The central nervous system sends out nerve impulses and analyzes information from the sense organs, which tell the brain about the things we see, hear, smell, taste, and feel. The peripheral nervous system includes the *craniospinal nerves* that branch off from the brain and the spinal cord. It carries the nerve impulses from the central nervous system to the muscles and glands. The autonomic nervous system regulates involuntary action, such as heartbeat and digestion.

Problems here can reflect trying to integrate too many activities in our lives, or not having enough activities to keep us occupied; being overly sensitive to criticism from self and others; not communicating our needs clearly, or interacting with others who are not communicating clearly with us; and being closed to new possibilities.

Sacral Animal Medicine

Blue Heron, Wolf, Ant, and Skunk Medicine are the Sacral's prescriptions.

Blue Heron teaches us how to go deep and look within to discover our gifts and overcome our challenges, without denying our true feelings and thoughts. Going deep within the emotional waters of our soul to learn of our value and true potential, Blue Heron assures us that with this newfound intimate self-knowing, we will be called upon to lead others in this same quest. Blue Heron's medicine unlocks the mysteries of life. As a divination symbol, when I see a Blue Heron I know this person is a spiritual teacher and leader, because he or she has the capability of looking deep within the emotional realms to bypass illusion and delusion.

Wolf is a teacher, pathfinder, and loyal companion, for wolves mate for life. Wolves have an enormous sense of family, yet still maintain an individualistic drive. The moon, associated with water and psychic energy, is the Wolf's ally. As a pathfinder, the Wolf is extremely skilled in intuition and therefore teaches us how to connect with our emotional intuition as we move forward along our path. As a divination symbol, when I see a Wolf, I know this person is involved in pathfinding, teaching, and healing work. Wolf knows how to go at it alone, as well as how to work with others. This healthy balance assures that Wolf is always on the right path and will always know how to track the next meal.

I like to work with Ant Medicine to encourage cooperation and breaking free of shyness. Ant teaches the strategy of patience, how to cooperate, and know its efficient role within the larger community. We associate Ant medicine with Earth and Fire elements, and the Root and Solar Plexus chakras. Ant says, "When the going gets tough, the tough get going. Time to hone my skills, I have a winning formula!"

I like to work with Skunk Medicine to encourage setting boundaries. Skunk teaches us that there is a time and place for sweetness and sternness. We associate Skunk medicine with the Air element and the Heart chakra. Skunk says, "I'm nice but don't take me for a fool."

Sacral Crystal Medicine

Carnelian, Orange Calcite, Copper, Moonstone, Picasso Marble

Crystals carry with them specific healing properties for humans and animals. They can be programmed through our intention for healing and divination. There are two ways we suggest you select your crystals; *intuitively* and *deliberately*.

Crystals call us. Therefore, allow yourself to browse a crystal selection and wait for the one that intuitively reels you in. When you research its medicinal properties, you will be amazed at how that stone spoke to you and your needs.

The second way is to deliberately select your stone based on the dis-ease or illness you wish to heal. For example:

When I have menstrual cramps, I will drink a Moonstone elixir; when my dogs have been cooped up in the home for too long due to weather conditions, to calm their nerves, they will drink an Orange Calcite elixir. Use the Internet to guide you in making your elixirs with crystals that are water soluble, photosensitive, sensitive to acid, and toxic.

Combining crystals with handpicked healing stones, aromatherapy, herbs, and animal medicine, I also work with my Guides as a medical intuitive using body scanning, remote viewing, and energy healing to detect and heal what is going on in the body. At the end of this chakra chapter, we show you how to conduct holistic health readings for yourself.

As a final note, you do not have to be an expert to conduct a healing session on yourself or your pet. You will learn as you practice so here are a few pointers:

Crystal Selection

When selecting your crystals and animal totems, know that each will resonate with specific chakras and assist in rebalancing and healing specific emotional, psychological, and physical dis-eases (energetic imprints). Often, one chakra will require the energy of another to recalibrate and heal so keep this in mind when you work with crystal and animal medicine.

Healing Session

When performing a healing session, combine love-based intention with the medicinal properties of the crystal(s) and animal spirit. Experiment with therapeutic ways to work with crystal and animal energies, they will teach you, so listen carefully.

Intuitive Nudges

Listen to the intuitive nudges from your Guides, they will direct you to the material you need.

Carnelian
Astrological Association: Cancer, Leo

Healing Qualities: Boosts personal power and self-esteem; dispels negative energy related to anger, jealousy, rage, envy, fear, and sorrow. Helpful in treating eating disorders, lethargy, laziness, confusion, by helping to see the links between emotional dis-ease and illness. Good for actors, musicians, and anyone involved in meditation and study.

Physical Benefits: Good for digestion, gallbladder, lungs, liver, kidneys, pancreas, spleen, thyroid gland, spine, tissue regeneration, voice, and speech. Boosts appetite, memory, and overall vitality. Helps asthma, bronchitis, hay fever, colds, infections, liver conditions. A topical elixir is good for cuts and scratches.

Orange Calcite
Astrological Association: Cancer, Leo

Healing Qualities: Balances sexuality, reduces aggression, promotes inspiration and creativity.

Physical Benefits: Calms excess physical energy, alleviates stress-related symptoms related to digestive disorders like IBS.

Copper
Astrological Association: Taurus, Sagittarius

Healing Qualities: Gets rid of exhaustion and lethargy; a "feel good" and "lucky" stone that boosts energy and balances emotions, preventing mood swings, irritability, excitability, and impatience.

Physical Benefits: Good for circulation. Stimulates metabolism. Aids detoxing. Good for infected wounds, joint inflammation, arthritis, bursitis, and rheumatism.

Moonstone
Astrological Association: Cancer, Libra, Scorpio

Healing Qualities: A soothing crystal that is good for inner awareness, balance, and bringing self-control to emotions. Promotes insight, intuition, creativity, confidence, peace of mind, and wisdom. Good to rid pessimism and oversensitivity. Helps to break patterns of suffering, to let go of the old, and to welcome new beginnings.

Physical Benefits: Helps with PMS, menstrual pain and cramps, fertility, pregnancy, childbirth, female hormones, menopausal symptoms, constipation, water retention, swelling, insect bites, and anaphylactic shock. Good for circulation, pituitary gland, eyes, and a youthful appearance. A topical elixir is good for hair and nails.

Picasso Marble
Astrological Association: Sagittarius, Cancer

Healing Qualities: Great for creative pursuits and careers in art and music, grounds the mind and thoughts, reduces anxiety, eases change, and encourages perseverance.

Physical Benefits: Circulation, digestion, metabolism, weight loss, detox, carpal tunnel syndrome.

Rainbow Medicine

Sacral Therapy

Sacral Chakra
Color Orange

Issue
Circle your issues:

- Sweetness
- Desire
- Dreams
- Sexuality
- Joy
- Creativity

Demon
Circle your demons:

- Guilt
- Selfishness
- Low self-esteem

Codependent Behavior
Circle your behaviors:

- Sexual addiction
- Excessive behavior, overindulgence

- Manipulation

Codependent Pattern
Circle your Avoidance patterns:

- Acting in ways that encourage rejection and shame
- Playing a cat and mouse *catch me if you can* game
- Using addiction to distract from accomplishing goals
- Judging others harshly
- Using indirect communication as a means to avoid confrontation
- Suppressing feelings so as not to feel vulnerable
- Engaging in an *I love you, I hate you* dualistic dynamic

Sacral Lesson
Since our chakras require regular maintenance, check in with each regularly by pulling two cards. I like to use a Tarot and an oracle deck but if you do not know Tarot, select two oracle decks, one with images and the other with words.

Begin each Tuesday by asking the question:

What lesson does my Sacral chakra want me to focus on today?

Shuffle and pull out one card from each deck. Analyze the cards in response to how they speak to the issues of this particular chakra.

Big Map
Take out two decks, one with images and one with words, and ask your Higher Self and Guides:

Show me my big picture story theme in my Sacral chakra?

Shuffle and pull out one card from each deck. Analyze the cards in response to how they speak to the issues of this particular chakra.

Sacral Issues
Continue with the same decks and pull two cards according to the following questions. Work with one question at a time. Once you receive

your cards, study them and write down every answer you are able to interpret. Remember to analyze the cards according to questions asked. If you need additional information or clarification for any question, pull more cards. When you move on to the next question, place all cards back into the decks. Sometimes you will see how the same cards will keep coming to you, this is Spirit's way of emphasizing the issue.

Since the Sacral relates to emotions and issues of guilt, selfishness, and avoidance, interpret your cards by looking for answers/responses to the following:

What is my dream?
What brings me joy?
What brings me sadness?
What do I value?
What do I feel guilty about?
Where do I need to set better boundaries for myself?
What message does my Sacral have for me?

Once you have reviewed all your channeled information, reconnect with your big picture theme. Connect all dots to identify the storyline, and write a brief paragraph summarizing your Sacral Reading.

Sacral Energy with Cards
Try this exercise by pulling cards for your Sacral and reading them psychically.

What energy is in my Sacral?

After you pull a couple of cards from your selected decks, don't look at them, place them together in one hand and face down hold them over your Sacral chakra. This will trigger information to come. You will feel the energy in that area, so it is important to write down everything you feel, taste, smell, sense, hear, think, and see.

Once you have completed the exercise, review your written material. Next, look at your cards to see how they relate to what you picked

up in meditation. The cards' meanings and images coupled with your channeled impressions will further inform your Sacral reading.

Psychic Sacral Scan

What Animal Medicine does my Sacral need?

Another way to pick up information about yourself or someone else is to scan your body using your mind and body sensations. Ask your Guide to give you the symbol of an animal that reflects the coping behavior you need to adopt.

Solar Plexus Chakra

Color Yellow
Element Fire
Issue Will, Power, Control, Intellect, Self-Assertiveness, Empowerment, Emotional Stability
Demon Shame, aggression, inferiority, clinginess
Balanced Archetype The Warrior
Imbalanced Archetype The Servant
Codependent Pattern Low Self Esteem, Denial
Codependent Behavior Fear of being alone, addiction, workaholic, judgmental
Complementary Chakra Third Eye
Intimacy Intellectual
Gland Pancreas
Body Part All digestive organs in the stomach area such as the liver, gall bladder, stomach muscles, gut, colon, intestines
Body System Endocrine, Digestive
Dis-ease and Illness Digestive problems, stomach ulcers, diabetes, eating disorders, phobias, chronic fatigue
Sense Sight (the stomach also has a Third Eye, known as gut instinct)
Spiritual Gift Clairvoyance (sight)
Glandular Prescription Nutrition, stable sugar levels, cooking, reading, study, teaching, tarot, boardgames, card games, crossword puzzles, tennis, martial arts, horseback riding, theatre, talks, bookstores
Animal Prescription Horse, Moose, Bee, Tigre
Crystal Prescription Amber, Citrine, Tiger's Eye, Sulfur, Golden Calcite

Just beneath the chest area, where we get heartburn, is the physical location of the Solar Plexus chakra; it is between the belly button and the upper abdomen. This third chakra is our power and control center. It is yellow like the sun, and associated with left-brain logic (intellect), the fire element (passion), and male yang energy (Emperor; Grandfather Sun; leadership, stability, organization, inner authority).

Solar Archetype

This chakra represents our emotional stability, the way we emotionally process intellectual information, and the way we communicate with others. When we are in balance, we feel confident to express our emotions and do not second-guess ourselves. We are assertive, emotionally stable, and operate from a place of empowerment. The way we know we are out of alignment, however, is that we use "illness" as a way to entertain people or as an excuse for our behavior. This is accompanied by aggression and/or clinginess, and it is the result of an inferiority complex. This form of theatrics is the cue that we need to bring ourselves back into balance. When this chakra is blocked, anger and irritation are constant, and this causes the body to attack itself. If too open, others draw our energy and deplete us, causing the immune system to weaken. Psychic vampires are able to get their energy fix by feeding on this chakra; hence they undermine our personal power and ability to think for ourselves.

When in balance, the archetype is that of the Warrior. This empowered person knows who he or she is in relation to the world, with neither an inflated nor a weak ego.

Balanced Solar Plexus qualities are self-esteem, confidence, and inner strength; ability to manifest abundance; being responsible and reliable; having a balanced and effective will; having a warm personality; ability to be spontaneous and playful; having a good sense of humor; ability to use appropriate self-discipline; having balanced ego-strength and a sense of personal power; ability to meet challenges.

The motto is "Ask no more from others than you would from yourself. Character, honor, loyalty, and humility."

When out of balance, the archetype is the Servant. This person is someone whose personal identity is anchored in the external world, seeking approval from others.

Imbalanced Solar Plexus qualities are difficulty digesting situations; lack of concentration; low energy; weak will; being easily manipulated; having poor self-discipline and follow-through; low self-esteem; being physically and emotionally cold; having poor digestion; being attracted to stimulants and/or sedatives; having a victim mentality; blaming others; being resentful, passive-aggressive, unreliable, overly aggressive; needing to be right; dominating controlling others; being manipulative, power hungry, and/or deceitful; having temper tantrums and violent outbursts; being stubborn; this is a Type A personality (driving ambition/perfectionism), competitive, arrogant, and hyperactive.

The motto is "You are not being genuine with yourself or others. You *can* learn how to love without being manipulative."

Yellow, the color of the Solar Plexus chakra, is the color of confidence, enthusiasm, intellectual activity, optimism, power, teaching, innovation (good at coming up with ideas); this person is a good conversationalist who will thrive in a career involved with the power of the mind, such as teaching. When an unpleasant yellow, this person may be disempowered, critical, timid, controlling, and egocentric.

Solar Psychology

The qualities this chakra is concerned with are part of personal identity, as in self-worth, inner knowing, and trusting our gut; self-esteem; confidence; freedom of choice; experiencing joy; and personal empowerment.

This chakra corresponds to the development we go through from adolescence to adulthood (ages fourteen to twenty-one). This is the time when we enter the world and develop our sense of self and individuality. Making positive choices, having the freedom to make choices, developing life experience, cultivating relationships with others, taking care of ourselves, handling work and financial responsibilities are all aspects through which our personal identity and sense of "who I am" is developed. The family environment is the first to teach us how to interact and negotiate with the world. Our sense of self-worth, our identity, and our ability to honor ourselves are formed through family relations.

The psychological function of the Solar Plexus chakra is willpower; its dysfunction is shame. Basic rights of this chakra are *a right to act as an individual and to be an individual.*

Psychological issues here relate to ego identity, as in how well we do or do not adjust to our environment. This ego identity is concerned with use of energy; activity; autonomy; individuation; will; proactivity; self-worth; self-esteem; confidence; personal power; freedom of choice; thoughts and beliefs; judgments; fear of the future; and work/career success. Attitudes of being well with the self and knowing self-worth, and the personal power that comes from an affirmed sense of selfhood, are rooted in the Solar Plexus chakra.

Childhood traumas and abuses to the Solar Plexus chakra are ego-based, and are caused by shaming, authoritarian parenting, volatile situations in the home, physical abuse, living in a dangerous environment, fear of punishment, domination of will, enmeshment, age-inappropriate responsibilities (child raises parent), and inherited shame from parent(s).

The life lesson of the Solar Plexus is to learn how to develop a strong and resilient ego, to know we are worthy simply because we exist.

The soul lesson is to recognize our humanness and to know we are loved by the Divine, regardless of error.

The motto is "I honor the power within me."

Solar Emotions

The ego/individuality resides in the Solar Plexus and perceives life as dualistic. This duality/opposition/contradiction found in this third dimension—the earth plane—is necessary for inner development to take place. Challenging situations exist in order for us to develop this chakra, and how we deal with life's ups and downs is reflected in either a balanced or imbalanced Solar Plexus chakra. The way that we handle and flow through resistance and opposition along our life path teaches us how to come into our personal power, and without such challenges we could never develop and mature. When we learn how to stand strong on our own two feet, it is called *walking the warrior's path.*

A sense of separateness that feeds loneliness is further encouraged when personal power, individuality, and self-worth have not been appropriately nurtured. Our reactions to circumstances manifest in a behavior called *shadowboxing,* the "mirror effect." This means that every battle we fight with someone else, we are actually fighting within ourselves, with the ego, for it was unhealthily developed as a result of the fears and abuses in the earlier chakras. As children, we were taught to cut something away within us (in our Sacral chakra), which made us vulnerable, and now we see it in someone else, and it aggravates us. This trauma results in a sense of halfness as opposed to wholeness, and the goal is to bring this part back, but in balance.

Intention is behind every thought and action, and all intention comes from either fear or love. An imbalanced Solar Plexus uses power from a place of fear, and manipulates others through a victim/martyr mentality, whereas a balanced Solar Plexus derives power from a place of love. When we work hard to win the approval of others, it means that we lack our own internal approval. This giving away of our power to please others is a sign/red flag that we do not know how to please ourselves, and it results in depleted energy and a less-resistant immune system.

Solar Pattern
Just as every chakra is interrelated with the one below and above it, each is also linked to its complimentary chakra. Look to the Third Eye and Crown chakras to heal the Solar chakra.

Low Self Esteem is the imbalanced behavior pattern found in the Solar Plexus chakra. It is characterized by judging the self as never good enough and un-loveable; needing to be right and resentful when wrong; unable to admit mistakes; a resistance to receiving help; not feeling comfortable in the limelight; looking for outside recognition valuing others' approval over one's own; expecting others to provide sense of safety; and, an inability to identify needs and wants, and set healthy priorities, deadlines, and boundaries to attain goals.

When in balance, we value the self and know we are lovable and worthy of praise; we recognize our responsibility to provide our own safety; we are honest about our motivations; we perceive ourself as equal; we let go of perfectionism and instead focus on progress; we don't procrastinate; we reach out for help when necessary; and we know how to identify opportunities, prioritize needs, and establish healthy boundaries to reach goals.

Solar Intimacy

The Solar Plexus chakra governs *mental intimacy*: sharing similar beliefs, cerebral curiosity, academic, scholarly or educational interests with our romantic partner. We want to have a shared belief system that is positive, "I am worth it."

Solar Dis-eases and Malfunctions

In the Solar Plexus chakra, physical and psychological dis-eases and illnesses are emotional and demanding. Body parts associated with the Solar Plexus chakra are all the digestive organs in the stomach area, such as the liver, gallbladder, stomach muscles, gut, colon, and intestines.

Physical dis-eases and illnesses that manifest from a blocked or overactive Solar Plexus chakra are a queasy or upset stomach; appendicitis; eating disorders, such as bulimia or anorexia; digestive disorders, such as IBS, Crohn's disease, gastritis, diverticulosis, colon cancer, gastric cancer, esophageal cancer, liver cancer, pancreatic cancer/failure, constipation, diarrhea, haemorrhoids, reflux, leaky gut, gallstones, ulcers, colitis, cirrhosis, diabetes and hypoglycaemia (high and low blood sugar levels); anemia; hypertension (high blood pressure); and stress-related skin conditions, such as eczema.

Psychological dis-eases and disorders that manifest from a blocked or overactive Solar Plexus chakra are failing memory; phobias; lethargy; chronic fatigue; and insomnia.

Solar Body Systems

Every chakra is related and positioned next to a gland, or glands, in the body. Just as every chakra is interrelated with the one below and above it, so are the glands and body systems. The body systems that affect the Solar Plexus chakra are the endocrine and digestive systems.

Endocrine System: Pancreas

The gland associated with the Solar Plexus chakra is the *pancreas*, it is both an organ and a gland that aids food digestion, influences nutritional absorption, controls carbohydrate metabolism, and produces hormones that regulate glucose and insulin (energy levels) in the blood. The pancreas is a large gland that lies alongside the stomach and the small intestine.

After we eat, enzymes (digestive juices) are released into the small intestine to break down and digest food. These enzymes make hormones that control blood glucose levels. When sugar (glucose) levels in the blood rise, the pancreas produces a hormone called *insulin*. Insulin then helps the body to lower blood glucose levels, and stores the sugar away in body tissues where it can be used for energy when required. Between meals, the pancreas does not produce insulin, which allows the body to release stored energy, gradually, back into the blood as needed. Stable glucose levels in the blood ensure that the body has a steady supply of energy needed for metabolism, exercise, and fueling parts of the brain, which runs on glucose.

Problems here reflect an inability to absorb the healthy aspects of life—such as joy, happiness, and peace—and, instead, to allow the unhealthy aspects to create imbalance and override the positive. Health issues here are indicators of how we respond to situations in our lives, such as overreacting to people and situations, or inhibiting our responses; basically, the problems reflect responding to life inappropriately.

Digestive System

The digestive system converts food and beverages into nutrients and energy, such as protein, vitamins, minerals, carbohydrates, and fats, all of which the body needs for energy, growth, and repair. Major organs include the esophagus, stomach, intestines, liver, pancreas, and gallbladder. After food is chewed and swallowed, it goes down the esophagus and enters the stomach, where it is further broken down by powerful stomach acids. From the stomach, the food travels into the small intestine. This is where food is broken down into nutrients that can enter the bloodstream through tiny hair-like projections. The excess food that the body doesn't need or can't digest is turned into waste that is eliminated from the body.

Primary functions of this system are ingestion and absorption; look to your habits to identify what you should and should not be ingesting and absorbing. This could indicate you are not using what you have available to you, are not absorbing new ideas, and/or are being wasteful.

Solar Animal Medicine

Horse, Moose, Bee, and Tiger Medicine are the Solar Plexus prescriptions.

Horse teaches us to recognize that our power is in our ability to move ourselves forward and into the unknown. Horse was the first vehicle that allowed man to travel and connect with his world. This new sense of freedom to traverse the land allowed him to share his medicine with those in need. Horse leads us on our path to our destiny. No wonder Spirit Guides often present themselves to us in our dreams and meditations as horses or on horseback! As a divination symbol, when I see a Horse, I know this is that person's Spirit Guide helping him or her. If I see a Donkey, then it is a message from this person's Spirit Guide to stop being stubborn. Like Horse, Donkey has a lot to share with others, so trust in your journey and power to make things happen for yourself, for you are never alone and are always transported forward, should you choose to move.

Moose teaches us about self-esteem; his tremendous pride in his maleness and desire to share his seed with others reminds us that by sharing our ideas and creations, we bring forth new ideas and creations. Moose medicine is often associated with elders and wisdom, as their joy lies in teaching children. Moose shows us how to be calm, how to learn, grow, and feel good about our accomplishments. As a divination symbol, when I see a Moose, depending on how high the antlers are, I will know how far along that person is on a five-year study/work plan.

I like to work with Tiger Medicine to encourage aligned action forward. Tiger teaches us how to take the lead, and lead with confidence. We associate Tiger medicine with the Fire element and the Solar Plexus chakra. Tiger says, "Go get them tiger! Just be reasonable and practical because people depend on you."

I like to work with Bee Medicine to soften anger and break free from shadow-boxing. Bee teaches us to cooperate and work in harmony with others for the sweet success of all involved. We associate Bee medicine with the Fire element and the Solar Plexus chakra. Bee says, "The Queen has arrived with a message: *Bee you*, beautiful! Recognize yourself!"

Solar Crystal Medicine

Amber, Citrine, Tiger's Eye, Sulfur, Golden Calcite

Crystals carry with them specific healing properties for humans and animals. They can be programmed through our intention for healing and divination. There are two ways we suggest you select your crystals; *intuitively* and *deliberately*.

Crystals call us. Therefore, allow yourself to browse a crystal selection and wait for the one that intuitively reels you in. When you research its medicinal properties, you will be amazed at how that stone spoke to you and your needs.

The second way is to deliberately select your stone based on the dis-ease or illness you wish to heal. For example:

When I lose my appetite, I will drink an Apatite elixir; when my dog's eyes are red, Savannah drinks a Tiger Eye elixir; When my dog's stomach is upset and he is lying down, I place a Citrine a few inches from Sam's side at the Solar Plexus area, and a Hematite a few inches away from his Root. Use the Internet to guide you in making your elixirs with crystals that are water soluble, photosensitive, sensitive to acid, and toxic.

Combining crystals with handpicked healing stones, aromatherapy, herbs, and animal medicine, I also work with my Guides as a medical intuitive using body scanning, remote viewing, and energy healing to detect and heal what is going on in the body. At the end of this chakra chapter, we show you how to conduct holistic health readings for yourself.

As a final note, you don't have to be an expert to conduct a healing session on yourself or your pet. You will learn as you practice so here are a few pointers:

Crystal Selection

When selecting your crystals and animal totems, know that each will resonate with specific chakras and assist in rebalancing and healing specific emotional, psychological, and physical dis-eases (energetic imprints). Often, one chakra will require the energy of another to recalibrate and heal so keep this in mind when you work with crystal and animal medicine.

Healing Session

When performing a healing session, combine love-based intention with the medicinal properties of the crystal(s) and animal spirit. Experiment with therapeutic ways to work with crystal and animal energies, they will teach you, so listen carefully.

Intuitive Nudges

Listen to the intuitive nudges from your Guides, they will direct you to the material you need.

Amber
Astrological Association: Leo, Aquarius

Healing Qualities: Traditionally worn by warriors as a good-luck talisman. Good for the mind; improves memory and heals absentmindedness. Helps to fulfill dreams by removing emotional blocks and negativity. Aids in treatment of abuse and schizophrenia. Sometimes burned as incense to cleanse spaces; removes negativity; balances yin/yang energy.

Physical Benefits: As a topical elixir, helps with treatment of bacterial infections (such as acne) and relieves teething in babies. To relieve constipation, drink as an elixir. Can also be used as a disinfectant and fumigator. Beneficial to the heart, kidneys, and bladder. Helps with hormone balance.

Citrine
Astrological Association: Gemini, Libra, Aries, Leo

Healing Qualities: Known as the "money" and "feel better" stone, bringing abundance on all levels. Aids with problem solving, eliminates emotional toxins, balances yin/yang energy. Great stone for teaching, writing, and studying.

Physical Benefits: As an elixir, good for digestive system, heart, liver, kidneys, and the thyroid and thymus glands; helps with anemia, jaundice, nausea, constipation, and diarrhea. Eliminates toxins; boosts tissue regeneration (good for surgery recovery); improves eyesight.

Tiger's-Eye
Astrological Association: Capricorn

Healing Qualities: Brings courage and calmness when dealing with life problems. Dispels introversion, intolerance, negativity, and prejudice. Supports intuition; balances yin/yang energy and right/left brain hemispheres; excellent for detective work or any profession that involves investigation. Helps to eliminate worry and sadness. A grounding crystal that is great for distant healing.

Physical Benefits: As an elixir, great for digestion issues, such as gas, nausea, bloating and diverticulosis. Can help with bone fractures and eye conditions.

Sulfur
Astrological Association: Leo

Healing Qualities: Good for mental balance, reasoning, and inspiration.

Physical Benefits: *No elixir. Good for insect bites, infections, tissue growth, painful joints and swelling. Good for fumigating.

Golden Calcite
Astrological Association: Leo

Healing Qualities: Gets rid of self-limiting beliefs, good for calm communication reducing likelihood of arguments. Great for divination, past-life recall, and healing visualizations. Can drink as an elixir to calm nerves.

Physical Benefits: Good to circulation, the nerves, physical energy, gallbladder, endocrine system, fights infection immediately.

Rainbow Medicine

Solar Plexus Chakra
Color Yellow

Issue
Circle your issues:

- Will power
- Control
- Intellect
- Self-assertiveness
- Empowerment
- Emotional stability

Demon
Circle your demons:

- Shame
- Aggression
- Inferiority
- Clinginess

Codependent Behavior
Circle your behaviors:

- Fear of being alone

- Workaholic
- Judgmental
- Addiction

Codependent Pattern

Circle your Low self esteem patterns:

- Judging the self as never good enough and unloveable
- Needing to be right and resentful when wrong
- Unable to admit mistakes
- Resistant to receiving help
- Not feeling comfortable in the limelight
- Looking for outside recognition valuing others' approval over one's own
- Expecting others to provide sense of safety
- Unable to identify needs and wants, and set healthy priorities, deadlines, and boundaries to attain goals

Solar Plexus Lesson

Since our chakras require regular maintenance, check in with each regularly by pulling two cards. I like to use a Tarot and an oracle deck but if you do not know Tarot, select two oracle decks, one with images and the other with words.

Begin each Wednesday by asking the question:

What lesson does my Solar Plexus chakra want me to focus on today?

Shuffle and pull out one card from each deck. Analyze the cards in response to how they speak to the issues of this particular chakra.

Solar Plexus Map

Take out two decks, one with images and one with words, and ask your Higher Self and Guides:

Show me my big picture story theme in my Solar Plexus chakra?

Shuffle and pull out one card from each deck. Analyze the cards in response to how they speak to the issues of this particular chakra.

Solar Plexus Issues
Continue with the same decks and pull two cards according to the following questions. Work with one question at a time. Once you receive your cards, study them and write down every answer you are able to interpret. Remember to analyze the cards according to questions asked. If you need additional information or clarification for any question, pull more cards. When you move on to the next question, place all cards back into the decks. Sometimes you will see how the same cards will keep coming to you, this is Spirit's way of emphasizing the issue.

Since the Solar Plexus relates to self esteem and issues of shame, aggression, self-assertion, self-empowerment, and emotional stability, interpret your cards by looking for answers/responses to the following:

What shame must I release?
In which area of my life do I need to take my power back?
In which area of my life do I need to release control?
What am I meant to be doing with my power?
What do I have to teach others?
What do others have to teach me?
What message does my Solar Plexus have for me?

Once you have reviewed all your channeled information, reconnect with your big picture theme. Connect all dots to identify the storyline, and write a brief paragraph summarizing your Solar Plexus Reading.

Sacral Energy with Cards
Try this exercise by pulling cards for your Solar Plexus and reading them psychically.

What energy is in my Solar Plexus?

After you pull a couple of cards from your selected decks, don't look at them, place them together in one hand and face down hold them over your Solar Plexus chakra. This will trigger information to come. You will feel the energy in that area, so it is important to write down everything you feel, taste, smell, sense, hear, think, and see.

Once you have completed the exercise, review your written material. Next, look at your cards to see how they relate to what you picked up in meditation. The cards' meanings and images coupled with your channeled impressions will further inform your Solar Plexus reading.

Psychic Solar Scan

What Animal Medicine does my Solar Plexus need?

Another way to pick up information about yourself or someone else is to scan your body using your mind and body sensations. Ask your Guide to give you the symbol of an animal that reflects the coping behavior you need to adopt.

Heart Chakra

Color Green, Pink (higher heart chakra)
Element Air
Issue Love, Peace, Healing, Social-the inner/outer Team
Demon Grief, possessiveness, jealousy, rootlessness
Balanced Archetype The Lover
Imbalanced Archetype The Actress/Actor
Codependent Pattern Control
Codependent Behavior Gives love for short periods of time then takes it away, excessively sympathetic, fear of rejection, rage
Complementary Chakra Root, Crown
Intimacy Social
Gland Thymus
Body Part Lungs, heart, arms, hands, shoulders
Body Systems Endocrine, Circulatory, Respiratory, Skeletal
Dis-ease and Illness Respiratory chest and lung infections, asthma, shoulder pain, arm/hand/finger injuries, ulcers
Sense Touch
Spiritual Gift Clairsentience (touch), Oneiromancy (Dreams)
Glandular Prescription Awareness of cause and effect, activities that make your heart sing, spending time with like-minded others, playing music in a band, team sports, group games, being part of a sisterhood/brotherhood, recovery group work
Animal Prescription Turtle, Scarab, Zebra
Crystal Prescription Jade, Malachite, Rose Quartz, Chrysocolla, Green Moss Agate, Ruby in Zoiste

The fourth chakra is the Heart chakra, which is located in the middle of the chest cavity, between the breasts. Its color is green, and it is also associated with the color pink, because of the Higher Heart chakra, just above it. Both Heart chakras represent our ability to be compassionate, and to be in harmony with ourselves and others. Its associated element is air (mind).

Heart Archetype

When we are in balance, we are loving and nurturing, we give love with no conditions attached, we are aware of our soul's purpose, and we know that everything happens according to a Divine plan. We know that we are out of alignment, however, when we exhibit neediness, possessiveness, and jealousy, and when we continue to blame others for things not working out the way we would like. Feeling like we are staring down a black hole and feeling pulled by it is the cue that we need to bring ourselves back into balance. When blocked, spiritual purpose is lost, and grief, disconnection, jealousy, and enormous resistance to change are common.

When in balance, the archetype is that of the Lover. This person is someone who is all-inclusive, who makes others feel accepted, embraced, and warm inside.

Balanced Heart qualities are an inner strength that requires the ability to change; a sense of brotherhood, sisterhood, and unity; purity and innocence; compassion and empathy; loving others and the self unconditionally; a sense of peacefulness; and a good immune system.

The motto is "Cooperation and compassion."

When out of balance, the archetype is that of the Actress/Actor. This person is someone who loves with limitation, who exhibits judgment and criticism, and who withholds love when the other doesn't fulfill expectation.

Imbalanced Heart qualities are being indecisive; displaying emotional confusion; exhibiting fear of rejection; displaying arrogance; being unable to express love; displaying an unloving and uncaring attitude; mistaking lust and longing for love; being antisocial and/or withdrawn; being critical, judgmental, and/or intolerant of others and the self; exhibiting narrow-mindedness; exhibiting loneliness, isolation, and/or depression; displaying fear of intimacy, fear of relationships, and/or relationship breakdown; exhibiting lack of empathy and/or narcissism; exhibiting codependency and/or poor boundaries; being demanding, clingy, and/or jealous; and overly sacrificing self for others, or the opposite (as in, doesn't give enough of self to others).

The motto is "Imprisonment is in the mind, but it is *you* who chooses powerlessness over change."

Green and pink, the colors of the Heart and Higher Heart chakras, respectively, are the color of healing, growth, and balance (green), and unconditional love (pink). Green is also the color of prosperity, team spirit, and humanitarian work (like teaching, medicine, and social work). When these colors are dull, the person may be indecisive and unhappy; he or she may also be filled with unresolved anger, resentment, guilt, and sadness, and likely has a hard time achieving goals.

[Throughout this chapter, we will examine the Heart and Higher Heart chakras together; if something applies specifically to one and not the other, or more to one than the other, we will stipulate that.]

Heart Psychology

The Heart chakra is the first of our *truth chakras,* which we mentioned briefly earlier. This chakra is the middle ground between the lower manifestation charkas and the higher truth chakras, and when the heart is blocked because of unresolved pain, sadness, and resentment, this leads to suffering, preventing the energy from flowing in balance, upward into our truth charkas and downward into our manifestation chakras.

The psychological function of the Heart chakra is love, and its dysfunction is grief. Basic rights are *a right to love and be loved.*

Psychological issues here relate to social identity; that is, all issues involving relationships and love. This social identity is concerned with love; balance; self-love; relationship intimacy; reaching out and taking in; and male (animus)/female (anima) integration and wholeness. Attitudes of happiness, joy and delight, knowing what makes your heart sing, and embracing life are rooted in the Heart chakra.

Childhood traumas and abuses to the Heart chakra are social, and are caused by rejection, abandonment, and/or loss; shaming and/or constant criticism; abuses to the lower chakras; unacknowledged grief, and grief over parents' divorce or the death of a loved one; lovelessness and a cold environment; conditional love; sexual or physical abuse; and betrayal.

The life lesson of the Heart chakra is to let love be the center of your life.

The soul lesson is brotherhood and sisterhood love.

The motto is "I am worthy of love."

Heart Emotions

The Heart chakra is where codependency lies. Codependency is the complete divorcing/splitting within one's self from whole to half. What does this mean? Simply stated, that within us we either have a well-developed feminine side, a well-developed masculine side, or a not-so-well-developed either side. It is a sense of lacking from within, so we go outward to find this half to fill us. This never works, and this is the cause of so many breakups of both friendships and romantic relationships, as well as problems at work and the overall rampant depressive and personality disorders diagnosed in today's society. This imbalance, which stemmed from the splitting that occurred in the Sacral chakra, manifests itself in matters of the heart. This heartbreak is actually grounded within a patriarchal ideology, where division, as opposed to wholeness, is central to "the dream" we are born into (money, financial success, fame, power, etc). We are taught by society that wholeness is something that is attainable from without and not from within. *If* we get the partner, *if* we have the children, *if* we get the great job, *if* we can afford the nice home, car, fancy restaurants, etc., etc., etc., *then* we are whole. Eventually, this system implodes, for it is not based on balance.

If we give more than we receive, this is a sign that we are dealing with control issues and an inferiority complex. If we receive more than we give, this is a sign that we do not know how to feed/nourish ourselves. A balanced, healthy Heart is exemplified by a balance of giving and receiving. It is both a gift to give and to receive; when we don't allow ourselves to receive from another, we not only deny ourselves the gift of the other's love, but we also deny the other the pleasure of giving. Do you see how it all goes hand in hand?

Peace, love, unity, joy, a sense of brotherhood and sisterhood, openness, sharing, touch, a heart-to-heart connection, and a sense of belonging are the qualities of the Heart chakra. The best way to feed the Heart is to choose to see life from love and joy, instead of from fear and hate. The Heart suffers when it feels separate and isolated. When we choose to forgive ourselves and others, and to release our sense of unworthiness, lack, and inferiority, as well as built-up pain from the past, we become healthier and happier. Going from divisibility and separateness to unity and belonging is what is necessary if you want to come into your truth so that you can live a healthier, more peaceful, and fulfilling life.

Heart Pattern

Just as every chakra is interrelated with the one below and above it, each is also linked to its complimentary chakra. Look to the Root and Crown chakras to heal the Heart chakra.

Control is the imbalanced behavior pattern found in the Heart chakra. It is characterized by a belief that people need others to manage them and tell them what to think, feel and do, *if I am needed, I am of value and valued*; buying influence; using sex to get things; demanding needs be met; offering advice without being asked and resentful when it is not taken; and, using blame and shame to emotionally manipulate outcomes.

When in balance, we realize people can manage their own lives and engage in relationships based on equality; we are aware of our motivations when we give gifts of any kind; We rely on our resources and ask for help without making demands; we do not use sex to get what we want; and, we do not use blame and shame to manipulate outcomes.

Heart Intimacy

The Heart chakra governs *social intimacy*: the people who surround us as well as the community inside of us. Within us is a template of every age and past life we have been, every *You* is there inside ready to paint the world with his/her special color.

The health of a romantic relationship depends on our ability to maintain a loving community within ourselves, and simultaneously, with everyone outside of ourselves to include relatives, friends, coworkers, children, pets, spirit guides, deceased relatives and the Divine itself. Social intimacy must nurture both our internal and external bonds. We are a stronger couple when surrounded by those who enhance goodness and love.

Heart Dis-eases and Malfunctions

In the Heart chakra, physical and psychological dis-eases and illnesses are psychosomatic and reactive. Body parts associated with the Heart chakra are the lungs, heart, arms, hands, and shoulders.

Physical dis-eases and illnesses that manifest from a blocked or overactive Heart chakra are a frozen shoulder; ulcers; chest infections; hypertension (high blood pressure); heart/coronary disease, such as heart attack, angina, heart arrhythmia, and arteriosclerosis; arm and hand troubles/ illnesses, such as Raynaud's disease, scleroderma, and rheumatoid arthritis; stenosis of the heart and lungs; lungs and respiratory troubles/ illnesses, such as asthma, pneumonia, chronic bronchitis, tuberculosis, repeated colds and respiratory infections; early physical signs of aging; and unrelated symptoms following one after the other.

Grief is the psychological dis-ease that manifests from a blocked or overactive Heart chakra.

Heart Body Systems

Every chakra is related and positioned next to a gland, or glands, in the body. Just as every chakra is interrelated with the one below and above it, so are the glands and body systems. The body systems that affect the Heart chakra are the endocrine, circulatory, respiratory, and skeletal systems.

Endocrine System: Thymus Gland

The gland associated with the Heart chakra is the *thymus gland,* which is located behind the breastbone in the upper chest area. The thymus forms part of the immune system; it is made up of two lobes, called *lymphoid tissues,* consisting of white blood cells and fat that join in front of the trachea. Its function is to transform white blood cells developed in the bone marrow into *T cells,* which are critical to human immunity. These cells are then transported to various lymph glands, where they play an important part in fighting infections and illness. Swelling of lymph glands and fever are signals that immune cells are multiplying to fight off invaders of the body, such as bacteria, fungi, viruses, or parasites.

The thymus gland is responsible for our emotional well-being. It secretes hormones that tone the heart and lungs, keeping the immune system balanced. When we are not happy, or have experienced trauma, loss, or rejection, this gland becomes underactive. Engaging in activities that make the Heart sing is the best way to ensure this hormonal flow.

Repetitive illnesses reflect our not recognizing that our actions have repercussions. This includes involving the self in issues and problems that do not concern us, infecting others with our thoughts and actions, allowing others' thoughts and actions to infect us, and losing the ability to find sweetness and benefit in life.

Circulatory System

The circulatory system is the body's transport system. It circulates blood and nutrients throughout the body through the heart and blood vessels, such as arteries, capillaries, and veins. The heart pumps the blood, and the arteries and veins transport it. Oxygen-rich blood leaves the left side of the heart and enters the biggest artery, called the *aorta.* The aorta branches into smaller arteries, which then branch into even smaller vessels that travel all over the body. When blood enters the smallest blood vessels, which are called capillaries and are found in body tissue, it gives nutrients and oxygen to the cells, and takes in carbon dioxide, water, and waste. The blood, which no longer contains oxygen and nutrients, then goes back to the heart through the veins. Veins carry waste products away from cells, bringing blood back to the heart, which pumps it to the lungs to pick up oxygen and eliminate carbon dioxide.

Problems here usually stem from lack of vitality in an area of life. Circulation problems are tied to how we allows our emotions to circulate and flow. When emotions flow too easily, this reflects no control. When emotions are not allowed to circulate, this reflects too much control; both conditions create blood pressure issues. Circulatory conditions reflect a person who is locked in the past, afraid to move on, unable to resolve old emotional issues, and harboring an attitude of self-defeatism.

Respiratory System

The respiratory system acquires oxygen and eliminates carbon dioxide. The major organs are the nose, lungs, larynx, trachea, and bronchial tubes. When we breathe in, air enters the nose or mouth and goes down a long tube called the *trachea* (windpipe). The trachea branches into two bronchial tubes, or *primary bronchi,* which go to the lungs. The primary bronchi branch off into even smaller bronchial tubes, or *bronchioles.* The bronchioles end in the *alveoli,* or air sacs. Oxygen follows this path, passes through the walls of the air sacs and blood vessels, and enters the bloodstream. At the same time, carbon dioxide passes into the lungs and is exhaled.

Breathing is essential for life; therefore, problems with breathing reflect issues of a right to life. Feeling undeserving or guilty about how you live, or feeling like you are not living your best life or not allowed to live your best life, and therefore are suppressing your life expressions and emotions, all can lead to respiratory issues. Unequal exchanges in the life process reflect grief, such as one-sided giving, or taking in too much, and this lodges in the lungs and manifests breathing dis-eases and disorders, such as asthma and pneumonia.

Skeletal System

The skeletal system includes bones, cartilage, and joints. This system has both mechanical functions and physiological functions. Mechanical functions relate to our bones, which support, protect, and move the body. Our bones are a rigid framework that protects soft tissues, such as our internal organs (the brain, heart, lungs, and the pelvic region organs). Physiological functions include blood cell production, and the supply and storing of important minerals. Blood-cell production converts chemical energy into mechanical through blood formation, providing a reservoir of minerals.

Bone problems reflect what we may or may not be protecting, the quality or lack of support or structure in our lives. The organ related to the broken bone will highlight what you are protecting, or not, and the significance of that organ in your life. Organs here are the heart and lungs.

Heart Animal Medicine

Turtle, Scarab Beetle, and Zebra Medicine are the Heart's prescriptions.

Turtle teaches us how to create boundaries in order to protect ourselves from hurt, jealousy, and the unconscious thoughts of others. Like the rib cage, Turtle's hard shell protects our Heart. When people bother us, Turtle reminds us when it's time to go inward, to ground ourselves, and to set boundaries. Because it is comfortable on land and in the water, Turtle knows how to flow harmoniously within its environment. Turtle buries its eggs in the sand, and allows the sun to hatch its children. From this behavior, Turtle teaches us to spend time with our thoughts and to nurture our ideas so that when it is time, they will shine. As a divination symbol, the Turtle is my sign for a mother or grandmother in spirit coming through with a message.

I like to work with Scarab Beetle to encourage emotional and intellectual balance. Scarab teaches us how to create and discern wisdom from dung. We associate Scarab and his mighty shield medicine with the Air element and the Heart chakra. Turtle says, "When you go within, you hear our wisdom of the Ages and Sages, clearly."

I like to work with Zebra Medicine to encourage building community with likeminded others. Zebra teaches us how to celebrate our individuality while still fitting in with others. We associate Zebra medicine with the Air element and the Heart and Throat chakras. Zebra says, "Sad nostalgia is when *you* take the knife and stab yourself in the heart. Mourned nostalgia is when you take our hand and realize you are moving on to smoother waters."

Heart Crystal Medicine

Jade, Malachite, Rose Quartz, Chrysocolla, Green Moss Agate, Ruby in Zoiste

Crystals carry with them specific healing properties for humans and animals. They can be programmed through our intention for healing and divination. There are two ways we suggest you select your crystals; *intuitively* and *deliberately.*

Crystals call us. Therefore, allow yourself to browse a crystal selection and wait for the one that intuitively reels you in. When you research its medicinal properties, you will be amazed at how that stone spoke to you and your needs.

The second way is to deliberately select your stone based on the dis-ease or illness you wish to heal. For example:

When I started working with crystals at a spiritual level, the first to wear me as jewelry was Ruby In Zoiste. I later discovered it helps with soul memories, loss, and healing, which, at that time, was the very issue I was working through; when my dogs are suffering with seasonal allergies, they will drink a Green Moss Agate elixir. Use the Internet to guide you in making your elixirs with crystals that are water soluble, photosensitive, sensitive to acid, and toxic.

Combining crystals with handpicked healing stones, aromatherapy, herbs, and animal medicine, I also work with my Guides as a medical intuitive using body scanning, remote viewing, and energy healing to detect and heal what is going on in the body. At the end of this chakra chapter, we show you how to conduct holistic health readings for yourself.

As a final note, you do not have to be an expert to conduct a healing session on yourself or your pet. You will learn as you practice so here are a few pointers:

Crystal Selection

When selecting your crystals and animal totems, know that each will resonate with specific chakras and assist in rebalancing and healing specific emotional, psychological, and physical dis-eases (energetic imprints). Often, one chakra will require the energy of another to recalibrate and heal so keep this in mind when you work with crystal and animal medicine.

Healing Session

When performing a healing session, combine love-based intention with the medicinal properties of the crystal(s) and animal spirit. Experiment with therapeutic ways to work with crystal and animal energies, they will teach you, so listen carefully.

Intuitive Nudges

Listen to the intuitive nudges from your Guides, they will direct you to the material you need.

Jade
Astrological Association: Aries, Gemini, Taurus, Libra

Healing Qualities: Helps in treatment of mental disorders, promoting balance, and promoting a sense of justice, modesty, and compassion. Place under the pillow while sleeping to enhance dreaming and dream recall. Offers inner and outer peace, and gives protection, especially from accidents. Great for problem solving, attainment of goals, and shamanic traveling.

Physical Benefits: A powerful muscle relaxant. Helps with bacterial and viral infections; good for high blood pressure and eye disorders; strengthens the immune system (especially lymphatic system); and promotes healing of the kidneys, bladder, gallbladder, and spleen. Helps with bones, joints, and muscles. Good for female reproductive organs, fertility, PMS, menstrual cramping and pains. An elixir used topically and ingested is great for kidneys and adrenals, blood disorders, asthma, and skin conditions (like acne); also benefits hair. Promotes longevity.

Rose Quartz
Astrological Association: Taurus, Libra

Healing Qualities: Known as the "love stone." Promotes love on all levels; eases the expression of unexpressed feelings of anger, fear, guilt, grief, inadequacy, jealousy, and resentment. Teaches self-love and self-acceptance, two lessons of the Heart chakra. Great for romance, sexual liberation, and reduction of frustration in all relationships. Relates to yin (female) energy and the nurturing of the inner child, soothing emotional wounds and bad childhood memories. Encourages forgiveness of self and others. Great for artists, musicians, and writers.

Physical Benefits: It energetically harmonizes the brain. When placed over Higher Heart chakra, it is known to calm breathing difficulties and asthma attacks. Great for lymphatic, circulation, and reproductive systems, as well as the thymus and adrenal glands. Balances sex drive, fertility, PMS, excessive bleeding, cramps, and menstrual cycle. Encourages healthy complexion, youthful appearance, and reduction of wrinkles. Great for adrenal glands, heart conditions, and varicose veins; helps with asthma, coughs, influenza, burns, sunburns, vertigo, kidney disorders, and general aches and pains.

Chrysocolla

Astrological Association: Gemini, Virgo, Taurus

Healing Qualities: Used as a powerful detoxifier and relaxant; excellent for a peaceful night's sleep. Helps with releasing feelings of guilt and the healing of a broken heart. Promotes female sexuality by helping you to let go of tension, phobias, and stressful situations. Helps with revitalizing relationships; encourages speaking our truth, curbing gossip, and showing compassion and forgiveness. When we feel better about ourselves, we release negative emotions and the need for gossip.

Physical Benefits: Helps to remove heavy metals from the body. Good for metabolism and digestion; promotes healing of arthritis and rheumatism; good for migraines, the eyes, throat, thyroid gland, PMS, menstrual pains, and menstrual cycle. Good for easing troubled breathing and increasing lung capacity by oxidizing the blood (helps with asthma, emphysema, bronchitis, and tuberculosis). Prevents ulcers; good for stress-related conditions. Promotes healthy development of the fetus. Great for pancreas gland function because it supports insulin production, which controls blood-sugar levels in diabetics. Prevents muscle cramping in arms and legs; reduces hypertension (high blood pressure); helps with restless leg syndrome. When used with other crystals, it speeds their effects. Good for past-life issues and problems in the past (in this lifetime); helps to relieve sexual traumas.

Green Moss Agate

Astrological Association: Virgo

Historical Uses: Traditionally associated with devas, nature spirits who watch over plant growth and agriculture. Midwives used it to ease pain during childbirth; Traditional Chinese Medicine used it to clear confusion and stabilize the mind; early Western medicine used it for the eyes. Today it is used to energetically heal skin and fungal infections, dehydration, and the lymphatic system.

Healing Qualities: Releases trapped emotions; relieves anxiety, stress, and tension. Great for healing plants and encouraging growth.

Physical Benefits: Helps people who are affected by seasonal allergies and environmental pollutants. Cleanses immune system after infection; eases cold symptoms. Good for digestion and eye care. When used as a topical elixir, great for skin disorders; helps with dehydration and fungal infections.

Ruby In Zoiste
Astrological Association: Leo, Scorpio, Cancer, Sagittarius

Colors: Green and red/fuchsia pink

Healing Qualities: It is a combination stone therefore it represents cooperation and balance. The stone encourages to talk about feelings and loss helping to see the purpose of experiences and embracing the gift in loss, it acts as a catalyst for soul healing. It brings soul memories to the surface for the sake of understanding and releasing. It helps to speak one's truth even when others try to block you. It is a stone that is good for speaking up against injustice and for those grieving the loss of a loved one. It also attracts new passion into life, and it reminds you to appreciate your individuality.

Physical Benefits: Detoxifies the blood, good for circulatory and elimination systems, testicles, ovaries, heart, pancreas, lungs, and acidification balance, reduces fever and stress, improves memory and sleeping disorders, and strengthens the aura encouraging multidimensional cellular healing.

Rainbow Medicine

Heart Therapy

Heart Chakra
Color Green, Pink (higher heart chakra)

Issue
Circle your issues:

- Love
- Peace
- Social-the inner/outer Team
- Healing

Demon
Circle your demons:

- Grief
- Possessiveness
- Jealousy
- Rootlessness

Codependent Behavior
Circle your behaviors:

- Short, intense periods of giving of love then taking it away
- Excessively sympathetic
- Fear of rejection

- Rage

Codependent Pattern
Circle your Control patterns:

- Belief that people need others to manage them and tell them what to think, feel and do
- *If I am needed, I am of value and valued*
- Buying influence
- Using sex to get things
- Demanding needs be met
- Offering advice without being asked
- Resentful when advice is not taken
- Using blame and shame to emotionally manipulate outcomes

Heart Lesson
Since our chakras require regular maintenance, check in with each regularly by pulling two cards. I like to use a Tarot and an oracle deck but if you do not know Tarot, select two oracle decks, one with images and the other with words.

Begin each Thursday by asking the question:

What lesson does my Heart chakra want me to focus on today?

Shuffle and pull out one card from each deck. Analyze the cards in response to how they speak to the issues of this particular chakra.

Heart Map
Take out two decks, one with images and one with words, and ask your Higher Self and Guides:

Show me my big picture story theme in my Heart chakra?

Shuffle and pull out one card from each deck. Analyze the cards in response to how they speak to the issues of this particular chakra.

Heart Issues

Continue with the same decks and pull two cards according to the following questions. Work with one question at a time. Once you receive your cards, study them and write down every answer you are able to interpret. Remember to analyze the cards according to questions asked. If you need additional information or clarification for any question, pull more cards. When you move on to the next question, place all cards back into the decks. Sometimes you will see how the same cards will keep coming to you, this is Spirit's way of emphasizing the issue.

Since the Heart relates to truth, grief, and control issues, interpret your cards by looking for answers/responses to the following:

What am I angry about?
What do I need to forgive in myself?
What does my Heart feel?
What does my Heart think?
What does my Heart want?
What does my Heart need?
What message does my Heart have for me?

Once you have reviewed all your channeled information, reconnect with your big picture theme. Connect all dots to identify the storyline, and write a brief paragraph summarizing your Heart Reading.

Heart Energy with Cards

Try this exercise by pulling cards for your Heart and reading them psychically.

What energy is in my Heart?

After you pull a couple of cards from your selected decks, don't look at them, place them together in one hand and face down hold them over your Heart chakra. This will trigger information to come. You will feel the energy in that area, so it is important to write down everything you feel, taste, smell, sense, hear, think, and see.

Once you have completed the exercise, review your written material. Next, look at your cards to see how they relate to what you picked

up in meditation. The cards' meanings and images coupled with your channeled impressions will further inform your Heart reading.

Psychic Heart Scan

What Animal Medicine does my Heart need?

Another way to pick up information about yourself or someone else is to scan your body using your mind and body sensations. Ask your Guide to give you the symbol of an animal that reflects the coping behavior you need to adopt.

Throat Chakra

Color Light blue, Turquoise
Element Ether
Issue Purification, Communication, Creativity, Expressing Truth
Demon Lies
Balanced Archetype The Communicator
Imbalanced Archetype The Silent One or Loud One
Codependent Pattern Avoidance
Codependent Behavior Prejudice, arrogance, over/under-talk-ative, one-sided communication and point of view
Complementary Chakra Sacral
Intimacy Verbal
Gland Thyroid
Body Part Throat, ears, mouth, shoulders, neck, jaw
Body System Endocrine, Respiratory, Digestive
Dis-ease and Illness Sore throat, jaw and teeth problems, constant colds and infections, thyroid imbalances, digestive problems
Sense Hearing
Spiritual Gift Clairaudience (hearing), transmediumship, channeling
Glandular Prescription Activities that encourage creative expression like writing, journalling, workbook exercises, singing, channeling, theatre, playing a musical instrument, mediation
Animal Prescription Cicada, Parrot, Caterpillar
Crystal Prescription Blue Lace Agate, Angelite, Apatite, Kyanite, Aquamarine, Turquoise, Blue Chalcedony, Aqua Aura

The fifth chakra is the Throat chakra, located in the Adam's apple area in the lower neck. Its color is turquoise (a combination of blue and green), or light/medium blue, and it represents truthful communication. Communication refers to thought, as well as the written and spoken word. Its element is Ether, the crossover between the physical and spirit world.

Throat Archetype

The Throat chakra represents our ability to communicate our truth. When we are in balance, we express ourselves truthfully without the fear of others judging us. We are verbally intimate with ourselves through talking to ourselves, writing in a journal, writing a poem, singing a song, listening to music, and so on—one way or another, we let it out verbally. The way we know we are out of alignment, however, is that we repeatedly second-guess what we say after we say it, or avoid speaking our truth for fear of not fitting in. Feeling like we are dependent on what others think and say about us, or being completely insensitive to others, are cues that we need to bring ourselves back into balance. When blocked, we cannot verbalize thoughts and feelings, and we cannot express our truth, so other people's opinions of us cause us great difficulty.

When in balance, the archetype is that of the Communicator. This person is someone who is skilled with words, and expresses his or her truth from a place of personal integrity.

Balanced Throat chakra qualities are using the inner voice to solve problems instantly; being able to express and communicate clearly; being a good listener; having a good sense of timing and rhythm; and being able to live creatively.

The motto is "Our character is what we are here to develop. I don't choose the easy road; I choose the just and honorable road."

When out of balance, the archetype is that of the Silent One or Loud One. This person is someone who either hides and suppresses his or her feelings at the expense of feeling ashamed, and even disliked or speaks impulsively without regard for others; both behaviors are often exercised simply to manipulate people and situations, and to have a way out. Sometimes yes means no to these individuals, and sometimes no means "I will do as I please when I feel like it." Either way, the behavior and attitude is not coming from an honest place.

Imbalanced Throat qualities are giving too much information (TMI) or too little information (TLI); speaking too softly (as in, a small weak voice), or talking too loudly (as in a dominating voice or a strained voice); stuttering when trying to get a point across; exhibiting a fear of speaking or too much talking; exhibiting a fear of speaking your mind: using talking as a defense mechanism; having the habit of interrupting others; having difficulty putting feelings into words; engaging in gossip; displaying introversion or shyness; having a lack of concentration; being tone deaf; having a poor sense of timing and/or rhythm; displaying an inability to listen; and having poor auditory comprehension.

The motto is "I choose not to end hostilities; instead I pretend I am blind to them, and I do/say what I please and what serves me in the moment."

Turquoise (blue/green), or light/medium blue, the colors of the Throat chakra, are cooling and relaxing colors. They represent clear communication, creative expression, clarity, serenity, tranquillity, peace, travel, freedom, honesty, sincerity, support, loyalty, adaptability, honesty, and intuition. These colors are "deep as the ocean" and "high as the sky." When these colors are dull, this person may be confused and find it hard to trust themselves and others.

Throat Psychology

The Throat chakra is considered the gateway to other dimensions. It is directly linked to our Higher Self and is connected to the back of the neck, near the *medulla oblongata* (the lowest part of the brain). When we channel Spirit, it is through this location that the energy enters.

Our Higher Self is responsible for guiding and protecting us; we receive these whispers from what is called our *internal auditory system.* When we are too dependent on the advice and approval of others, at the expense of honoring our own truth, our internal auditory system becomes polluted by exaggeration, lies, and negativity.

The ability to express our highest truths is dependent upon how we honor our individuality, maintain our sense of self, and live by integrity. When we fear being different, and, instead, aim to fit in, we say things that do not necessarily reflect our truth. Being able to stand apart, being able to mean what we say and to stand up for ourselves, despite the risk of rocking the boat and/or not fitting in, is critical not only to a healthy Throat chakra but also to being a healthy and mature adult.

The psychological function of the Throat chakra is communication, and its dysfunction is lying. Basic rights of this chakra are *a right to speak and be heard.*

Psychological issues here relate to creative identity: how we communicate, listen, speak, and offer guidance. This creative identity is concerned with truthful communication, having a sense that expressing truth is the key to individuality, and finding our voice. Speaking the truth, gossiping, lying, exaggerating, creativity, and integrity are rooted in the Throat chakra.

Childhood traumas and abuses to the Throat chakra are creative, and are caused by lies, mixed messages, verbal abuse, constant yelling, excessive criticism (which blocks creativity), secrets, threats for "telling," having authoritarian parents who don't let kids talk back, and being part of an alcoholic/chemically dependent family who operates from a "don't talk, don't trust, don't feel" dynamic.

The life lesson of the Throat chakra is to harness your will, to express your highest truth, to live creatively.

The soul lesson is to express Divine will.

The motto is "I hear and speak the truth; I express myself with clear intent."

Throat Emotions

Gossip, lies, verbal abuse, emotional abuse, substance abuse, eating disorders, grief, unexpressed feelings (such as anger, sadness, and fear), and an absence of loving words all can block this chakra. These unhealthy factors pass through the Throat area and block the flow of energy from the lower chakras to the higher chakras. Furthermore, substance abuse clouds and disorients the mind and emotions, preventing us from expressing our highest truths. This blockage results in fatigue, an underactive thyroid gland, and a variety of physical ailments (as mentioned above).

In order to avoid these problems and come into greater selfhood, we must exercise our Throat chakra, at the expense of our fears of not being liked or approved of by others. It is a domino effect: The more we express our truth in loving ways, the more we become aware of how people perceive us, the more we come into our sense of self, and the stronger and more resilient to life's adversities we become. The Throat chakra is therefore the interdimensional center for the vital energy that flows throughout our physical, mental, emotional, and spiritual bodies.

We can only speak our truth to the extent that we are free in the Heart. Our communication reflects "the state of mind" of our Heart. Self-love and integrity are cornerstones of a healthy Heart, which show themselves up here. The way we treat others reflects the way we see ourselves. If we are blocked in our Heart, we are blocked in our truth. If we deny our feminine or masculine side, we are denying our wholeness, our truth. [*See* Chapter 17 for more details about the Heart chakra.]

Throat Pattern
Just as every chakra is interrelated with the one below and above it, each is also linked to its complimentary chakra. Look to the Sacral chakra to heal the Throat chakra.

Avoidance is the imbalanced behavior pattern found in the Throat and Sacral chakras. It is characterized by a belief that displaying emotion is a sign of weakness; a lack of intimacy with others to avoid feeling vulnerable, often using a *push-pull* dynamic to draw people in, then push them away; an *I love you, I hate you* relationship; and, passive aggressive indirect ways of expressing feelings.

When in balance, we trust our feelings and express vulnerability; we engage in close connections and maintain healthy boundaries; we share feelings openly and calmly; and we express appreciation.

Throat Intimacy

The Throat chakra governs *verbal intimacy*: talking, writing, singing, one way or another, we let it out. The partnership is fruitless unless we know how to express our emotions, needs, opinions, and love with the other. Talking at our partner won't do it. We must talk with them and this requires listening. A healthy relationship will compel us to share and to listen, to speak and to hear. When both hearts are willing to hear spiritual guidance the relationship evolves into one that is rich with the wealth of understanding.

Throat Dis-eases and Malfunctions

In the Throat chakra, physical and psychological dis-eases and illnesses relate to root beliefs and blocked communication. Body parts associated with the Throat chakra are the throat, ears, mouth, shoulders, neck, and jaw.

Physical dis-eases and illnesses that manifest from a blocked or overactive Throat chakra are a sore throat; laryngitis; a stiff neck; shoulder pain; constant colds; sinus problems; viral infections; thyroid problems/imbalances; hearing problems; ear infections; tightness of the jaw, jaw pain, and temporomandibular joint (TMJ) syndrome; skin rashes; hypertension (high blood pressure); heart attacks; digestive problems; speech impediments; and problems with the mouth and teeth.

Psychological dis-eases and disorders that manifest from a blocked or overactive Throat chakra are attention deficit disorders (ADD and ADHD) and autism.

Throat Body Systems

Every chakra is related and positioned next to a gland, or glands, in the body. Just as every chakra is interrelated with the one below and above it, so are the glands and body systems. The body systems that affect the Throat chakra are the endocrine, respiratory, and digestive systems.

Endocrine System: Thyroid Gland

The gland associated with the Throat chakra is the *thyroid*, the body's thermostat, which governs our metabolic rate. The thyroid is located at the front of the neck, just below the Adam's apple and along the front of the trachea (windpipe). The thyroid is rich with blood vessels and nerves that are important for voice quality.

The thyroid gland is responsible for regulating our body's growth, such as tooth development, muscle tone, mental development, and the functioning of our sexual organs and adrenal glands. The thyroid secretes several hormones influencing metabolism, growth and development, and body temperature. Adequate thyroid hormone produced during infancy and childhood is crucial for brain development. The main hormone secreted is called *thyroxine*, also known as T4.

Here is a list of thyroid conditions:

Goiter
Thyroiditis
Hyperthyroidism (overactive thyroid)
Hypothyroidism (underactive thyroid)
Graves' disease (a common form of hyperthyroidism)
Thyroid cancer
Thyroid nodule
Thyroid storm (a rare form of hyperthyroidism)

Problems here reflect issues of proper expression. Hyperactivity is often a reflection of an imbalance in the Throat chakra. A sluggish metabolism can reflect being sluggish in using creative expression; not expressing ourselves; not doing what we need and want to do; and not claiming our power, or claiming it in an inappropriate manner.

Digestive System

The digestive system converts food and beverages into nutrients and energy, such as protein, vitamins, minerals, carbohydrates, and fats, all of which the body needs for energy, growth, and repair. Major organs include the esophagus, stomach, gut, intestines, liver, pancreas, and gallbladder. After food is chewed and swallowed, it goes down the esophagus and enters the stomach, where it is further broken down by powerful stomach acids. From the stomach, the food travels into the small intestine. This is where food is broken down into nutrients that can enter the bloodstream through tiny hair-like projections. The excess food that the body doesn't need or can't digest is turned into waste that is eliminated from the body.

Primary functions of this system are ingestion and absorption; look to your habits to identify what you should and should not be ingesting and absorbing. This could indicate that you are not using what you have available to you, are not absorbing new ideas, and/or are being wasteful.

Respiratory System

The respiratory system acquires oxygen and eliminates carbon dioxide. The major organs are the nose, lungs, larynx, trachea, and bronchial tubes. When we breathe in, air enters the nose or mouth and goes down a long tube called the *trachea* (windpipe). The trachea branches into two bronchial tubes, or *primary bronchi,* which go to the lungs. The primary bronchi branch off into even smaller bronchial tubes, or *bronchioles.* The bronchioles end in the *alveoli,* or air sacs. Oxygen follows this path, passes through the walls of the air sacs and blood vessels, and enters the bloodstream. At the same time, carbon dioxide passes into the lungs and is exhaled.

Breathing is essential for life; therefore, problems with breathing reflect issues of a right to life. Feeling undeserving or guilty about how you live, or feeling like you are not living your best life or not allowed to live your best life, and therefore are suppressing your life expressions and emotions, all can lead to respiratory issues. Unequal exchanges in the life process reflect grief, such as one-sided giving, or taking in too much, and this lodges in the lungs and manifests breathing dis-eases and disorders, such as asthma and pneumonia.

Throat Animal Medicine

Cicada, Parrot, and Caterpillar are the Throat's prescription.

Cicada teaches us about nurturing ourselves through patience and creative activity. After laying their eggs, they remain underground for many years—some for thirteen years, and some for seventeen years—until they have reached maturity and are ready to come out of the closet, so to speak. By spending quality time honing our unique creative voice that is both heart- and mind-centered and -driven, Cicada medicine guarantees that once we share our true voice, invitations and opportunities will be offered. As a divination symbol, Cicada is my sign that a person has a seven-month wait for something beautiful that will emerge from within, and it involves creative expression.

I like to work with Parrot Medicine to discourage passive aggressive communication and encourage speaking truth from a place of alignment. Parrot teaches us how to access and harness our true colors, and share them proudly and loudly. We associate Parrot medicine with the Air element and the Throat chakra. Parrot says, "Sometimes what we have to say is pretty, and sometimes it's not. Either way, it needs to be shared and heard."

I like to work with Caterpillar Medicine to discourage bullying tactics and aggressive communication. Caterpillar teaches us that there is a time and place for everything. We associate Caterpillar medicine with the Water element and the Sacral chakra. Caterpillar says, "Connect with us before you open your mouth. Count to ten, then let us speak through you."

Throat Crystal Medicine

Blue Lace Agate, Angelite, Apatite, Kyanite, Aquamarine, Turquoise, Blue Chalcedony, Aqua Aura

Crystals carry with them specific healing properties for humans and animals. They can be programmed through our intention for healing and divination. There are two ways we suggest you select your crystals; *intuitively* and *deliberately.*

Crystals call us. Therefore, allow yourself to browse a crystal selection and wait for the one that intuitively reels you in. When you research its medicinal properties, you will be amazed at how that stone spoke to you and your needs.

The second way is to deliberately select your stone based on the dis-ease or illness you wish to heal. For example:

When I work as a Channel, I always wear a Kyanite crystal; when my dogs and I need insect repellant, we will use an Angelite elixir. Use the Internet to guide you in making your elixirs with crystals that are water soluble, photosensitive, sensitive to acid, and toxic.

Combining crystals with handpicked healing stones, aromatherapy, herbs, and animal medicine, I also work with my Guides as a medical intuitive using body scanning, remote viewing, and energy healing to detect and heal what is going on in the body. At the end of this chakra chapter, we show you how to conduct holistic health readings for yourself.

As a final note, you do not have to be an expert to conduct a healing session on yourself or your pet. You will learn as you practice so here are a few pointers:

Crystal Selection

When selecting your crystals and animal totems, know that each will resonate with specific chakras and assist in rebalancing and healing specific emotional, psychological, and physical dis-eases. Often, one chakra will require the energy of another to recalibrate and heal so keep this in mind when you work with crystal and animal medicine.

Healing Session

When performing a healing session, combine love-based intention with the medicinal properties of the crystal(s) and animal spirit. Experiment with therapeutic ways to work with crystal and animal energies, they will teach you, so listen carefully.

Intuitive Nudges

Listen to the intuitive nudges from your Guides, they will direct you to the material you need.

Blue Lace Agate
Astrological Association: Pisces

Healing Qualities: Gentle and calming. Provides emotional stability. Improves communication on all levels. Helps to attune to spiritual energies.

Physical Benefits: Good for eyesight, speech, nails, and pancreas. Helps with fluid retention, skin growths, and bone fractures. As an elixir, can be used to soothe tired eyes (soak gauze in the elixir and then place over eyes.)

Angelite
Astrological Association: Aquarius

Healing Qualities: Known as the "angel stone," it helps with connecting to the angelic realm, including your Spirit Guides, animal totems, and Guardian Angels. It also promotes feelings of security. Great for spiritual awareness and communication, channeling, and telepathy. When drunk as an elixir, it helps with spirit protection, psychic work, and spiritual healing. Good to help people who work with numbers, such as accountants.

Physical Benefits: Benefits all five senses. As a topical elixir, works as an insect repellant. Fights infectious diseases. Good for hemoglobin production and blood vessels.

Apatite
Astrological Association: Gemini

Healing Qualities: Calms the Throat chakra, promoting clear communication. Great for teachers, healers, writers, publishers, presenters, actors, performers, and singers. Clears mental confusion, allowing you to see the truth. Promotes psychic abilities and past-life recall. Great for meditation. Facilitates good understanding of the inner self. Balances yin/yang energy.

Physical Benefits: When drunk as an elixir, it settles the stomach and heals energy blockages. Great for tissue regeneration and repair. Helpful for weight loss, as it acts as an appetite suppressant. Also good for arthritis.

Kyanite
Astrological Association: Taurus, Libra, Aries

Healing Qualities: Helps you to "talk your talk." Aligns all the chakras, releasing energy blockages, and promoting tranquillity, calmness, perseverance, and reason. Creates a great internal space for meditation. Helps to connect with Spirit Guides. Facilitates dream recall. Increases psychic awareness. Balances yin/yang energy.

Physical Benefits: Good for the Throat chakra; improves health of the throat. Excellent for channeling and singing. Benefits muscles, all glands, the brain, and the elimination system.

Turquoise
Astrological Association: Sagittarius, Pisces, Scorpio

Healing Qualities: Great for public speaking and creative expression. Provides protection through any kind of journey, physical and metaphysical. Enhances romance, friendship, and love. Helps you to see your path and "walk your walk," by bringing spiritual and mental clarity, peace of mind, and ability to see the beauty in life. Protects property; prevents accidents; encourages writing and astral travel; enhances spiritual contact and all psychic abilities; promotes wisdom; balances yin/yang energy.

Physical Benefits: Great for circulation, lungs, throat, muscles, weight gain, detoxing, and postoperative recovery. Aids in nutritional absorption. Helps with headaches, backache, arthritis, asthma, gas, cataracts, wounds, and whiplash injuries. When drunk as an elixir, it heals stress-related skin disorders.

Blue Chalcedony
Astrological Association: Sagittarius

Healing Qualities: Great for dealing with childhood issues as it promotes emotional expression and eases communication. In combination with therapy, it can assist healing alcoholism helping you to let go of emotional baggage and material things.

Physical Benefits: Good for weight loss.

Aqua Aura
Astrological Association: Leo

Healing Qualities: Enhances psychic abilities, boosts aura, gives protection, dispels negativity, depression, sadness, loss, and grief. Excellent for treating shock and emotional trauma.

Physical Benefits: Helps relieve physical trauma and tension to the throat, neck and shoulder area.

Rainbow Medicine

Throat Chakra
Color Light blue, turquoise

Issue
Circle your issues:

- Purification
- Communication
- Creativity
- Expressing truth

Demon
Circle your demon:

- Lies

Codependent Behavior
Circle your behaviors:

- Prejudice
- Arrogant
- Over talkative
- Under talkative
- One sided communication and point of view

Codependent Pattern
Circle your Avoidance patterns:

- Showing emotion is a sign of weakness
- Avoiding intimacy with others to avoid feeling vulnerable
- Using a *push-pull* dynamic to draw people in, then push them away
- Engaging in an *I love you, I hate you* relationship
- Using passive aggressive indirect ways of expressing feelings

Throat Lesson
Since our chakras require regular maintenance, check in with each regularly by pulling two cards. I like to use a Tarot and an oracle deck but if you do not know Tarot, select two oracle decks, one with images and the other with words.

Begin each Friday by asking the question:

What lesson does my Throat chakra want me to focus on today?

Shuffle and pull out one card from each deck. Analyze the cards in response to how they speak to the issues of this particular chakra.

Throat Map
Take out two decks, one with images and one with words, and ask your Higher Self and Guides:

Show me my big picture story theme in my Throat chakra?

Shuffle and pull out one card from each deck. Analyze the cards in response to how they speak to the issues of this particular chakra.

Throat Issues
Continue with the same decks and pull two cards according to the following questions. Work with one question at a time. Once you receive your cards, study them and write down every answer you are able to interpret. Remember to analyze the cards according to questions asked. If you need additional information or clarification for any question, pull

more cards. When you move on to the next question, place all cards back into the decks. Sometimes you will see how the same cards will keep coming to you, this is Spirit's way of emphasizing the issue.

Since the Throat relates to expression, avoidance, truth and lies, interpret your cards by looking for answers/responses to the following:

What do I need to express and get off my chest?
What do I need to keep to myself?
What does my Throat suppress?
What is my Throat's strength?
What is my Throat's weakness?
What form of creative expression do I need?
What message does my Throat have for me?

Once you have reviewed all your channeled information, reconnect with your big picture theme. Connect all dots to identify the storyline, and write a brief paragraph summarizing your Throat Reading.

Throat Energy with Cards
Try this exercise by pulling cards for your Throat and reading them psychically.

What energy is in my Throat?

After you pull a couple of cards from your selected decks, don't look at them, place them together in one hand and face down hold them over your Throat chakra. This will trigger information to come. You will feel the energy in that area, so it is important to write down everything you feel, taste, smell, sense, hear, think, and see.

Once you have completed the exercise, review your written material. Next, look at your cards to see how they relate to what you picked up in meditation. The cards' meanings and images coupled with your channeled impressions will further inform your Throat reading.

Psychic Throat Scan

What Animal Medicine does my Throat need?

Another way to pick up information about yourself or someone else is to scan your body using your mind and body sensations. Ask your Guide to give you the symbol of an animal that reflects the coping behavior you need to adopt.

Third Eye Chakra

Color Indigo
Element Light
Issue Intuition, Imagination, Envisioning Goals
Demon Delusion
Balanced Archetype The Wise Elder
Imbalanced Archetype The Intellectual Skeptic
Codependent Pattern Denial
Codependent Behavior Impatient, egotistical
Complementary Chakra Solar Plexus
Intimacy Visual
Gland Pituitary
Body Part Eyes, brow, base of skull
Body System Endocrine, Nervous
Dis-ease and Illness Obsessions, migraines, headaches, sinuses, ear infections, eye problems, high blood pressure
Sense Sight, mindful knowing
Spiritual Gift Clairvoyance (sight)
Glandular Prescription Positive thinking, choosing the good in your life, sewing, knitting, puzzles, chess, activities that encourage leadership and self-celebration
Animal Prescription Blue Jay, Magpie, Salmon
Crystal Prescription Lapis Lazuli, Sodalite, Sapphire, Apophyllite, Prehnite, Celestite

The sixth chakra is the Third Eye chakra. Its color is indigo, cobalt, or dark blue, and it is located in the area between the eyes and slightly above them, in the middle of the forehead. Its element is Light.

Third Eye Archetype

The Third Eye chakra represents our ability to use intuition, and to make mental connections between intuitive perceptions, thoughts, and actions in a way that helps us to move forward. When we are in balance, these connections bring understanding and direction. The way we know we are out of alignment, however, is that we become paranoid and delusional, allowing other people's thoughts and beliefs to control our own thoughts, actions, and perceptions of the world. Feeling unable to make healthy decisions for ourselves, and/or to commit to following through on our choices, are cues that we need to bring ourselves back into balance. When blocked, we allow other people's opinions of us override our own view of ourselves, as we allow their mental hooks to affect, control, and coerce our minds.

When in balance, the archetype is that of the Wise Elder. This person is someone who trusts in Source and offers cultivated wisdom from his or her life experience.

Balanced Third Eye qualities are clairvoyance, intuition, imagination, and a sharp memory; ability to think symbolically; ability to visualize desired outcomes and goals; ability to trust; ability to reason well; displaying perceptiveness, wisdom, discernment, and knowledge; exhibiting good dream recall.

The motto is "With Spirit working through me, I direct my energy and drive, and use my available resources to accomplish my goals."

When out of balance, the archetype is that of the Intellectual Skeptic. This person is someone who relies solely on the rational left-brain thinking mind.

Imbalanced Third Eye qualities are getting caught up in details and/or in denial (as in, can't see what's really going on; considering luck and fate as the reasons for why things happen; needing to dominate and control situations and people; exhibiting trust issues; exhibiting insensitivity; having poor vision and poor memory; having difficulty envisioning the future; displaying lack of imagination and lack of ambition; having poor dream recall;

being monopolarized (only seeing one right way); having hallucinations, delusions, obsessions, difficulty concentrating, and frequent nightmares.

The motto is "I feel sorry for myself, I am angry at the world, and I blame others for why my life is the way it is."

Indigo (and cobalt and dark blue), the color of the Third Eye chakra, is the color of sedation, altered states of consciousness, envisioning goals, and seeing self; it represents peace, calmness, acceptance, tolerance, understanding, a desire to help and nurture others, humanitarianism, psychic potential, and high sensitivity. This is the color of enjoying learning and discovering the mysteries of life, and working with like-minded people. When this color is dull, the person may have a negative outlook on life or may tend to withdraw from others.

Third Eye Psychology

The Third Eye chakra represents seeing truth, and when we meditate, this Third Eye, our Higher Self, is a portal. It represents clarity of thinking that comes from clear seeing and seeing truth; it uses the intellect to think about and see our goals. If our Heart is unforgiving and angry, that means we have a veil over the Third Eye, keeping ourselves in states of denial about certain aspects of the self. This self-deception inhibits the ability to break patterns of suffering, which prevents us from manifesting our highest potential. Dream recall is an indication that truth wants to be revealed; lack of dreaming means we are not yet ready to see our truths, for we are still afraid.

When the Third Eye is fully activated, it stimulates both the right and left brain hemispheres to create a harmonious vision of reality, including both the creative and imaginative, and the logical and rational. Its role is to cultivate positive beliefs of self and other: the more positive we are, the more resilient and joyful we become. To fully implement our dreams, it is important to address self-limiting ideas about ourselves and the world. The Third Eye is the catalyst and channel for allowing this energy to revitalize us. Its purpose is to help us to develop wisdom, discernment, imagination, knowledge, and intuition.

The psychological function of the Third Eye chakra is intuition, and its dysfunction is delusion. Its basic right is *a right to see.*

Psychological issues here relate to holistic personal identity; how we each relate to seeing ourselves as a spiritual, emotional, psychological, and spiritual being. This holistic identity is concerned with pattern recognition, sight, intuition, inner vision, strategy, self-mage, visualization, insight, dreams, long-range goals, developing understanding for our own limitations and those of others, and cultivating and practicing gratitude. Attitudes that are self-affirming, accepting, and inclusive are rooted in the Third Eye chakra.

Childhood traumas and abuses to the Third Eye affect holistic integration, and are caused when what you see doesn't go with what you are told, when intuition and psychic occurrences are invalidated, and when you grow up in ugly or frightening environments, such as domestic violence or war zones.

The life lesson of the Third Eye chakra is to learn to focus your intelligence, to know who and what are for your highest good and greatest joy, to distill wisdom from your life experiences (both pleasant and difficult), and to choose life, health, joy, and fulfillment in every aspect of your life.

The soul lessons are detachment and intuition.

The motto is "I see all things clearly; I can manifest my visions and goals."

Third Eye Emotions

Exercising the Third Eye helps us to develop sensitivity and open-mindedness, replacing oversensitivity (and/or insensitivity) and close-mindedness. When our mind functions well, we are open to the power of healing. Confirming our worth and ability to think and intuit at the same time feeds the Third Eye; this is like cultivating seeds in our subconscious, allowing them to grow and harvest into conscious manifestation, bringing us greater possibility for emotional and physical well-being. As the mind becomes healthier, so does the body. When we think more positively, we let go of destructive and sabotaging ways, and then we can detach from this form of spinning. Ultimately, with consistent practice, we become accustomed to choosing love over fear, and once we get used to thinking, behaving, acting, and manifesting from love, the possibilities of more positivity become endless.

The ultimate lesson of the Third Eye chakra is "To become wise we must learn from the whys."

Third Eye Pattern

Just as every chakra is interrelated with the one below and above it, each is also linked to its complimentary chakra. Look to the Solar Plexus chakra to heal the Third Eye chakra.

Denial is the imbalanced behavior pattern found in the Third Eye chakra. It is characterized by an inability to identify one's feelings; minimizing the feelings of others; wearing a mask; projecting one's negative traits on to others; misinterpreting the feelings of others; and, perceiving the self as a savior, helping others but not accepting the help of others.

When in balance, we identify our thoughts and feelings, and can discern the difference; we embrace our feelings and value them; we recognize that the mirror goes both ways; we know that caretaking is self-motivated whereas caring is not; we feel compassion for the other's needs; we express our pain appropriately and communicate directly and calmly; and we are able to participate in healthy, loving relationships.

Third Eye Intimacy

The Third Eye governs *visual intimacy*: holding a common vision to assure a long term dedicated relationship. The longterm goal in the relationship serves as the foundation for the decisions we make for and within that relationship. The assumption of a lasting promise provides us the assurance we need to hang on when the going gets tough. However, we must be careful to avoid obligations that force either person to sacrifice a vital part of the Self.

Visual intimacy begins and ends with self-knowledge. If we see ourselves accurately, we can perceive others accurately. From this place, we can pursue goals and plans that will suit both partners, not only one or the other. Once we have established our longterm agenda, we can orient our daily life around joint goals and objectives. Our everyday interactions should include everything from making career decisions together to lovingly splitting the household chores.

Third Eye Dis-eases and Malfunctions

In the Third Eye chakra, physical and psychological dis-eases and ill-nesses are intuitive and metaphysical. Body parts associated with the Third Eye chakra are the eyes, brow, and the base of the skull.

Physical dis-eases and illnesses that manifest from a blocked or overactive Third Eye chakra are eye problems and conditions, such as blurred vision, cataracts, and glaucoma; sinus problems and infections; ear problems and infections; spinal disorders; and headaches and migraines.

Psychological dis-eases and disorders that manifest from a blocked or overac-tive Third Eye chakra are a negative mind state; being mentally overwhelmed; experiencing all kinds of irritations; exhibiting mental illness, such as schizo-phrenia and personality disorders; and displaying neurological disorders.

Third Eye Body Systems

Every chakra is related and positioned next to a gland, or glands, in the body. Just as every chakra is interrelated with the one below and above it, so are the glands and body systems. The body systems that affect the Third Eye chakra are the endocrine and nervous systems.

Endocrine System: Pituitary Gland

The gland associated with the Third Eye chakra is the *pituitary gland,* also known as the "governor gland" or "master gland," because it secretes hormones that control the activities of the other glands and various bodily functions, affecting the entire immune system. The pituitary gland is lo-cated at the base of the brain, below the hypothalamus. Pituitary hormones control skeletal growth, sexual development and maturation, milk secretion in women, thyroid and adrenal function, and blood pressure; the pituitary is necessary for physical and psychological growth.

The pituitary gland feeds energy to the brain, eyes, ears, nose, and mouth, activating positive thought and action. We impede this gland when we have self-limiting beliefs, and we maximize the use of this gland when we trust ourselves and use our inner knowing. Positive thinking and choosing the good we want in our lives secretes the pituitary hormone, which stabilizes blood pressure and heart rate, helping us to withstand pain and create healthier realities. Negative thinking blocks the secretion of the hormone.

Health problems here reflect how we govern our lives, as well as how we let others govern us. Issues of control and balance are what need to be considered, such as constantly making decisions for others, having others overactive in our lives and constantly making decisions for us, or our not being active enough in choosing what is best for us and therefore wanting others to make decisions for us.

Nervous System

The nervous system is responsible for communication and control; it integrates the activities of all the organs. It is made up of the brain, the spinal cord, and nerves. It stores information, responds to the environment, and transmits messages between the brain, spinal cord, and peripheral nervous system. There are three parts of your nervous system that work together: the *central nervous system,* the *peripheral nervous system,* and the *autonomic nervous system.*

The central nervous system sends out nerve impulses and analyzes information from the sense organs, which tell the brain about the things we see, hear, smell, taste, and feel. The peripheral nervous system includes the *craniospinal nerves* that branch off from the brain and the spinal cord. It carries the nerve impulses from the central nervous system to the muscles and glands. The autonomic nervous system regulates involuntary action, such as heartbeat and digestion.

Problems here can reflect trying to integrate too many activities in our lives, or not having enough activities to keep us occupied; being overly sensitive to criticism from self and others; not communicating our needs clearly, or interacting with others who are not communicating clearly with us; and being closed to new possibilities.

Third Eye Animal Medicine

Blue Jay, Magpie, and Salmon Medicine are the Third Eye's prescriptions.

Blue Jay teaches us how to recognize proper choices and how to become responsible for these choices. Taking into consideration the highest good of all players, Blue Jay leads us to the door that opens other doors. When we choose poorly, life becomes complicated; when we act with integrity and personal accountability, royal opportunities await. As a divination symbol, Blue Jay is my sign that a decision is needed in order to move forward. One day while lost on a country road, a blue jay appeared to show me which path to take.

I like to work with Magpie Medicine to discourage self-deception. Magpie teaches us how to access hidden secrets and fears so as not to deceive the self with false truth. We associate Magpie medicine with the Air element and the Third Eye chakra. Magpie says, "Better the devil you know than the one you don't. Not."

I like to work with Salmon Medicine to encourage overcoming obstacles. Salmon teaches us that with a disciplined attitude, *the only way is up*. We associate Salmon medicine with the Water element and the Sacral and Crown chakras. Salmon says, "At the end of the day, we know how to put it all into perspective, and still dance and have fun."

Third Eye Crystal Medicine

Lapis Lazuli, Sodalite, Sapphire, Apophyllite, Prehnite, Celestite

Crystals carry with them specific healing properties for humans and animals. They can be programmed through our intention for healing and divination. There are two ways we suggest you select your crystals; *intuitively* and *deliberately*.

Crystals call us. Therefore, allow yourself to browse a crystal selection and wait for the one that intuitively reels you in. When you research its medicinal properties, you will be amazed at how that stone spoke to you and your needs.

The second way is to deliberately select your stone based on the dis-ease or illness you wish to heal. For example:

When I have a fever combined with nausea, I will drink a Sapphire elixir; after a long week of exercise with my dogs, Savannah, Sam, and I will drink a Lapis Lazuli elixir to help repair muscles and bones. Use the Internet to guide you in making your elixirs with crystals that are water soluble, photosensitive, sensitive to acid, and toxic.

Combining crystals with handpicked healing stones, aromatherapy, herbs, and animal medicine, I also work with my Guides as a medical intuitive using body scanning, remote viewing, and energy healing to detect and heal what is going on in the body. At the end of this chakra chapter, we show you how to conduct holistic health readings for yourself.

As a final note, you do not have to be an expert to conduct a healing session on yourself or your pet. You will learn as you practice so here are a few pointers:

Crystal Selection

When selecting your crystals and animal totems, know that each will resonate with specific chakras and assist in rebalancing and healing specific emotional, psychological, and physical dis-eases (energetic imprints). Often, one chakra will require the energy of another to recalibrate and heal so keep this in mind when you work with crystal and animal medicine.

Healing Session

When performing a healing session, combine love-based intention with the medicinal properties of the crystal(s) and animal spirit. Experiment with therapeutic ways to work with crystal and animal energies, they will teach you, so listen carefully.

Intuitive Nudges

Listen to the intuitive nudges from your Guides, they will direct you to the material you need.

Lapis Lazuli
Astrological Association: Sagittarius

Healing Qualities: Great for promoting psychic abilities. Brings clarity to dreams; relieves insomnia and depression. Helps to clear a cluttered mind, enabling you to become more organized. Improves yin/yang energy for balance within and with others.

Physical Benefits: Helps repair muscles and bones. Good for detoxing. Helps with dizziness, vertigo, hearing loss, and backache. Boosts the immune system. Boosts energy; good for thyroid and thymus glands.

Sodalite
Astrological Association: Sagittarius

Healing Qualities: Good for healing oversensitivity, feelings of inadequacy, and mental confusion; great for group work communication.

Physical Benefits: Good for diabetes, hypertension (high blood pressure), and calcium deficiency. Good for the metabolism and the lymphatic system. Combats signs of aging. Good for healthy development of infants.

Sapphire
Astrological Association: Virgo, Libra, Sagittarius

Healing Qualities: A record keeper that helps to access the Akashic Records; excellent for communication with Spirit. Helps relieve depression and narrow-mindedness; promotes emotional balance.

Physical Benefits: Has astringent properties; good for all glands and hormones. Helpful for treating nausea, boils, and infections. Reduces bleeding, signs of aging, fevers, and backache pain.

Apophyllite
Astrological Association: Libra, Gemini

Healing Qualities: Great for meditation, psychic abilities, spirit communication, and astral travel, helps with seeing 'truth.'

Physical Benefits: Helps to rejuvenate the body and eyesight.

Prehnite
Astrological Association: Libra

Healing Qualities: Good for divination, prophesy, dream recall and visualization of dreams and goals, helps you to let go of thoughts and feelings no longer needed, helps remove frustration and increase flow, great for helping you find your spiritual path.

Physical Benefits: Kidneys, bladder, anemia, and gout.

Celestite
Astrological Association: Gemini

Healing Qualities: Great for angelic communication, dream recall, astral travel, and to prevent nightmares, it relieves stress and helps for clear thinking when involved with working through complex ideas.

Physical Benefits: Good for eye, ear, and speech conditions. Good for detoxing and pain relief.

Rainbow Medicine

Third Eye Chakra
Color Indigo

Issue
Circle your issues:

- Intuition
- Imagination
- Envisioning goals

Demon
Circle your demon:

- Delusion

Codependent Behavior
Circle your behaviors:

- Impatient
- Egotistical

Codependent Pattern
Circle your Denial patterns:

- Unable to identify one's feelings

267

- Minimizing the feelings of others
- Wearing a mask
- Projecting one's negative traits on to others
- Misinterpreting the feelings of others
- Perceiving the self as a savior
- Helping others but not accepting the help of others

Third Eye Lesson

Since our chakras require regular maintenance, check in with each regularly by pulling two cards. I like to use a Tarot and an oracle deck but if you do not know Tarot, select two oracle decks, one with images and the other with words.

Begin each Saturday by asking the question:

What lesson does my Third Eye chakra want me to focus on today?

Shuffle and pull out one card from each deck. Analyze the cards in response to how they speak to the issues of this particular chakra.

Third Eye Map

Take out two decks, one with images and one with words, and ask your Higher Self and Guides:

Show me my big picture story theme in my Third eye chakra?

Shuffle and pull out one card from each deck. Analyze the cards in response to how they speak to the issues of this particular chakra.

Third Eye Issues

Continue with the same decks and pull two cards according to the following questions. Work with one question at a time. Once you receive your cards, study them and write down every answer you are able to interpret. Remember to analyze the cards according to questions asked. If you need additional information or clarification for any question, pull more cards. When you move on to the next question, place all cards back into the decks. Sometimes you will see how the same cards will keep coming to you, this is Spirit's way of emphasizing the issue.

Since the Third Eye relates to longterm and envisioned goals, uncertainty, and delusion, interpret your cards by looking for answers/responses to the following:

What is my goal?
What am I seeing clearly?
What am I not seeing clearly?
What will help me to see more clearly?
What does my mind want?
What does my mind need?
What message does my Third Eye have for me?

Once you have reviewed all your channeled information, reconnect with your big picture theme. Connect all dots to identify the storyline, and write a brief paragraph summarizing your Third Eye Reading.

Third Eye Energy with Cards
Try this exercise by pulling cards for your Third Eye and reading them psychically.

What energy is in my Third Eye?

After you pull a couple of cards from your selected decks, don't look at them, place them together in one hand and face down hold them over your Third Eye chakra. This will trigger information to come. You will feel the energy in that area, so it is important to write down everything you feel, taste, smell, sense, hear, think, and see.

Once you have completed the exercise, review your written material. Next, look at your cards to see how they relate to what you picked up in meditation. The cards' meanings and images coupled with your channeled impressions will further inform your Third Eye reading.

Psychic Third Eye Scan

What Animal Medicine does my Third Eye need?

Another way to pick up information about yourself or someone else is to scan your body using your mind and body sensations. Ask your Guide to give you the symbol of an animal that reflects the coping behavior you need to adopt.

Crown Chakra

Color Violet, White

Element Pure Spirit, inner Light

Issue Thought, Consciousness, inspiration from and connection to Source

Demon Attachment, arrogance

Balanced Archetype The Guru

Imbalanced Archetype The Egotist

Codependent Pattern Low Self Esteem

Codependent Behavior Manic depression, alienation, feeling like the world is against you

Complementary Chakra Solar Plexus, Root

Intimacy Spiritual

Gland Pineal

Body Part Head, Central Nervous System, Cerebral Cortex

Body System Endocrine, Nervous

Dis-ease and Illness Confusion, neurosis, forgetfulness, sleep disturbances, migraines, depression

Sense Thought, bliss

Spiritual Gift Claircognizance (thought)

Glandular Prescription Psychic and mediumship development, meditation, visual arts practices, interior design, gardening, landscaping, snorkelling, scuba diving, flying

Animal Prescription Hawk, Eagle, Octopus

Crystal Prescription Amethyst, Charoite, Labradorite, Selenite, Rutilated Quartz

The seventh chakra is the Crown chakra. Its colors are purple and white, it is located at the top of the head, and it spins at the fastest vibrational rate. Its element is pure Spirit, inner Light.

Crown Archetype

This chakra represents our ability to communicate with Source for inspiration and guidance. When we are in balance, we have a sense of spirituality and are able to ground our ideas and manifest them. The way we know we are out of alignment, however, is that we become obsessed by our thoughts, are overly sensitive to our environment, and/or are arrogant, believing that everything we do is the result of our own efforts, with no Higher Power working through us. Feeling confused and experiencing loss of memory are cues that we need to bring ourselves back into balance. When blocked, we control others; if too open, we obsess.

When in balance, the archetype is that of the Guru. This person is someone who knows who he or she is.

Balanced Crown qualities are understanding, grace, beauty, serenity, and oneness with Source, All That Is; ability to manifest easily; ability to release old patterns; exhibiting compassion for self and others; having intuitive understanding; ability to perceive, analyze, and assimilate information; displaying intelligence, thoughtfulness, awareness, and open-mindedness; the ability to question thoughtfully and truthfully; being spiritually connected; displaying wisdom, mastery, and broad understanding.

The motto is "I am inspired. I feel that what I contribute matters, and although I am vulnerable, I am capable of inner strength and am able to give my love with no fear that I will lack."

When out of balance, the archetype is that of the Egotist. This person is someone who thinks he or she is responsible for all outcomes.

Imbalanced Crown qualities are feeling victimized and persecuted; exhibiting anger; holding on to old patterns; inability to sympathize or feel compassion toward others; being anxious; inability to sleep well; manifesting headaches, spiritual cynicism, learning difficulties, rigid belief systems, spiritual addiction, overintellectualization, confusion, dissociation from body, apathy, and excess in the lower chakras (i.e., materialism, greed, and domination of others).

The motto is "I treat myself as though I have a gangster community living inside me. I torment myself, I bully myself, and I operate from shame rather than confidence and self-respect."

Violet and white are the colors of the Crown chakra. Violet (or purple) is the color of Divine wisdom, spiritual evolution, psychic abilities, sensitivity, creativity, and charisma. This color represents having unique solutions and insights, and seeking truth and education as lifelong interests. When this color is dull, a person may be obsessive, may have an addictive personality, and will seldom be happy with achievements, always seeking perfection. White is the color of Angelic presence and receiving angelic communication; it represents innocence, purity, faith, and the soul (white light).

Crown Psychology

The Crown chakra represents our Higher Self and our Divine connection. The interdimensional channels into higher consciousness become more available to us when we are working on healing the Heart by understanding what happened to us and releasing the pain. Once involved in this process, we begin to vibrate at higher frequency rates and are able to tap into higher intelligence. It is from this place that we experience group consciousness: oneness, peace, and no fear, only love.

When in balance, we recognize that life moves through us, and we allow our experiences to take us to deeper levels of consciousness. Psychological maturity and spiritual development facilitate the opening of this chakra. Its lesson is oneness through acceptance of one's self.

The psychological function of the Crown chakra is understanding, and its dysfunction is attachment. Basic rights of this chakra are *a right to know and to learn.*

Psychological issues here relate to universal identity: a sense of oneness with All That Is. This universal identity is concerned with consciousness, transcendence, spiritual purpose and destiny, and contact with spiritual realms. It is about developing holistic and universal principles of acceptance and respect, and knowing that we never do anything without the help of our Higher Self and Source.

Childhood traumas and abuses to the Crown chakra are anticonnective, and are caused by withheld information, forced religion, invalidation of ours beliefs, blind obedience (as in, having no right to question or think for ourselves), misinformation, lies, and spiritual abuse.

The life lesson of the Crown chakra is to learn of your connection with the greater whole of life, and how to create a vital and spiritual context for holding, understanding, and discerning the meaning of your life experiences.

The soul lesson of the Crown chakra is to be at one with Source, All That Is.

The motto is "I am open to new ideas, I embrace my divinity, I trust that the information I need comes to me, and I am guided by my inner wisdom and a Higher Power."

Crown Emotions

Healing becomes possible only when the mind is loving, allowing, embracing, and accepting, aware that we have purpose, and are loved, guided, protected, and never alone. A sign that we are operating from a strong Crown chakra is the realization of our humility and gratitude for being alive and for our life being just the way it is. We understand and accept our hardships as life lessons that we are here to learn and gifts that help us manifest desires and dreams. With this transformed attitude and new appreciation, we become more resilient, able to work through the negativity, and are thus able to live with greater joy, harmony, and peace.

Crown Pattern

Just as every chakra is interrelated with the one below and above it, each is also linked to its complimentary chakra. Look to the Heart, Solar Plexus, and Root chakras to heal the Crown chakra.

Low Self Esteem is the imbalanced behavior pattern found in the Crown chakra. It is characterized by judging the self as never good enough and unloveable; needing to be right and resentful when wrong; unable to admit mistakes; a resistance to receiving help; not feeling comfortable in the limelight; looking for outside recognition valuing others' approval over one's own; expecting others to provide sense of safety; and, an inability to identify needs and wants, and set healthy priorities, deadlines, and boundaries to attain goals.

When in balance, we value the self and know we are lovable and worthy of praise; we recognize our responsibility to provide our own safety; we are honest about our motivations; we perceive ourself as equal; we let go of perfectionism and instead focus on progress; we don't procrastinate; we reach out for help when necessary; and we know how to identify opportunities, prioritize needs, and establish healthy boundaries to reach goals.

Crown Intimacy

The Crown chakra governs *spiritual intimacy*: both parties share common values, ethics, and beliefs about the Divine; they share living values and, if spiritual, support the other in achieving enlightenment. If their living values are too disparate, it makes it difficult for the couple to succeed.

Crown Dis-eases and Malfunctions

In the Crown chakra, physical and psychological dis-eases and illnesses arise from disconnection. Body parts associated with the Crown chakra are the central nervous system and the cerebral cortex.

Physical dis-eases and illnesses that manifest from a blocked Crown chakra are migraines, brain tumors, coma, dementia, Alzheimer's, amnesia, sleep pattern disturbances (such as too much sleep or insomnia), as well as no known causes of physical or mental illness.

Psychological dis-eases and disorders that manifest from a blocked or overactive Crown chakra are nervous system disturbances and disorders, cognitive delusions, environmental sensitivity, confusion, alienation, boredom, apathy, depression, and inability to learn.

Crown Body Systems

Every chakra is related and positioned next to a gland, or glands, in the body. Just as every chakra is interrelated with the one below and above it, so are the glands and body systems. The body systems that affect the Crown chakra are the endocrine and nervous systems.

Endocrine System: Pineal Gland

The gland associated with the Crown chakra is the *pineal gland*, which is situated in between the right and left cerebral hemispheres, attached to the third ventricle. The pineal gland is involved in several functions of the body: it secrets the hormone *melatonin*, which regulates the endocrine functions by converting nervous system signals to endocrine signals, causing feelings of sleepiness so that the body slows down and falls asleep; it also influences sexual development and the sexual functions of the ovaries and testes. The pineal gland is light sensitive. Considered the doorway to Spirit and Source, it releases endorphins that affect our physical and emotional happy place. I refer to it as *the real G-Spot*.

Problems here relate to physical and spiritual growth; not using and honoring our sexual, mental, and spiritual energies appropriately; not seeing what is right in front of us; not honoring all our energies and aspects of ourselves as spiritual; and not being sympathetic to others (nor finding others sympathetic to us).

A dysfunctional Crown chakra is exhibited by an egotistical attitude of separateness, whereby we think that life carries us through simply by our own efforts, unaware of the greater whole. When the ego gets involved and functions on the premise that it is "doing life" alone, it functions on arrogance, false pride, exploitation and manipulation, and this closes the Heart to love and healing. This imbalanced thinking creates problems with learning, perception, and spiritual understanding. Some of the physical problems that manifest are nervous disorders, neurosis, insomnia, alcoholism, color blindness, and epilepsy.

Meditation, yoga, and simple appreciation for beauty in life stimulate the release of melatonin. This hormone promotes compassion, gratitude, acceptance, and having the spiritual context in which to understand life's challenges. This last quality is also known as *transcendence*, a state of bliss that is achieved once we truly embody this connection with the Divine. When we open up this conduit to channel—be it through mediumship, the creative arts, the culinary arts, or the healing arts—we begin to experience more and more frequently this state of joyful bliss, and then we can make the necessary life adjustments that allow this feeling to be more constant in our life, including letting go of the people in our life who reject peace.

Nervous System

The nervous system is responsible for communication and control; it integrates the activities of all the organs. It is made up of the brain, the spinal cord, and nerves. It stores information, responds to the environment, and transmits messages between the brain, spinal cord, and peripheral nervous system. There are three parts of your nervous system that work together: the *central nervous system,* the *peripheral nervous system,* and the *autonomic nervous system.*

The central nervous system sends out nerve impulses and analyzes information from the sense organs, which tell the brain about the things we see, hear, smell, taste, and feel. The peripheral nervous system includes the *craniospinal nerves* that branch off from the brain and the spinal cord. It carries the nerve impulses from the central nervous system to the muscles and glands. The autonomic nervous system regulates involuntary action, such as heartbeat and digestion.

Problems here can reflect trying to integrate too many activities in our lives, or not having enough activities to keep us occupied; being overly sensitive to criticism from self and others; not communicating our needs clearly, or interacting with others who are not communicating clearly with us; and being closed to new possibilities.

Crown Animal Medicine

Hawk, Eagle, and Octopus Medicine are the Crown's prescriptions.

Hawk and Eagle teach us to rise above all situations, and to take a bird's-eye view of life in order to develop the ability to move beyond petty details, see the greater picture at play, envision a strategy, and put things into perspective. As a divination symbol, both Hawk and Eagle are my signs for native Spirit Guides, and as you have read in Chapter 7, Hawk is also a sign of a passed-over loved one making contact. Why are birds associated with Spirit Guides? Because Spirit Guides help us to understand the larger picture at play.

I like to work with Octopus Medicine to discourage tunnel vision. Octopus teaches us how best to keep an eye out for adjacent opportunities. We associate Octopus medicine with the Air and Water elements, and the Sacral, Third Eye and Crown chakras. For seizing opportunity, Octopus says, "The opportunity has arrived, take the call!"

I also like to work with Octopus Medicine to encourage flexibility and adapt-ability. Octopus teaches us how best to adapt to environments and flow through tight squeezes. Octopus says, "Get your heart out of your head and stop obsessing over your losses. Free your mind of the past and let yourself ascend into this new future."

Crown Crystal Medicine

Herkimer Diamond, Amethyst, Charoite, Labradorite, Selenite, Rutilated Quartz

Crystals carry with them specific healing properties for humans and ani-mals. They can be programmed through our intention for healing and divi-nation. There are two ways we suggest you select your crystals; *intuitively* and *deliberately*.

Crystals call us. Therefore, allow yourself to browse a crystal selection and wait for the one that intuitively reels you in. When you research its medicinal properties, you will be amazed at how that stone spoke to you and your needs.

The second way is to deliberately select your stone based on the dis-ease or illness you wish to heal. For example:

When I have a headache related to PMS, I will combine drinking an Amethyst elixir with a topical elixir compress placed over my Crown; when my dog's skin is dry, Savannah drinks a Selenite elixir; When she has a wart, we will treat it with a Labradorite topical elixir. Use the Internet to guide you in making your elixirs with crystals that are water soluble, photosensitive, sensitive to acid, and toxic.

Combining crystals with handpicked healing stones, aromatherapy, herbs, and animal medicine, I also work with my Guides as a medical intuitive using body scanning, remote viewing, and energy healing to detect and heal what is going on in the body. At the end of this chakra chapter, we show you how to conduct holistic health readings for yourself.

As a final note, you don't have to be an expert to conduct a healing session on yourself and/or your pet. You will learn as you practice so here are a few pointers:

Crystal Selection

When selecting your crystals and animal totems, know that each will resonate with specific chakras and assist in rebalancing and healing specific emotional, psychological, and physical dis-eases (energetic imprints). Often, one chakra will require the energy of another to recalibrate and heal so keep this in mind when you work with crystal and animal medicine.

Healing Session

When performing a healing session, combine love-based intention with the medicinal properties of the crystal(s) and animal spirit. Experiment with therapeutic ways to work with crystal and animal energies, they will teach you, so listen carefully..

Intuitive Nudges

Listen to the intuitive nudges from your Guides, they will direct you to the material you need.

Herkimer Diamond
Astrological Association: Sagittarius

Healing Qualities: Helps to attune energies to people, animals, deities, and places, removes tension and fear, helps with relaxation.

Physical Benefits: Great for detoxing, removes radiation and toxins, helps with injury recovery, good for DNA and RNA replication, and metabolism.

Amethyst
Astrological Association: Pisces, Virgo, Aquarius, Capricorn

Healing Qualities: Helps relieve obsessive/compulsive disorder (OCD), as well as all addictive behaviors, including alcoholism; reduces anger and violent tendencies; increases ability to make decisions. Great for public speaking and negotiation. Eases insomnia, oversensitivity, grief, and homesickness. Helps you to move forward in life, and to make changes in home and business. When near other crystals, it amplifies their powers to help heal dis-ease and remove negative energy blocks.

Physical Benefits: Drinking the elixir can bring relief to arthritis, is good for the immune system, blood clots, hormones, stomach problems, skin, bones, teeth, headaches, migraines, asthma, and detoxing.

Charoite
Astrological Association: Sagittarius, Scorpio

Healing Qualities: Helps with autism and ADD/ADHD; promotes being in the moment and seizing opportunities to move forward in life, to release old relationships, and to ground during spiritual experiences.

Physical Benefits: As an elixir, good for detoxing, eyes, heart, pulse rate, headaches, aches and pains, pancreas and liver damage.

Labradorite
Astrological Association: Sagittarius, Leo, Scorpio

Healing Qualities: Reduces insecurity, anxiety, and stress, by promoting mental sharpness, originality, and intuition. Great for divination work, linking right and left brain hemispheres, and helping the connection between magic and science. Stabilizes the aura and energy flow between the chakras, allows mental flow of thoughts to enable the ability to see many possibilities at once.

Physical Benefits: As a topical elixir helps with treating warts; great for digestion and eyes.

Selenite
Astrological Association: Taurus, linked to the Moon

Healing Qualities: Good for abuse recovery, menstrual cycle, and releasing emotional patterns and behaviors.

Physical Benefits: Helps with skin conditions like psoriasis, eczema, and acne; encourages a youthful appearance, preventing hair loss, wrinkles, increased skin elasticity; removes free radicals associated with cancer, tumors, and age spots. Boosts fertility and sex drive.

Rutilated Quartz
Astrological Association: All signs in the zodiac

Healing Qualities: Great for mental health, breakdowns, depression, despair, negativity, and healing emotional blockages. Encourages calmness and balance.

Physical Benefits: Reduces signs of aging and helps to maintain a youthful appearance; great for tissue regeneration, weight gain, Parkinson's disease, and boosting the immune system.

Rainbow Medicine

Crown Chakra
Color Violet, white

Issue
Circle your issues:

- Thought
- Consciousness
- Inspiration from & connection to Source

Demon
Circle your demons:

- Attachment
- Arrogance

Codependent Behavior
Circle your behaviors:

- Manic depression
- Alienation
- Feeling like the world is against you

Codependent Pattern

Circle your Low Self Esteem patterns:

- Judging the self as never good enough and unloveable
- Needing to be right and resentful when wrong
- Unable to admit mistakes
- Resistant to receiving help
- Not comfortable in the limelight
- Looking for outside recognition valuing others' approval over one's own
- Expecting others to provide sense of safety
- Unable to identify needs and wants, and set healthy priorities, deadlines, and boundaries to attain goals

Crown Lesson

Since our chakras require regular maintenance, check in with each regularly by pulling two cards. I like to use a Tarot and an oracle deck but if you do not know Tarot, select two oracle decks, one with images and the other with words.

Begin each Sunday by asking the question:

What lesson does my Crown chakra want me to focus on today?

Shuffle and pull out one card from each deck. Analyze the cards in response to how they speak to the issues of this particular chakra.

Crown Map

Take out two decks, one with images and one with words, and ask your Higher Self and Guides:

Show me my big picture story theme in my Crown chakra?

Shuffle and pull out one card from each deck. Analyze the cards in response to how they speak to the issues of this particular chakra.

Crown Issues

Continue with the same decks and pull two cards according to the following questions. Work with one question at a time. Once you receive your cards, study them and write down every answer you are able to interpret. Remember to analyze the cards according to questions asked. If you need additional information or clarification for any question, pull more cards. When you move on to the next question, place all cards back into the decks. Sometimes you will see how the same cards will keep coming to you, this is Spirit's way of emphasizing the issue.

Since the Crown relates to enlightenment, attachment, self esteem, and a win/lose dual mentality, interpret your cards by looking for answers/responses to the following:

How do I self sabotage?
How can I heal my self-sabotage?
What triggers me to doubt myself?
What message does my Crown have for me?
What message does my Higher Self have for me?
What message does my Spirit Guide have for me?
What message does my passed-over loved one have for me?

Once you have reviewed all your channeled information, reconnect with your big picture theme. Connect all dots to identify the storyline, and write a brief paragraph summarizing your Crown Reading.

Crown Energy with Cards

Try this exercise by pulling cards for your Crown and reading them psychically.

What energy is in my Crown?

After you pull a couple of cards from your selected decks, don't look at them, place them together in one hand and face down hold them over your Crown chakra. This will trigger information to come. You will feel the energy in that area, so it is important to write down everything you feel, taste, smell, sense, hear, think, and see.

Once you have completed the exercise, review your written material. Next, look at your cards to see how they relate to what you picked up in meditation. The cards' meanings and images coupled with your channeled impressions will further inform your Crown reading.

Psychic Crown Scan

What Animal Medicine does my Crown need?

Another way to pick up information about yourself or someone else is to scan your body using your mind and body sensations. Ask your Guide to give you the symbol of an animal that reflects the coping behavior you need to adopt.

Part IV

Coming Full Circle

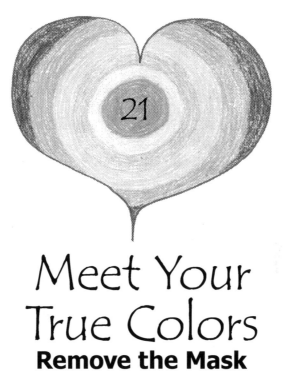

Meet Your
True Colors
Remove the Mask

As I contemplated how to end this book, I received one more piece of the puzzle on my journey to explain yet again why Spirit show themselves to me through the rainbow. This is what I heard them sing to me in the shower:

I see your true colors, and that's why I love you.
So *don't be afraid to let them show,*
Your true colors are beautiful like a rainbow.

—"True Colors"
Cyndi Lauper (1986)

Thank you, my beautiful A-Team, for showing me and all those we touch the way into the Light.

Final Message

Unbury yourself to live your true potential and power.

It is never too late to invest in yourself or shall we say, "it's not over until it's over." No matter your age or circumstance, you can take advantage of the *now* and tend to your garden of plenty. Only through *self-awareness*, *conflict resolution,* and *self-acceptance* can we come into greater *self-love* so don't fear what you may find when you go beneath the surface to confront your illusions of what you thought your life should look like. There is no competition or comparison with others needed to identify who you are and where you are meant to be, simply sportsmanship and mirrors to help you see where you are and guide you to your next adventure. Let go, free yourself in your heart and like a good facial or shave, peel away the layers that hide your truth so that you may shine bright and attract more Light. On behalf of *your* A-Team who love and cherish *you*, we hope you commit yourself to cohealing and cocreating your best life for when consciousness is raised, change becomes possible, and life shows you *real* magic and dreams!

G-d bless.

Rainbow Medicine

Decoding
Discomfort

Appendix 1. Self-Diagnosis Form

This exercise is to help you decode your discomfort, injury, accident, cold, fever, infection, disease, and mental illness. Photocopy and work with this printer friendly form. Circle everything in the form that relates to the condition you are diagnosing. After you have diagnosed your discomfort and understand its energetic imprint i.e. underlying emotional and psychological issues driving it, read the corresponding chakra chapters to learn how your imbalances come to be, how these puzzle pieces unite to create the *you* that you are, engage in the exercises at the end of the chapters, and follow the glandular prescriptions suggested in *Chapter 12*.

Every dis-ease and disease is an opportunity to learn a life lesson, break a pattern, heal, and thrive. When you discover its consciousness, bring your patterns into balance, and heal intimacy issues, you will be amazed at the power you have to prevent dis-ease and maximize holistic health. Once you learn how to identify specific components that create your discomfort, you are able to intervene in your pathological behavior, heal the condition, and bring yourself into greater harmonic health within and without.

Body Conditions

- Chills and Fevers
- Congestion
- Cramps
- Fatigue
- Infection
- Inflammation
- Irritations
- Nausea
- Pain
- Swelling

Chills and Fevers

Chills occur when the body needs to realign with the physical. Chills cause a contraction, a pulling inward, and can represent:

- Pulling away from others, or a need to pull away to ground yourself
- Being involved in too many activities
- Being scattered
- A need to take enough time for yourself
- Feeling insecure and left out in the cold

Fevers occur when the body needs to realign with Spirit. A fever in the body means that the body is trying to shake off, burn off, and realign itself. A fever is designed to burn off toxins in the body and eliminate them through the condensation the body produces. A fever happens when a sudden temperature raise occurs and the pulse quickens, converting matter to spirit. The subtle bodies separate from the physical in order to transmute the toxins and make room for healing:

- Losing touch with the spiritual, representing a toxic congestion with physical matters
- The body needs to be stimulated into greater activity, it needs its pulse raised
- Being lazy, neglecting activities and self, putting things off

- Suppressing/holding in and onto anger
- Desires heating up inside but not being expressed

Congestion

Congestion happens in the sinuses and lungs, and also in the form of *constipation*. Congestion is an excess of blood and mucus. The place in the body where congestion appears will explain which area of your life is congested as a result of being overburdened:

- Head congestion relates to thought processes, such as irritation, worry, doubt, and fear, all of which fill our head and congest it.
- Lung congestion points to holding in feelings and emotions, so a good cry will eliminate this congestion. It also reflects people who prevent good things and good people from entering their lives, or who feel deserving of taking up more space and therefore congested in their current space. Being afraid to take in and breathe life, feeling depressed and sad, feeling stifled, and stifling others, all can fill and congest the heart with unexpressed emotion, which can manifest as lung congestion.
- Constipation usually points to a person who refuses to eliminate old ideas, emotions, and patterns, who is stuck in the past, refusing to change.

Cramps

Cramps come from muscle contractions, they can represent:

- A response to fear
- A holding on too tightly to something or someone you don't want to let go of
- The body is telling you to relax and let go
- Hand cramps relate to Heart chakra issues and holding on too tightly
- Leg cramps relate to Root chakra issues and could mean you are moving too much or working too hard (workaholic and perfectionist)
- Menstrual cramps could reflect issues around a woman's femininity

- Look for a pattern between the relationship of your activities, emotions, and life experiences and the severity of cramps
- The location of your cramps and the body part and system they are associated with will tell you more about the underlying causes

Fatigue

Fatigue means we are really tired of something in our lives:

- A job
- Relationship
- constant family stress
- A signpost to encourage play

Infection

Infections are poisons in the body derived from:

- Toxic thoughts
- Negativity
- Anger
- Fears
- Disharmony and negativity in surroundings—such as unhealthy people, situations, and environments.
- Our bad habits also foster infection, affecting the quality, character, and condition of our lives unfavorably. Look to who or what is currently affecting you.

Inflammation

Inflammation manifests as redness, swelling, pain, tenderness, and heat, and can represent:

- A reaction to an injurious agent, such as a person, condition, attitude, and negativity in your life
- Harboring annoyance and aggravation
- No healthy outlet to offload the anger and frustration of life conditions
- Preventing peacefulness and calmness
- Being overly critical or criticized

- Not approving of self
- Refusing to change old patterns

Irritations

Irritations are burning sensations and itches, they can represent:

- Something that is burning or eating you up
- An unexpressed desire or unfulfilled wish
- Itching to do something but not acting upon it
- A fear of unfulfilled needs and desires
- Unhappiness with your present life situation and position

Nausea

Nausea represents what we are sick of in our lives:

- An attitude you are exposed to but do not want to digest
- Something you are trying to expel from your life
- A fear of rejection
- A rejection to someone or something
- Not feeling safe and secure
- Having difficulty swallowing something

Pain

Pain relates to feelings of:

- Guilt
- Nursing old hurts
- Overly critical attitudes by others or yourself
- Longing
- Resistance to new moves and changes
- Feeling a lack of freedom
- Chronic pain that recurs and persists can relate to a refusal to change, reflecting long-standing fears and outworn behavior patterns. Look for something or someone that is always a pain in your life.
- Throbbing pain could reflect punishing self or feeling guilty
- Steady pain could reflect lack of self-approval and/or approval by others

- Acute sharp pain could reflect sensitivity to criticism, or being overwhelmed by ideas
- Achy pains can reflect a longing for something or someone, a longing for love

Swelling

Swelling in the body can represent:

- A blocked attitude/clogged process related to going forward in life
- Stuck in old patterns and outworn ideas
- Refusing to let go and grow
- Too emotional and not practical
- Clogged internally
- Inflating things out of proportion
- Allowing emotions to override common sense and practical thinking
- Invading others' lives or space where you should not

Germs

Bacteria

Bacteria in the body can represent:

- Unbalanced emotions
- Compulsively angry and fearful
- Unexpressed negative emotions
- Guilt

Virus

Virus in the body can represent:

- A Lack of self-worth
- Fear issues
- A belief that illness is a punishment and that you deserve to be ill
- The need to punish the self
- What you resist shall persist

Fungus

Fungus in the body can represent:

- Anger, resentment
- Procrastination
- Feeling undeserving of love and appreciation

Parasite

Parasites in the body can represent:

- Feeling like a victim
- Allowing others to take advantage of you
- Not being able to say no
- Allowing yourself to get sucked dry
- An imbalanced belief system

Skeletal System

Problems here represent:

- Bone problems reflect what we may or may not be protecting, the quality or lack of support or structure in our lives. The organ related to the broken bone will highlight what you are protecting, or not, and the significance of that organ in your life.

Eliminative System

Problems here represent:

- A refusal to let go and difficulty releasing emotions, thoughts, patterns, people, situations, and memories that no longer serve your growth and well-being
- Holding on to anger and unhealthy memories
- A fear of no longer being needed
- A fear of letting go of someone or something
- A fear of how people will perceive you if you change
- A fear of what the new may bring

Gland

Root *Adrenal issues* represent:

- Long-standing anxieties and worries
- A refusal to care for the self in healthy ways
- A resistance to responding to important issues in your life or in the lives of those closest to you
- How you perceive others' responses or lack thereof to your issues

Reproductive System

Problems here represent:

- Inability to be creative and productive in your own life
- Not participating in activities that are creative and fun, that rejuvenate and regenerate your mental, emotional, physical, and spiritual bodies
- Sexual performance problems can relate to problems with self-expression, such as feeling unable to fully express sexuality, or not being happy with the self's gender and/or sexual orientation.

Gland

Sacral *Testes and ovaries issues* represent:

- Inability to be creative and productive in your own life
- Not participating in activities that are creative, fun, rejuvenating and regenerating mentally, emotionally, physically, and spiritually.
- Problems with self-expression

Digestive System

Problems here represent:

- Habits you should and should not be ingesting and absorbing
- Not using what you have available to you
- Not absorbing new ideas
- Being wasteful

Gland

Solar *Pancreas issues* represent:

- What you should and should not be ingesting and absorbing
- Inability to absorb the healthy aspects of life—such as joy, happiness, and peace
- Allowing the unhealthy aspects to create imbalance and override the positive
- Inappropriate responses to life situations such as overreacting or inhibiting

Circulatory System

Problems here represent:

- Lack of vitality for an area in one's life
- How you allow your emotions to circulate and flow
- Locked in the past, afraid to move on, unable to resolve old emotional issues, and harboring an attitude of self-defeatism.

Respiratory System

Problems here represent:

- Issues of a right to life
- Feeling undeserving or guilty about how you live
- Feeling like you are not living your best life or not allowed to live your best life

- Suppressing your life expressions and emotions
- Unequal exchanges in the life process such as one-sided giving, or taking in too much

Gland

Heart *Thymus issues* represent:

- Not recognizing that your actions have repercussions
- Involving the self in issues and problems that do not concern you
- Infecting others with your thoughts and actions
- Allowing others' thoughts and actions to infect you
- Losing the ability to find sweetness and benefit in life

Gland

Throat *Thyroid issues* represent:

- Proper expression
- Hyperactivity
- Sluggish in using creative expression
- Not expressing yourself
- Not doing what you need and want to do
- Not claiming your power
- Claiming your power in an inappropriate manner

Nervous System

Problems here represent:

- Trying to integrate too many activities in your life
- Not having enough activities to keep you occupied
- Being overly sensitive to criticism from self and others
- Not communicating your needs clearly
- Interacting with others who are not communicating clearly with you
- Closed to new possibilities

Gland

Third Eye *Pituitary gland issues* represent:

- How you govern your life
- How you let others govern you
- Being overactive in people's lives making decisions for them
- Having overactive people in your life making decisions for you
- Not being active enough in choosing what is best for you

Gland

Crown *Pineal gland issues* represent:

- Physical and spiritual growth
- Not using and honoring your sexual, mental, and spiritual energies appropriately
- Not seeing what is right in front of you
- Not honoring all your energies and aspects of yourself as spiritual
- Not being sympathetic to others nor finding others sympathetic to you.

References

Alexander S. *Angels Among Us*. UK & USA: A David & Charles Book, 2011.

_____. *The Secret Power of Spirit Animals*. Avon, Massachusetts: Adams Media, 2013.

Andrews, T. *The Animal Wise Tarot*. Jackson, Tennessee: Dragonhawk Publishing, 2012.

Andrews, T. *The Healer's Manual*. Woodbury, Minnesota: Llewellyn Worldwide, 1993, 2006.

Balaban, N., and J. Bobick. *The Handy Anatomy Answer Book*. Canton, MI: Visible Ink Press, 2008.

Beattie, M. *Codependent No More: How to Stop Controlling Others and Care for Yourself*. Center City, Minnesota: Hazelden Foundation, 1992.

_____. *The Language of Letting Go: Daily Meditations on Codependency*. Center City, Minnesota: Hazelden Foundation, 1990.

Bethards, B. *The Dream Book*. Petaluma, California: NewCentury Publishers, 1983, 2003.

Choquette, S. *The Answer Is Simple: Oracle Cards*. Carlsbad, California: Hay House, 2008.

Co-Dependents Anonymous. *Patterns and Characteristics of Codependency*. Coda.org

Dale, C. *Beyond Soulmates: Open Yourself to Higher Love Through the Energy of Attraction*. Woodbury, Minnesota: Llewellyn Worldwide, 2013.

Dale, C. *The Complete Book of Chakra Healing*. Woodbury, Minnesota: Llewellyn Worldwide, 1996, 2009.

Hall, J. 101 *Power Crystals*. Beverly, Massachussetts: Fair Winds Press, 2011.

Hall, J. *The Crystal Wisdom Oracle*. UK: Watkins Publishing, 2013.

_____. *Saints and Angels*. Carlsbad, California: Hay House, 2005.

John, E. and Rice, T. "Circle of Life" [BOP Recording Studios]. *The Lion King* Soundtrack [CD, Track 1]. Mmabatho, South Africa: Walt Disney, 1994.

Judith, A. *Eastern Body, Western Mind*. New York: Random House, 1996, 2004.

Judith, A. *Wheels of Life*. Woodbury, Minnesota: Llewellyn Worldwide, 1987, 1999, 2012.

Kübler-Ross, E. *On Death and Dying*. New York: Macmillan, 1969.

Lauper, C. Steinberg, B. and Kelly, T. *True Colors* [EPIC]. *True Colors* [Vinyl]. New York: Portrait, 1986.

Lebo, M. and Rifkin, J. "They Live in You" [BOP Recording Studios]. *The Lion King* Soundtrack [CD, Track 7]. Mmabatho, South Africa: Walt Disney, 1994.

Linn, D. *Gateway Oracle Cards*. Carlsbad, California: Hay House, 2012.

Permutt, P. *The Complete Guide to Crystal Chakra Healing*. New York: CICO Books, 2008.

Sams, J. and Carson, D. *Medicine Cards*. New York: St. Martin's Press, 1988, 1999.

————. *Dancing the Dream: The Seven Sacred Paths of Human Transformation*. New York: Harper Collins, 1998.

Stibal, V. *Theta Healing: Diseases and Disorders*. Carlsbad, California: Hay House, 2008, 2011.

Taylor, S. *The Hidden Power of Your Past Lives*. Carlsbad, California: Hay House, 2011.

Taylor, S. *Energy Oracle Cards.* Carlsbad, California: Hay House, 2013.

Virtue, D. *Healing with the Angels*. Carlsbad, California: Hay House, 1999.

————. *Magical Unicorns*. Carlsbad, California: Hay House, 2005.

————. *The Healing Miracles of Archangel Raphael*. Carlsbad, California: Hay House, 2010.

Virtue, D. and Van Praagh, J. *Talking to Heaven: Mediumship Cards*. Carlsbad, California: Hay House, 2013.

Waite, A.E. *The Key to the Tarot*. London: Random House, 1993.

Wauters, A. *The Complete Guide to Chakras*. London: Quarto Publishing, 2002, 2010.

Weiss, B. *Only Love Is Real*. New York: Grand Central Publishing, 1997, 2000.

Weiss, B. *Many Lives, Many Masters*. New York: Fireside, 1988.

Williams, L. *The Survival of The Soul*. Carlsbad, California: Hay House, 2011.

Rainbow Medicine
Acknowledgments

To our teachers, students, clients and friends above and below, thank you for our shared memories, healing and celebrations, and for holding me within your loving embrace. I am blessed and honored to be touched and moved by your experiences, knowledge, and love.

To my loved ones above and below, I am grateful for our lives, thank you for holding my hand every step of the way through this adventurous terrain. I love you and cherish us.

May peace be with us all.

About
The Author

Dr. Leanne Levy is a women's rights advocate and leading authority on the development of authentic self-empowerment. As an educational therapist and psychic medium teacher, she brings to her Empowerment Transpersonal Practice and School (*Whitewolf Academy*) the body of media-rich research and years of experience as a teacher and therapist in one-on-one and group settings with females in crisis.

From 2002-2006, while engaged in her doctoral studies at *Concordia University*, Dr. Leanne Levy developed a pattern recognition methodology to understand how people use signs, symbols, and patterns to construct and communicate identity. Shortly thereafter, in 2008, she was awarded a postdoctoral fellowship by the *Social Sciences and Humanities Research Council of Canada* in conjunction with *Steinhardt's New York University* to pursue her research with children under youth protection, on the healing and empowering benefits of arts-based tools for crisis intervention.

Dr. Leanne Levy has lectured extensively, both locally and internationally, about her female empowerment work; published in top-tier peer-reviewed journals, authored two girlhood social justice books, and produced and directed numerous girl-centered educational documentary films, namely *This Is My Body* (2007), a *National Film Board of Canada* distribution.

Regarding her chosen educational path, she states: As life unfolds, we begin to see the links and snowball effect.

At the various times I decided to pursue my academic degrees in the area of Art Education—B.Ed., M.Ed. (*McGill University*), Ph.D., and Postdoctorate in Art and Art Professions—my goal was never to be a classroom art teacher, but, rather, to use art as a healing tool for personal growth and social awareness. Now I clearly see how my visual literacy education, coupled with my methodical pattern recognition ability, are foundational to my particular method of communicating with the spirit world. If you wait long enough, you will discover how one hand does indeed wash the other.

The author divides her time between Montreal, Quebec; Boca Raton, Florida; and online where she gives readings, therapy, and teaches the language of spirit communication and holistic healing. Her clients and students come from all walks of life, with varying professional backgrounds. Please visit her at www.rainbowmedicine.co and whitewolfacademy.co